THE HERO WITHIN

THE HERO WITHIN

SIX ARCHETYPES WE LIVE BY

Third Edition

Carol S. Pearson, Ph.D.

HARPER**ELIXIR**

HARPER**ELIXIR**

Designed by Interrobang Design Studio

First HarperOne edition published in 1986

Library of Congress Cataloging-in-Publication Data

Pearson, Carol
   The hero within : six archetypes we live by / Carol S. Pearson.—3rd ed.
Includes bibliographical references
ISBN: 978–0–06–251555–1
   1. Archetype (Psychology).   2. Self-actualization (Psychology).
3. New Age movement.   I. Title.
BF175.5.A72P43   1998
150.19'54—dc21   98–17531

19 20 21 LSC(C) 40 39 38

For Amalie Frank

Contents

Preface   *ix*

Changes from the Second Edition   *xiv*

Uses of This Book   *xix*

Acknowledgments   *xxi*

Part One: The Heroic Journey: The Map

    Introduction: Making a Difference:
The Heroic Journey   *3*

1. Choosing Freedom: The Guides   *17*

2. Surviving Difficulty:
From the Innocent to the Orphan   *33*

3. Finding Yourself: The Wanderer   *65*

4. Proving Your Worth: The Warrior   *95*

5. Showing Generosity: The Altruist   *123*

6. Achieving Happiness: The Innocent's Return   *151*

7. Transforming Your Life: The Magician   *181*

Part Two: Personal Mastery: The Guidebook

    Introduction: Personal Mastery:
Inner Resource Development   *217*

8. Honoring Your Life: The Route   *229*

9. Troubleshooting When You Get Lost
or Stuck: The Compass   *247*

10. The Ethics of the Journey: The Code   *275*

Appendix A: The Heroic Myth Self-Test

Part I: How I See Myself   *289*

Part II: How Others See Me   *292*

Part III: The Influence of My Family of Origin   *295*

Part IV: The Influence of My Current Family   *298*

Part V: The Influence of My Current
          Workplace (or School)   *301*

Part VI: Putting It All Together   *304*

Appendix B: Guidelines for Heroic Journey Groups *307*

Appendix C: Creating Heroic Environments

Heroic Families   *311*

Heroic Schools   *312*

Heroic Workplaces   *313*

Heroic Psychotherapy, Coaching, and Counseling   *315*

Heroic Recovery   *316*

Heroic Politics, Economics, and Government   *318*

Appendix D: The *Awakening the Heroes Within* Twelve-Archetype Model: Notes and Resources *321*

About the Author *325*

Bibliography: Suggested Reading *327*

Notes *331*

Preface

A computer expert once complained to me that many people, after buying their first PC, call the hot-line number outraged because their computer won't work. What they mean is that they do not know how to work it. He noted that when we buy a car, we do not expect it to drive itself. We have to learn to use it—and then get a license to drive.

All of us have tremendous richness within us—potential that, when tapped, can help us find greater success and fulfillment in our lives. However, few people today learn how to access their own inner potential. *The Hero Within* is a primary text for the emerging field of inner resource development (IRD)—a field devoted to giving the keys to the kingdom back to ordinary people so they can live extraordinary lives.

Most of us know that when we buy a computer, we at least should read the instruction manual, if not take a course. However, when it comes to our psyches, we often simply expect that they will run themselves. It is tacitly assumed in our culture that we need to look within ourselves only when something goes wrong. Then we call in an expert (psychiatrist, psychologist, minister, guru, etc.) to identify what is sick, inadequate, or sinful about us that is causing the problem—just as we would look for a defective part in a machine, so it can be replaced.

The success of self-help books in our time reflects a constructive desire on people's parts to take responsibility for their own mental health and spiritual development. However, most such books also focus on teaching us what is wrong with ourselves and then telling us how we can get better. Just as with a computer, we may not need to be fixed; we simply may need to learn to understand what we have going for us and how to use it in the current stage of our journey.

The Hero Within can be thought of as an operating manual for the psyche, or as a map or guidebook for the journey. It describes six inner guides, or archetypes, that help us on our way. With their assistance, we can traverse the predictable dilemmas of the maturation process—a process that continues throughout our lives. When we learn how to access this inner support, we also become less fearful about the future. It becomes clear that we have within us everything we need to handle whatever challenges we encounter on the path.

Moreover, life has become too complex to cede ownership of knowledge about our inner resources to psychologists and other experts. Success in today's workplace requires all of us to develop emotional and spiritual intelligence. Archetypes—the fundamental structures of the psyche—can help us decode our own inner workings, as well as the inner lives of other people, groups, and social systems, so that we can rise to the challenge of contemporary life.

Work on archetypes was pioneered by the Swiss psychiatrist C. G. Jung, who also formulated theories about psychological type, the individuation process, transference, projection, and synchronicity. Jung described archetypes as deep and abiding patterns in the human psyche that remain powerful and present over time. These may exist, to use Jung's terminology, in the "collective unconscious," or "objective psyche"; they may even be encoded into the makeup of the human brain. Jung discovered these archetypes in patients' dreams as well as in art, literature, and sacred myths. He developed treatment strategies such as dream analysis, active imagination exercises, and awareness of the archetypal dimension of waking life to heal his patients, sometimes from very serious emotional or mental illness. But whereas

Jung's work was motivated by a desire to heal dysfunction, *The Hero Within* employs Jungian ideas and approaches to help well people learn to *thrive*.

In much of the world today, ordinary people face choices beyond those available to all but the most privileged in the past. For most of human history, specified sex roles, set career patterns, and predictable behaviors determined by one's class or ethnic group defined how people lived and even what they thought. Sex roles are now much more blurred, and ethnicity no longer limits who and what we can be. The pace of economic and social change will cause many of us to pursue several careers in one short lifetime. Moreover, we have the freedom to choose to live out very different lifestyles. All of this requires more of us. We need to be more flexible, to be able to keep more balls in the air, and to make an infinite number of choices—small and large—about who we are and how we want to live.

The modern world is so complex that we all must understand our own psyches and their potential. Unfortunately, it remains true that most of us receive no systematic training to acquaint us with our inner desires and resources. In fact, most people do not gain any real self-knowledge until or unless they get depressed or have some other difficulty great enough to send them to a psychotherapist for help.

Today, many of us realize that we bear some responsibility for our own physical health. It is not enough to trust the doctor to make you well when you get sick. It is at least equally important to exercise, eat well, and live a healthy lifestyle to prevent illness. When we are ill, most of us know we should read up on our illness, seek a second opinion when it seems warranted, and not simply give our power over to the physician, however competent she or he might be.

The same principle applies to mental health. Psychospiritual fitness is just as important as physical health. In providing expert information to the lay public, *The Hero Within* gives knowledge of the inner life back to readers. The point is that we can be safe and at home in our own psyches, and we also can learn the basics of what we need to know so that we can have access to the richness of our inner lives.

The Hero Within model can be used to increase people's emotional and spiritual intelligence. It is appropriate in a variety of settings because it allows for communication that is deep and authentic without prying into the details of people's personal lives or histories. It also can help individuals connect to their spirits and souls in a way that neither promotes nor violates their particular religious commitments (or lack thereof). Through this approach, they can go inward to find out not what is wrong with them but what is potentially very right, thus contributing to higher self-esteem and better functioning.

PUBLICATION HISTORY OF THIS BOOK

This third version of *The Hero Within* builds on the framework of the first and second editions. I was inspired initially to write *The Hero Within* out of a concern that we would not be able to solve the great political, social, and philosophical problems of our time if so many of us persisted in seeing the hero as "out there" or "up there," beyond ourselves. The book was meant as a call to the quest, a challenge to readers to claim their own heroism and take their own journeys. This call is not about becoming bigger or better or more important than anyone else. We *all* matter. Every one of us has an essential contribution to make, and we can make it only by taking the risk of being uniquely our own selves.

Underneath the frantic absorption in the pursuit of money, status, power, and pleasure and the addictive and obsessive behaviors so prevalent today are, we all know, a sense of emptiness and a common human hunger to go deeper. In writing *The Hero Within*, it seemed to me that each of us wants and needs to learn, if not the "meaning of life," then the meaning of our individual lives, so that we can find ways of living and being that are rich, empowered, and authentic.

Yet, even though I knew this, the massive cultural response to Bill Moyers's interviews with Joseph Campbell on the PBS series *The Power of Myth*, along with the enthusiastic reader response to *The Hero Within*, was a pleasant surprise. More people than I ever dared imagine seem prepared and even eager to respond to the call to the heroic quest with an enthusiastic "Yes!"

The first edition of *The Hero Within* sold almost entirely by word of mouth. I was fascinated to learn how many readers bought multiple copies to give to their friends and co-workers as a way of calling them to the quest and, at the same time, creating a sense of community that would support their own journeys. Readers frequently complained that copies of the book had a way of disappearing from their offices and living rooms, by way, I gather, of friends, lovers, relatives, clients, and colleagues.

Many readers also have written or called to say how *The Hero Within* either named their own experience or in some other way empowered them. I was particularly touched by a man from Perth, Australia, who called three times, long distance, to thank me for writing the book, apparently undeterred by always getting my answering machine. But most of all, I have been moved by stories of personal transformation. One young man from the Pacific Northwest told me that he had been on drugs and had lost everything. He was living alone in the woods, he said, when he read the book, believed it, and it changed his life. By the time he brought his tattered copy of the book to a lecture for me to sign, he was an executive in a small company and generally doing well. Such *is* the power of myth.

The second edition of *The Hero Within* was prompted by the question asked most frequently by readers: "Is it possible to do something to encourage the development of an archetype in one's own life?" The answer is yes, and the exercises I added to the second edition were designed to do just that.

This third edition was inspired by the understanding that the world has changed a great deal since *The Hero Within* was first published. The original version provided a title format and an approach that became a model spawning many similar books—"The (fill in the blank) Within." It also was part of a much larger movement of books and workshops helping people to recognize and awaken their inner resources. This abundance has made people much more sophisticated than they were just a decade ago about understanding their inner resources. Today, the president of the United States refers unself-consciously to our nation's "journey." Business books tell executives that they have to go on their heroic journeys to make the changes required in today's competitive environment. Virtually all of us understand that we are entering a time so challenging that qualities we once expected to find only in exceptional people now are required in everyone.

I am thankful to Harper San Francisco for asking me to prepare this completely revised and expanded edition. Writing it helped me not only to see how my own ideas had evolved, but also to understand more clearly the way the collective consciousness of our culture was and is changing. I come away from this writing project ever more optimistic about the potential for individual and societal transformation. The seeds have been planted and new growth has begun to sprout. We can water this new life by our attention. Whatever we focus on tends to build and grow.

CHANGES FROM THE SECOND EDITION

My primary purpose in revising *The Hero Within* has been to make it more accessible. So many readers have shared with me how transformative this material is that I simply wanted to make it available to a greater number of people. This necessitated major revision and expansion of the introduction to explain key concepts in a simpler, clearer way. (The original introduction has been replaced by two chapters.) It also required the addition to three chapters at the end of the book to help readers know how to use the archetypal approach in their everyday lives. Because people have been working with this material for more than a decade, we now have a rich trove of resources to draw upon that show readers how they can consciously employ the hero's journey as a model to take charge of their own.

Much of my knowledge comes from confidential situations. In Chapters 2 through 7, which describe archetypes, I frequently cite literary examples, augmenting them with a few true stories. In chapters exploring ways to use archetypal awareness in readers' lives (Chapters 1 and 8 through 10), I have used more illustrations from real people's lives. However, so as not to breach confidentiality, these generally are either composites or have been fictionalized enough that the original model for the story cannot be traced. I also have included a few incidents from my own life.

I began revising this book because the sex role revolution and its archetypal impact had dated some of the examples. When I wrote the original version of *The Hero Within*, I was concerned about the fact that women did not see themselves as heroes because the society saw them as "other." This is why I did not use the term "heroine." Women's journeys often differ in style and sometimes in sequence from those of men, but the hero's journey is essentially the same for both sexes. In the past decade, men's and women's lives have become more similar. As I returned to revise this work, I therefore updated many of the gender examples.

In the past, gender limited people, circumscribing the lives of both sexes. Men tried to be manly, but they also struggled not to be, or seem, like sissies. Women strove to be feminine and nurturing and not to seem masculine in any way. Now, an increasing number of men expect to nurture children, help "make a home," and share their feelings with their partner and even their friends.

More and more women expect to earn a living, work out, and show toughness when it is needed.

Many of the changes I was advocating in *The Hero Within* have now come to pass, at least for the young. In the original edition of this book, I encouraged women to act on the world as Warriors, but I also encouraged men to expand their own sense of heroism to encompass the traditional heroism of women—as Martyrs/Altruists—whose caring function has, in many ways, held our families and neighborhoods together. Women have been faster to embrace traditionally male forms of heroism than men have been to embrace female modes—largely because the culture still respects male models of behavior more than female ones. The last archetype discussed is the Magician, not only because it presides over the transformation of the kingdom, but also because it is intrinsically androgynous, bringing together the best of the male and female traditions. I believe the emergence of this archetype inevitably will bring about an empowering balance in which both the masculine and the feminine are honored equally within the individual psyche and society as a whole.

The greatest challenge I encountered in revising the book was the evolution in the way archetypes have been expressed in the past decade. This cultural shift necessitated major conceptual changes in the book influencing the naming of an archetype, the order in which the archetypes are presented, and the descriptions of each archetype.

When I wrote the first edition of *The Hero Within*, I was concerned that the Warrior archetype, with its need to conquer, would destroy the world. The cold war was heating up; the stockpiling of nuclear weapons was accelerating; racial tensions were increasing; and environmental catastrophe, fueled by unbridled competitiveness, seemed imminent. Since then, the Berlin Wall has come down, apartheid has ended in South Africa, environmental awareness has increased substantially, and the men's movement (with its critique of the macho Warrior role) has erupted. Archetypes are eternal forms, but their expression is shaped by the level of consciousness of a particular historical time. For most of recorded history, men proved themselves in battle. Beginning with Vietnam, war became suspect.

With the advent of nuclear weapons, war has become too dangerous for civilization to use it as a rite of passage into manhood. As a result, the expression of the archetype is forced to move to a higher level. Today, we send our young men and women into corporate "jungles" with admonitions to make something of themselves. The Warrior energy is primarily channeled into the will to achieve—on the athletic field, in schools, and in the workplace.

We can see an equally radical shift in the Altruist archetype. Writing in the 1980s, I called this archetype the Martyr, noting in particular how women were expected to sacrifice for their husbands and children. Since then, women's roles have changed markedly, the men's movement has exposed the self-sacrifice inherent in the traditional male as well as female role, and the psychological literature on codependence has identified the Martyr with pathology. As a result, martyrdom now is socially unacceptable. Indeed, the word "martyr" has taken on such negative connotations that it seemed wise to change the name of the Martyr archetype to "the Altruist" for this new edition. This is not simply a matter of renaming. The use of the term "Altruist" honors the evolution of the archetype that has occurred during the past decade. We are struggling to express altruism and care without being martyrs. In the process, the archetype is being suppressed. Faced with homelessness in the streets, neglected children in our homes, and a growing discrepancy between the incomes of not only the rich and the poor, but the rich and the middle class, we never have needed the Altruist more than we do today.

The Innocent archetype also has evolved. When I wrote *The Hero Within*, the reawakening of spirituality in the culture had only just begun. When spirit is denied, the Innocent expresses itself in childlike dependence, "me"-generation narcissism, materialism, and a massive cultural inability to pick up after ourselves (especially in the areas of environmental pollution and social injustice). When spirit enters a life, however, the Innocent becomes a mystic, experiencing the essential goodness of the universe. The return of spirit to the culture means that although innocence still is being evidenced in its spoiled-little-child aspect, the more hopeful sign is how many people today are experiencing the consciousness of the Innocent's return to Eden. The massive cultural emergence of the returned Innocent caused me to move the Innocent chapter to the penultimate position—after the Altruist and before the Magician. Working with the higher form of the archetype also allowed me to differentiate between the high-level Innocent and the Magician. The hero finds the treasure and recaptures innocence and then, as the Magician, transforms the kingdom. What this means is that we do not transform the world in order to be happy. We find happiness first, and then we transform our world.

I am aware that some readers may be displeased by so many changes in the book, especially if they liked the previous edition the way it was. I anticipated this, because at a speech I gave after *Awakening the Heroes Within: Twelve Archetypes to Help Us Find Ourselves and Transform Our World* was published, a man in the audience stood up during the question-and-answer period to tell me how furious he was that I had written that book. He explained that he liked *The Hero Within* just as it was and resented my expanding the number of archetypes and describing them in a different way! He wanted me to leave well enough alone.

I ended the preface to the 1986 edition by saying, "If you happen to see me after a lapse of several years, do not ask me to defend ideas in this book. Very likely I will know more and may no longer agree with what I have said. Tell me what you think, and ask me, if you wish to ask me something, what I have learned since writing it." This revised edition—as well as *Awakening the Heroes Within*—answers that question. I look forward to learning even more from reader responses to this edition and to the continued influence such interactions will have on my ideas and my life.

USES OF THIS BOOK

The Hero Within is written primarily for individual readers seeking greater self-knowledge and success on their journeys. It also is appropriate for use in:

- *parenting:* to encourage children to become successful, ethical, and happy;
- *psychotherapy:* as a means to identify archetypal strengths that can help with the therapeutic process as well as to know what archetypes may need to be developed for more successful functioning;
- *schools:* in character development and school-to-work programs, staff/teacher renewal programs, and student motivation efforts;
- *counseling:* to enhance career and life fulfillment, marriages and families, and out-placement efforts;
- *recovery programs:* to help people pick up life lessons missed because their families of origin were dysfunctional and/or because their own alcohol or drug use interfered with their development;
- *organizations:* as a tool for team building, diversity training, leadership development, and organizational change efforts;
- *executive and transition coaching:* to encourage leadership excellence from the inside out;

- *churches, synagogues, and other religious groups:* as an aid to spiritual development;
- *mediation, cultural diversity, and political organizing:* to help people understand each other's divergent perspectives and common ground; and
- *scholarship, journalism, and other forms of analytical thought:* to recognize (archetypally based) biases that undermine objectivity and what paradigms or mental maps are operating in different accounts of "reality."

Acknowledgments

I am inspired to revise and expand this work by the many readers who have shared with me the stories of their heroic journeys and anecdotes about ways *The Hero Within* touched their lives. I have been moved, encouraged, and occasionally challenged by the mail, phone calls, and e-mail I daily receive. I have learned not only from readers, but also professionals whom I have trained in the use of this model and other similar ones. It is fascinating to me that although I have been working with these materials for years, others using them always come up with some nuance or even breakthrough insight I have missed. I am particularly grateful for insights from what I call my training faculty "dream team": Patricia Adson, whose book *True North* provides practical guidance for psychotherapists on the uses of these and other archetypes with their clients; Eileen and Patrick Howley, who apply these models to the training of educational leaders; Chris Saade, who integrates these ideas with existential philosophy/psychology and whose emphasis on the importance of existential choice strongly influenced this revision; and Suzanne Guy, who edits *Heroes Ink*, a newsletter to support people who are using the hero's journey model in their lives and work.

A number of theories positively influenced the development of these models. The three major philosophical traditions this book integrates and develops are: Jungian psychology, scholarship on the hero's journey, and new-thought spiritual principles. In the Jungian world, I wish to acknowledge particularly C. G. Jung, who provided the pioneering studies of archetypes, without which this book could not have been written; James Hillman, whose archetypal theories were essential to its development; and Frances Parks, whose skillful analytical training provided guidance in understanding my own inner archetypal life. For the hero's journey material, of course, this book would not have been possible without the scholarly achievement of Joseph Campbell and the practical applications of these theories by David Oldfield, whose example was extremely helpful in developing the exercises herein. For insight into new thought spiritual traditions, I am particularly indebted to the work of Eric Butterworth.

Other theoretical perspectives that influenced my thinking include gestalt therapy, the fields of women's and ethnic studies, cognitive psychology, learning theory, family systems theory, and organizational development/systems theory.

I also am grateful to a series of editors who treated this book with professionalism and care: Pat Lassonde, who edited the first edition; Tom Grady, who edited the second edition and proposed this third edition; my agent, Angela Miller, who convinced me to take it on; Mark Chimsky, who edited this edition and provided invaluable guidance during the writing process; and Ann Moru for copyediting. I also thank Edith Lazenby for her work typing revisions for this book and my husband, David Merkowitz, for his substantial help in the writing/editing process and for his unfailing love and support.

THE HERO WITHIN

PART 1

The Heroic Journey: The Map

Introduction
Making a Difference: The Heroic Journey

> . . . We have not even to risk the adventure alone, for the heroes of
> all time have gone before us. The labyrinth is thoroughly known.
> We have only to follow the thread of the hero path, and where we
> had thought to find an abomination, we shall find a god. And where
> we had thought to slay another, we shall slay ourselves. Where we
> had thought to travel outward, we will come to the center of our
> own existence. And where we had thought to be alone, we will be
> with all the world.
>
> —Joseph Campbell, *The Power of Myth*

You are a hero—or could be.

Heroes—in myth, literature, and real life—take journeys, confront dragons (i.e., problems), and discover the treasure of their
true selves. Although they may feel very alone during the quest, at
its end their reward is a sense of community: with themselves,
with other people, and with the earth. Every time we confront
death-in-life, we confront a dragon. Every time we choose life
over nonlife and move deeper into the ongoing discovery of who
we are, we bring new life to ourselves and to our culture.

The need to take the journey is innate in the species. If we do
not risk, if we play prescribed social roles instead of taking our
journeys, we may feel numb and experience a sense of alienation,
a void, an emptiness inside. People who are discouraged from

slaying dragons internalize the urge and slay themselves by declaring war on their fat, their selfishness, their sensitivity, or some other attribute they think does not please. Or they suppress their feelings in order to become successful performance machines. Or they become chameleons, killing off their uniqueness to serve an image they think buys success or just will keep them safe. When we declare war on our true selves, we can end up feeling as though we have lost our souls. If this goes on long enough, we are likely to become ill and have to struggle to get well. In shying away from the quest, we experience nonlife and, accordingly, we call forth less life in the culture. This is the experience of the wasteland.

TRANSFORMING THE WASTELAND

At the beginning of the classic hero myth, the kingdom is a wasteland. Crops are not growing, illness is rampant, babies are not being born, and alienation and despair are pervasive. The fertility, the sense of life, has disappeared from the kingdom. This dilemma is associated with some failure on the part of the ruler, who is impotent, or sinful, or despotic. The old king or queen represents anachronistic ways that are hamstringing the culture.[1]

Therefore, a more youthful challenger goes on a journey, confronts a dragon, and wins a treasure, which may be riches or a more clearly symbolic object, such as the grail in the Grail myths or a sacred fish in the Fisher King myths. The journey transforms the challenger, whose treasure is the discovery of a new and life-affirming perspective. When the hero returns to the kingdom, this insight also changes life for everyone. For this reason, the returned hero becomes the new ruler. Because new answers have been found, fertility and abundance are restored. Rain falls, nourishing parched ground. Crops spring up, babies are born, the plague is cured, and people feel hopeful and alive once more.

In this story, you may notice generational conflicts. If you are a young person, you might identify the old ruler as parents and other authority figures. They are not necessarily bad; it is just that their truths come from another time. That is why you must take your own journey.

At any age, you may experience this pattern when you become dissatisfied with your family system, your organization, your community—or even just the way you are living your own life. As you go on a quest to find greater vitality and aliveness for yourself, you also seek answers that contribute to a collective transformation.

In fact, any time you identify a wasteland element in your life—illness, boredom, lethargy, alienation, emptiness, loss, addiction, failure, anger, or outrage—it is time to take a journey. You can be called to the quest by such dissatisfaction or simply by a desire for adventure. The journey you take inevitably will transform you. Systems theory tells us that when any element of a system changes, the whole system has to reconfigure. Therefore, simply by experiencing your own metamorphosis, you can contribute to the transformation of all the social systems of which you are a part: family, school, workplace, community, and society as a whole.

Heroes, then, are not only people who grow and change and take their journeys; they also are agents of change. In *The Hero: Myth/Image/Symbol*, Dorothy Norman maintains that "myths of the heroes speak most eloquently of man's quest to choose life over death."[2] Joseph Campbell, in *The Hero with a Thousand Faces*, defines the hero as "the champion not of things to become but of things becoming; the dragon to be slain by him is precisely the monster of the status quo: Holdfast the keeper of the past."[3] The hero's task always has been to bring new life to an ailing culture.

In ancient times, societies were governed by kings and queens. Most people had little power over their lives. Today, however, we prize the achievement of democracy. Yet living in an egalitarian society carries with it responsibilities. Instead of only exceptional people going on the quest, we all need to be doing so. Heroism today requires us all to find the treasure of our true selves and to share that treasure with the community as a whole—through doing and being fully who we are. To the degree that we do so, our kingdoms are transformed.

THE CALL IN THE CONTEMPORARY WORLD

Many people put off their journeys, expecting to be cared for, but in the contemporary world this desire soon is thwarted. Most of us would like to count on being safe, but the world has a way of throwing us out of the secure nest. The result is that we learn to fly or fall to the ground to try again. The following are just a few of the many ways the world requires us to be willing to face uncertainty:

- Many young people feel alienated, if not bitter, because it has dawned on them that they may not achieve the same level of prosperity as their parents. In the United States, we had come to expect that progress was automatic: each generation would have it better than the previous one. Now it looks as though this may not be true, at least for many. No matter how angry one feels about this, it still is necessary to grapple with making one's way in the world.

- In the past, people assumed that when they married, it would be for life. Now divorce has become common. Some people whose spouses walk out on them are unprepared—emotionally or financially—and find themselves at a loss. Others who are more worldly-wise develop backup plans, but also know that doing so puts a slight wedge between them and their partner. Still, most are willing to risk loss to gain the joys of intimacy.

- In many companies, employees formerly believed that if they worked hard and were loyal, they always would have a job. Now this loyalty contract has broken down. The result is that workers not only are anxious, but feel that they alone are responsible for their futures. Yet if they are smart, they do not hunker down in fear. They find their own vocational purpose and develop a commitment to their own work and its quality—whether they stay with their present employer, move to another job, or start their own company.

When the heroic journey was thought to be for special people only, the rest of us just found a secure niche and stayed there. Now we have no secure places in which to hide and be safe. In the contemporary world, if we do not choose to step out on our quest, it will come to get us. We are being thrust on the journey. That is why we all must learn its requirements.

A WORLD IN TRANSITION

Times of rapid change require a heroic spirit. Management consultant and business professor Robert Quinn, describing the pressures of a quickly shifting global economy, concludes that organizations today must learn to move into unknown territory, continually reinventing themselves. Doing so, he notes, "can be a terrifying experience, with the possibility of failure or death a reality rather than a metaphor." Organizations cannot make this heroic journey without the individuals in them also doing so, Quinn says, because there "is an important link between deep change at the personal level and deep change at the organizational level."

To make deep personal change, Quinn continues, is to develop "a new paradigm, a new self, one that is more effectively aligned with today's realities." Individuals and organizations cannot succeed unless they are willing to embark on the hero's journey—a story of individual and group transformation. This requires us, in Quinn's words, to "step outside our old paradigms" to "think differently." On the journey, we reinvent ourselves, to "realign ourselves with the surrounding environment."[4]

By taking us down into the deep recesses of our souls, the hero's journey allows us to adapt to a changing world without becoming chameleons. Instead, we go inward to find an authentic response to the challenges that face us. In so doing, we become more authentic.

We are witnessing a paradigm shift of epic proportions. It is affecting every possible field of study and endeavor, even as it raises the bar on the level of consciousness required to live a successful life. The threat of nuclear or environmental catastrophe, the advent of technology that has ushered in the global age, and the exponential rate of change in our society have created a crisis that requires humankind to participate consciously in its evolution.

Heroism today requires consciousness, which means that we virtually are required to deprogram ourselves from negative and anachronistic scripts. This is why, for instance, deconstructionism has been the dominant modality in recent scholarly endeavor; why millions of people are in therapy and recovery groups working hard to free themselves from negative messages they received from their parents; why women and racial minorities must work so hard to rid themselves of internalized sexist and racist attitudes; and why men are beginning to refuse to go to war, overwork themselves to an early death, or pretend they have no vulnerable feelings. It also is why youth today take longer to reach maturity than prior generations. Not only do they need time to develop the technological sophistication and the communication skills required to thrive in a demanding economic climate, they also recognize that so much in the world today is not working. It takes time to move through alienation into heroic engagement.

As we deprogram ourselves from outmoded habits and traditions, however, the temptation is to see ourselves as victims, not heroes, especially if we have a conscious or unconscious sense of entitlement. If we did not come from a healthy family, if there are few jobs in our field, or if we fear we will not surpass our parents' prosperity level, we then can become demoralized. It is important to remember that heroes of myth and legend hardly ever have perfect parents or perfect lives. Think, for instance, of Oedipus, left to die as an infant on the hillside, or Oliver Twist, growing up in a cruel orphanage. Even Jesus of Nazareth was born, humbly, in a manger.

Heroes have the esteem that comes from personal responsibility, but they have little or no sense of entitlement. To claim the hero within, we must let go of our belief that we are victimized if we do not have perfect parents or a perfect job, a perfect government or unending affluence. The very nature of heroism requires us to face the dragon, not sit around and complain that dragons exist and someone should do something about them. It never was, and it undoubtedly never will be, popular or easy to challenge "Holdfast the keeper of the past."

Actually, the heroic part of each of us fundamentally does not mind that the world is imperfect. This part does not live for comfort; it loves a good adventure. King Arthur of the Camelot stories illustrates this wonderfully. In one tale, just as the knights and ladies begin to sit down for their evening feast, Arthur declares that they cannot eat yet: they have had no adventure that day. So off they go in search of one!

Box-Car Bertha, the heroine of *Sister of the Road*, has a spirit to match King Arthur's. At the close of her autobiography, Bertha looks back over a life that has included abandonment by her mother at a very young age, a dehumanizing stint as a prostitute (culminating in a case of syphilis), and the experience of looking on helplessly when one lover was hanged and another run over by a train. She declares: "Everything I had ever struggled to learn I found I had already survived. I had achieved my purpose—everything I had set out in life to do, I had accomplished. I had wanted to know how it felt to be a hobo, a radical, a prostitute, a thief, a reformer, a social worker and a revolutionist. Now I knew. I shuddered. Yes, it was all worthwhile to me. There were no tragedies in my life. Yes, my prayers had been answered."[5] While I admit I would not want my daughter or son to adopt her lifestyle, we all can benefit from her attitude. Bertha takes responsibility for her choices and is thankful for the gift of her life.

Many people subscribe to the false idea that being heroic means you have to suffer and struggle to prevail. The fact is, most of us will experience difficulty whether or not we claim the heroic potential within us. Moreover, if we avoid our journeys, we also may feel bored and empty. It is not so much that we take our journeys in order to attain happiness. Rather, when we follow our real bliss, our journeys *are* our treasures. Mystic Annie Dillard in *Pilgrim at Tinker Creek* surmises that life "is often cruel, but always beautiful—the least we can do is try to be there," to be fully in life. She imagines that "the dying pray at the last not 'please,' but 'thank you,' as a guest thanks his host at the door. The universe," she explains, "was not made in jest but in solemn, incomprehensible earnest. By a power that is unfathomably secret, and holy, and fleet. There is nothing to be done about it, but ignore it, or see."[6] The emerging heroic ideal does not see life as a challenge to be overcome, but a gift to be received.

ANTI-HEROIC CULTURAL FORCES

We are just emerging from an anti-heroic time. On the one hand, people in our society today yearn for heroes, bemoaning the lack of greatness in our leaders as scandal—and image-mongering become commonplace. Too often, cynicism is seen as a sign of sophistication. People then excuse their own misdeeds, saying, "Everyone does it," because they do not believe they make a difference. The increased complexity of life, moreover, makes people feel powerless, leading them to believe it doesn't matter what they do. In this context of resigned nihilism, many use the word "hero" pejoratively. For example, a young man who is outraged by an ethical lapse in his corporation becomes a whistleblower and is warned by his boss, "We don't need any heroes here." What he is, in fact, being told is that it is unsophisticated and unwise to take a risk for your values. It is much safer, and much better for one's career, to wink at shady dealings. In such cases, people make light of the heroic ideal because they want to excuse their own moral laxity.

Women and people of color are often actively discouraged from seeing themselves in a heroic light. A psychologist practically sneers as he chides a young artist for her desire to make a transformative mark on the world, asking, "What are you trying to be? A hero?" He goes on to suggest that her ambition shows she is in flight from her genuine femininity. "Give up the art for the time being," he counsels, "and concentrate on raising your children," the implication being that her ambition somehow makes her a bad mother and a deficient woman.

Whoever you are, do not be surprised if others actively discourage you from taking your own life seriously. In fact, people may even ridicule or demean you for thinking of yourself as a hero. Those who are hiding out in cowardice want company! In addition, you may have your own inner blocks to imagining that you can make a difference. You may think you do not count as much as those of a different gender, race, family background, income level, or level of accomplishment. Perhaps you do not see yourself as being as talented, smart, strong, or advantaged enough to matter to the world. If so, you run the risk of giving away your power and letting others carry the day, while you sink into the background. If you do so, it is not only you who loses; the society loses, because the gift only you can bring to the transformation of the kingdom will be lost.

Your own self-doubt can be reinforced by people who have a strong need for control. Controlling heroic people is a bit like herding cats. Therefore, bosses, psychologists, teachers, politicians, and even friends who want to get their own way may discourage the journey in others. Groups can discourage people from taking themselves seriously because they want to maintain group solidarity. The fear is that the heroic journey encourages individualism (which it does), so that heroes will not be loyal to the group. In fact, people who are on their journeys can be excellent group members because they are willing to stand their ground against the lowest-common-denominator tendency of group thinking. Groups in which people recite the party line tend to operate at an intelligence level well below that of the individuals involved. However, when a group encourages its members to share their real wisdom, the collective intelligence is likely to surpass that of any individual.

Sometimes people are suspicious of the heroic idea because they have anachronistic notions of what heroism means. They think of the hero in terms of the single, heroic act involving enormous risk—like saving someone from a burning building. Or they consider people to be heroes only if they achieve something extraordinary—for example, winning a gold medal in the Olympics or a Nobel Prize. In fact, such modes of heroism are rare. The first is a necessity born out of extreme conditions; the second results from exceptional talent combined with favorable conditions and great effort. Moreover, it is important to remember that heroism is not the same as celebrity. No matter how much we enjoy following the lives of the rich and famous, we know that the world is affected more deeply by quiet, even invisible acts of integrity, kindness, and generosity than by fame and fortune.

When we define heroism as larger than life (or at least larger than our lives), we project it outside ourselves, expecting, for example, our political and organizational leaders (and sometimes also therapists, mentors, and spouses) to prove their worth—heroism—by saving us from difficulty. When they fail or when we see their vulnerable side, we turn on them; we become increasingly cynical as, one by one, our saviors let us down. The truth is, these are not the times for the great man or woman to save us; these are the times for each of us to do his or her own part.

THE EVERYDAY HEROISM OF ORDINARY PEOPLE

Heroism does not require us to live up to a larger-than-life image of the hero as superman or superwoman, only to become burned out, exhausted, and demoralized. Real heroism is not showing that you can handle anything and everything that comes your way. Rather, it is doing your own part, however humble that might be. Indeed, the heroic journey does not require you to become something greater than you are. It merely requires absolute fidelity to your own authentic path.

Anytime we say that "someone should do something about" whatever problem is bothering us, we are giving away our own heroic power. Of course, we do so because the problems seem so overwhelming and we do not feel powerful enough to live up to the larger-than-life images of the hero we have in our heads. But the reality is that if we all contribute, no one has to do anything quite so extraordinary! Think of walking along a sidewalk littered with trash. It may seem overwhelming to clean up the whole neighborhood, but it's easy enough to clean up after yourself and the immediate area in front of where you live.

Many of us also are aware of the danger of identifying the heroic only with the public world of achievement. We know the problem inherent in wanting to make a difference, because we have seen people—perhaps ourselves included—who are so obsessive about making a mark on the world that they have no meaningful private lives. The day of the award dinner honoring them for their great contributions to society, their spouse leaves them because they are never home and their chronically neglected child is caught shoplifting.

Heroism in an achievement-oriented culture includes holding out against workaholism, so that we can be good parents, neighbors, and citizens and so that we can "have a life." It also requires us to take time to go inward and reflect and time to move outward to follow our genuine curiosity and interests, so that we can find our own wisdom and depth. Most of us have read about too many wealthy, successful people living lives of quiet desperation who confuse success, by itself, with the heroic ideal. Therefore, the kind of heroism detailed here holds out the promise that we can achieve the balance necessary to enjoy our lives, not be run by them.

THE RIPPLE EFFECT OF HEEDING THE CALL

Heroism is contagious—just as villainy is. I once was extremely touched by the story of a woman who had come to one of my workshops. She told me that not long ago before, she had been homeless and addicted to drugs. By what seemed to her the most improbable of accidents, she was panhandling on a corner near a drug treatment clinic. A counselor leaned out the window to read a few paragraphs at a time of *The Hero Within* to this poor, desperate soul. After each passage, this caring counselor would say something like: "The way you are today is just one stage of your journey. It is not how you will always be. You are not how you appear. You are a hero on a journey." Eventually, the young woman went inside, and by the time I met her was well into recovery. She had a job, an apartment, and, if her rosy cheeks were any indication, her health.

I was touched to be part, even a small part, of this woman's metamorphosis. Then I thought back to when I was in my early twenties. I was very different from the young woman in my workshop. If anything, I was too good, having grown up in a fundamentalist Southern family with little license for youthful experimentation. I had been taught a gender role that emphasized selfless sacrifice and a religious role that stressed being good and avoiding sin. Because we had little money, I believed it prudent to be cautious in life to avoid ending up poor. In college, I read Joseph Campbell's *The Hero with a Thousand Faces* and believed him when he said that heroes followed their own bliss. Doing so changed the course of my life.

When Campbell was in his twenties, he dropped out of graduate school because it was boring. He was cautioned by his elders and contemporaries to settle down and get a job. Instead, he spent five years playing in a jazz band and reading heroic myths from around the world. His books (not to mention Bill Moyers's wonderful television interviews) encouraged many people to claim their own journeys, setting in place a ripple effect whose limits are unknowable.

If you examine your life, you may notice that this same pattern has been true for you. A family member, a friend, a teacher—anyone at all—who has exemplified the heroic life blazes a path that makes yours easier. You also may notice that every time you take the risk to be true to your own soul—whether or not you name your action as heroic—your example helps others to do likewise. When you notice this pattern, it becomes easier to have absolute fidelity to your own path without fear that doing so is selfish. We can do nothing better for others than model the authentic life.

We all know that when people constrict and sacrifice their inner call to conventional wisdom, to ambition, or to addiction, their actions can cause harm that similarly radiates out, affecting their children, employees, and many others. We all are affected by life-denying as well as life-affirming patterns in the culture. The heroic task is to allow such life-defeating patterns to stop with us, instead of taking the easy road of excusing our own behavior by blaming our current actions on past influences.

When we strike out to face the unknown, it is quite natural to experience a combination of terror and exhilaration. In some versions of the ancient Grail stories, the seeker gets to a point at the top of a mountain from which the Grail castle can be seen off in the distance. There does not appear to be any way across. The hero looks down into the chasm below, which goes down for miles. He looks across to the other side, realizing that the space is much too wide to jump. Then he remembers an ancient Grail teaching that says to step out in faith. As he puts one foot out into what appears to be empty space, a bridge suddenly appears and he is saved. Similarly, when the Israelites, who were slaves in Egypt, left to find the promised land, the Red Sea parted, but not before Moses (and his sister, Miriam) stepped bravely forward, trusting they would not drown.

These stories sound very exotic and unlike our everyday lives, but they share in mythological language experiences that we all have. Anyone who has ever left a job or even school not knowing what would come next has put his or her foot out into the abyss. The same is true when we leave relationships that are not working for us; we leave not knowing if, or when, we will ever love again. It even is true when we let go of ideas that are not working, allowing ourselves to risk the terror of uncertainty until a new truth emerges. Fortunately, we all have access to six inner guides that, like the invisible bridge over the mountain chasm or the path between the waters of the Red Sea, can provide us with safe passage, even when the next step on our journey looks perilous indeed.

CHAPTER 1

Choosing Freedom: The Guides

> Let us then imagine archetypes as the deepest patterns of psychic functioning, the roots of the soul governing the perspectives we have of ourselves and the world. . . . They are similar to other axiomatic first principles, the models or paradigms that we find in other fields.
>
> —James Hillman, *Revisioning Psychology*

Most of us are slaves of the stories we unconsciously tell ourselves about our lives. Freedom begins the moment we become conscious of the plot line we are living and, with this insight, recognize that we can step into another story altogether. Our experiences of life quite literally are defined by our assumptions. We make up stories about the world and to a great degree live out their plots. What our lives are like, then, depends on the scripts we consciously or, more likely, unconsciously have adopted.

Each of the six archetypal perspectives described in this book is like the central character in its own movie, which has its own plot structure.

Archetype	Plot Structure	Gift
Orphan	How I suffered or how I survived	Resilience
Wanderer	How I escaped or found my own way	Independence
Warrior	How I achieved my goals or defeated my enemies	Courage
Altruist	How I gave to others or how I sacrificed	Compassion
Innocent	How I found happiness or the promised land	Faith
Magician	How I changed my world	Power

To discover which archetypal plots dominate your life, pay attention to your conversation for a few days, noticing the stories you tell yourself and others about what happens to you. Then notice which archetypes dominate in these recurring story lines.

You might think what six different people, each with a different archetype dominant in their lives, might say about going for a job interview but not getting the job. For example:

"It was so unfair. I was the most qualified candidate. You just can't win." (Orphan)

"Soon after I got there I realized I wouldn't like it there. It seemed so confining, I could hardly wait to escape." (Wanderer)

"I was definitely the best qualified candidate. I'm going to convince them to hire me." (Warrior)

"I felt really happy for the person who got the job." (Altruist)

"I'm sure the right job for me will be there at the right time." (Innocent)

"I didn't get the job, but I learned something very important about landing the position that really is right for me." (Magician)

As you can see, how you tell the stories about your life reflects your self-image and also predicts, to some extent, how much or how little you expect in the future.

The word "archetype" can seem intimidating to some. Actually, archetypes are nothing more than the deep structures in the psyche and in social systems. Scientists talk about the deep structures of nature as "fractals." For example, every snowflake is unique. Yet there is something similar in the deep structure of snowflakes that allows us to recognize them as snowflakes. Archetypes are fractals of the psyche. For instance, every person who displays the Warrior attributes of courage and valor is different—yet we recognize the Warrior essence in each.

You can think of archetypes as inner potentialities, allies, or guides that always are available to you. There are many more than the six described here. In fact, I have written other books with other configurations of archetypes: *Awakening the Heroes Within: Twelve Archetypes to Help Us Find Ourselves and Transform Our World* and *Magic at Work: Camelot, Creative Leadership, and Everyday Miracles*. Those discussed in this book preside over stages in the *heroic* journey, that is, the journey of finding and expressing your true self in a way that makes a genuine contribution to the world. These also are archetypes that appear not simply in our dreams, but during the day, in our waking action. They help us become successful and fulfilled and contribute to our families, workplaces, and communities.

The story goes like this. We all begin in infancy and early childhood as Innocents, trusting that we will be cared for and still in awe of the beauty of the world. Soon we fall from this state of grace, as Adam and Eve fell from the Garden of Eden. Being Orphans, we are forced to face disappointment and pain. From these experiences, we learn realism and how to tell the difference between guides and tempters.

Growing older, we often experience our lives as confining and limiting, even oppressive. As Wanderers, we take off to find ourselves and seek our fortunes. Then, as Warriors, we gain the courage to face our dragons and to develop the discipline and skill necessary to succeed in the world. As Altruists, we discover that our existence is more meaningful if we commit to something greater than ourselves by, for example, giving back to others and to life itself.

As returned Innocents, we can find the treasure of true happiness, once again trusting in the process of being alive. Finally, as Magicians, we become capable of transforming our lives and our kingdoms.

These same archetypes also help us with the major developmental tasks of the maturation process:

Archetype	Task
Orphan	Survive difficulty
Wanderer	Find yourself
Warrior	Prove your worth
Altruist	Show generosity
Innocent	Achieve happiness
Magician	Transform your life

Although quite a large number of archetypal plots may be available to us, most do not influence our development as much as these six. For an archetype to have a major impact upon our lives, some external duplication or reinforcement of the pattern must take place: an actual event in one's life and/or exposure to stories (books, movies, other people's real life events) that embody the plot within us. Therefore, both our personal histories and our culture influence the archetypes that will be dominant in our lives. The archetypes included in this book are active in our culture today. They are important not only to our individual journey, but to the future of democracy because they prepare us for life in a free society, where each of us must be capable of making wise choices—as individuals, parents, workers, and citizens.

HOW ARCHETYPES HELP YOU ON YOUR JOURNEY

Archetypes help us on our journey in *eight* major ways.

One: When an archetype is activated in your life, it provides a structure that makes immediate growth possible. When we feel frustrated and experience what is defined as failure, it is often because, without being aware of it, we are living a story in a way that is inappropriate to our current situation or untrue to who and how we are at heart. Tapping into other inner resources restores our ability to act effectively, even when faced with genuinely new challenges:

- Perhaps you have always been very independent and like to explore the world, but then you have a baby. Now you must sacrifice some of that desire for exploration in order to care for your child. To do it well, how can you access a more nurturing potential within yourself?
- Because of your technical competence and because you are a good team player, you have been very successful in your work—so much so that now you have risen to a major leadership position in your workplace. Your company is in a process of change, and everyone around you is in turmoil. You need to exercise power independently in order to lead them through

the turmoil—and you must do so without much support or help from colleagues. How can you tap into that spirit of independence and leadership?

• You are accustomed to being successful and in charge, but suddenly you find yourself in a situation you cannot control: perhaps you develop a very serious illness, your spouse walks out, your child dies in an accident, your company takes a nose dive, or your job is eliminated. How do you connect with the part of you that knows how to be okay when faced with a problem that is not something you can fix just by working harder, or longer, or even smarter?

• You have a relationship problem in which you see the world very differently from your friend, spouse, boss, or colleague. This difference in perception might even threaten the relationship itself. How do you learn to understand where someone else is coming from?

Each of these circumstances can be seen as a call to awaken an archetype that has been dormant in your life so far.

I remember as a child playing a game called "Chutes and Ladders." Players rolled the dice and then moved ahead slowly and incrementally, inching through the number of spaces thrown—except, of course, if you landed on a ladder or a chute. The ladder zoomed you toward the finish line with delightful speed, while the chute ruthlessly shot you back toward the starting line, undoing your former progress. Recently, I saw a science fiction film about wormholes in the universe, cosmic shortcuts through which a spaceship can move through space much faster than the speed of light.

Both of these examples can help us understand how archetypes work. If I want to develop courage, I can try persistently, gradually taking greater risks and incrementally becoming less afraid. Or I can call up the Warrior archetype within me (who offers me the power of the ladder or the wormhole). That Warrior, an inner ally, is in touch with the accumulated fighting power of all the warriors who ever have been. Put another way, that inner archetypal Warrior holds the full potential of the Warrior as evidenced in my time. Although I still may have to learn skill, practice discipline, and differentiate between courage and bravado, through the archetype I can gain the Warrior's gifts much faster than if that archetype did not already exist within me. My task is simply to awaken that energy and find my expression of it.

It also is important to realize that under stress, any of us can be taken over temporarily by an archetype, since we have within us its entire negative as well as positive potential. We see this archetypal possession by the Warrior in those extreme cases in which a person "loses it," gets a gun, and goes on a shooting spree. More typically, we see it in lawsuits or corporate competition in which people begin to act as if they are at war with their opponent. The only help for this archetypal possession is consciousness. Understanding archetypes and their positive manifestations operates as a kind of psychological inoculation against their sides (which are often called shadow sides); by being exposed to archetypes and becoming aware of how they operate in us, we can learn to balance, and sometimes even supplant, their more negative aspects. Anything we repress, including archetypes, forms a shadow that can possess us in its negative or even demonic form. Freedom comes with consciousness. I encourage you to think of archetypes as inner allies who can help you to grow and to develop in definable ways, as long as you remain awake and responsible for your actions as they influence you.

Another helpful way to view archetypes is to look at parallels between the ways archetypes work in the psyche and how software works on our computers. My word processing program can help me write a book, but it cannot help me do my taxes or design a house. For either of those, I need a different software package.

Similarly, the Warrior archetype can help me fight a war or even close a deal, but it cannot help me learn to care for others or to be intimate with them. For that, I need to access my Altruist archetype.

Furthermore, I actually might have software packages on my hard drive but not know how to access them for specific use. In this case, they may be useful to me someday, but they are not at the moment. Similarly, the inner allies described here are in you right now—at least potentially. As you read through the book, you may recall times when you have lived out their stories. You also may notice an ally or two you have not expressed in your life thus far. Reading about your inner potential with an awareness of the dynamics of archetypes helps you to access one when you need it and to understand the behavior and motivations of others influenced by these patterns in humanity.

Two: Archetypes help you grow and develop. We all know that software packages are upgraded continually. The program on which I am writing this book, I have learned, is about to become outmoded; an even more advanced version is now available. Similarly, archetypes also develop, but in a somewhat different way. As archetypes are expressed in our lives, they evolve as we do. For example, Attila the Hun was once considered the epitome of the Warrior archetype. Today, given the level of his ruthlessness, he would have been charged with war crimes. Now, we are more likely to respect the martial arts teacher who knows how to block an assailant without unduly hurting him. In fact, the more common advanced form of the Warrior in our culture today—in the corporate world or on the playing field—replaces actual violence with competition. At this level, the Warrior substitutes a laser focus on the goal for any undue concern with a competitor. Thus, archetypes also help us to evolve as different inner allies awaken in us.

Three: Understanding the archetypes can help you make peace with your life. Many of us have ideas of who we should be that are at odds with how we are. Different archetypes dominate at different stages in our lives—and in different situations. Each gives a gift. When we stop beating ourselves up for not living up to how we think we should be, we can begin to notice what gifts we have developed.

For example, a woman complained to me about feeling like a failure. She kept exploring new options and never maintained any commitments. Thus, she had neither career success nor a husband and 2.4 children. As we discussed this, however, she began to realize that her true soul hunger always had been for adventure. She had sacrificed other possibilities for the Wanderer archetype's emphasis on independence and the chance to try new things. She came to see that although she had not lived the kind of life she thought she should have, she actually had exactly the life she really wanted. Once she accepted her previous choices, of course, she also was able to make some new ones for her future.

Similarly, a young man regretted having his childhood cut short because of an abusive father. As he worked on these issues in therapy, he realized that he had gained the gifts of the Orphan archetype—realism, compassion, and empathy. As he put it, "I did not have the wrong life. It was my life, my movie. It produced who I am."

Four: Recognizing archetypes can provide you with the freedom to choose the life you want. Perhaps your life has been defined by the Warrior archetype. You can appreciate that this archetype has given you courage, taught you to take big risks, and made you competitive and ambitious enough to become very successful in a worldly way. At the same time, you are beginning to feel burned out, too one-sided: every challenge is a mountain to be climbed, every business deal a chance to make it big. You start noticing that you are spending little time with your family—except the time you spend trying to shape them up so they will amount to something.

You can appreciate the gift of the Warrior without thinking that it defines who you are. Gaining an awareness of other archetypes helps you to awaken other possibilities within yourself. Perhaps you want to awaken the Wanderer and take some time to explore what you really want at this time in your life. Or perhaps it would be more satisfying to move to the Altruist and give up the focus on achievement for a time in favor of becoming more generous and caring.

In addition, the ability to determine which archetype is operating within you can save you from a bad job match, or it can help you to know whether to stay, leave, or try to change the situation. For example, Sally works as a nurse in a large hospital. The Altruist archetype is strong in her. She currently is suffering because managed care, with its Warrior focus on the bottom line, has undercut the quality of patient care. If she operates entirely out of her Altruist's motivation, all she can do is give more and more of herself to compensate for the Altruist deficit in the organization, until she burns out. She realizes she can either awaken her Wanderer archetype to seek a more satisfying environment for her work or develop her own Warrior and organize the nurses to fight for change in the system. In this case, she decides that fighting would create an overload for her, so she opens up to the adventure of finding out what else she might do or how else she might be.

Roberta, on the other hand, dislikes her Warrior-archetype insurance company, but recognizes that her distaste comes from her own almost total lack of warrioring ability. She decides to stay in order to learn from this environment how to activate her inner Warrior.

Five: Recognizing archetypes can help you achieve balance and personal fulfillment. Anytime we feel our lives are out of balance, it means that the archetype or archetypes currently dominating our behavior no longer coincide with those active in our inner lives. To correct our course, we can go inward and observe the yearnings that are our first indication that some new aspect of consciousness wants to be expressed. For instance, perhaps the Altruist archetype has been dominant in your life for some time. At first, you gained great satisfaction from giving to others. Now, however, some part of you feels dissatisfied. You wonder when it will be your turn. Your Wanderer wants time for self-exploration, creative expression, and just hanging out. Listening to that inner voice allows you to adjust your behavior to more accurately reflect your inner truth.

When your outer behavior matches the archetypes active within, you will feel a sense of meaning and fulfillment and no longer experience your life as out of balance. People today tend to define the balance issue as a product of external factors. For example, we blame the boss who makes us work overtime. However, that person cannot really control us. He or she might be able to hire or fire us, but the boss cannot physically chain us to the desk and whip us into submission. Actually, we are being controlled by buying into the belief that we have to sacrifice essential parts of ourselves—or our children—to succeed upon accepted terms.

I vividly remember giving a speech to such a large group that questions from the audience had to be written down on cards and submitted. I opened one card that said: "I have been taking care of people all my life. When will it be my turn? I'm eighty years old." My answer was: "Right now!"

After my speech, I counseled the man who submitted this question. As we talked, we realized that he thought it was the outside world that always made him be the responsible one. But that was not the whole truth. His dominant archetype for most of his life had been the Altruist. This inner Altruist sided with outside voices and helped him to keep his Wanderer shut down. In his eighties, he realized that he needed to take control of his life and embark upon that long awaited journey of self-discovery.

Six: Awareness of the archetypal plot lines that determine your life can give you the freedom to avoid making mistakes—or making the same mistakes over and over. Perhaps the Orphan archetype has been activated in your life many times. You have been abandoned, betrayed, and victimized. As a result, you have become very cautious. You enter a situation and get that old feeling. Quickly you recognize that you are about to get conned. Now you simply walk away and refuse to play! Or if you don't, at least you notice more consciously than before the pattern of victimization that unfolds. Noticing this allows you to walk away the next time. At some point, when the cosmos offers us one more similar challenge, we can say no—refuse the date, the job, the friendship and move on down the road to learn a new lesson.

Many of us lose our center when we begin to reexperience a new version of the archetypal plot that was most difficult for us in our family of origin. For example, my family was dominated by the Altruist archetype, so we were always generous and nice to other people as well as to each other. This kind of upbringing often encourages compassionate behavior, but typically it also suppresses people's awareness of what they want for themselves. So when I enter an environment in which altruism seems required, I immediately fear people will expect me to take care of them—at my expense.

We can reenter an archetypally similar situation as many times as it takes to move to a higher level of the archetype. The gift for me of taking several jobs in organizations with Altruist values is that I was forced to learn boundaries and to give no more than is suitable for me. I also had to learn not to care overly much if others held it against me when I refused to sacrifice myself unnecessarily for their benefit.

If you develop an understanding of your inner mythic landscape, you also can recognize the kinds of people who are likely to be able to manipulate you. For example, one woman realized that the Altruist archetype was very dominant in her life: she never met a person in need whom she did not yearn to help. A couple of years before, a younger woman preyed on this vulnerability and convinced her to sign over control of part of her business. The Altruist within her was so busy trying to save this younger woman, it took her a year or more before she even realized that she had been conned. However, now she is conscious of this weakness. She still helps people, but she has antennae that alert her when she is likely to be taken advantage of by them.

Seven: Archetypal recognition can help you better understand others and how they see the world. We can use archetypal insights to increase our ability to get along with our bosses, co-workers, spouses, partners, children, and parents. We can do this simply by recognizing the archetypes that dominate our cognitive maps. If I try to share with my husband and he always has to have the last word, it helps me to realize that the Warrior is present. Rather than trying to change him, I might remind him that we are on the same team—and we succeed or fail together. Thus, he has no reason to triumph at my expense.

If my child is feeling sorry for himself and (unfairly) blames me, I do not have to become defensive. I simply can empathize with his (Orphan) feelings of powerlessness and listen while he vents. If my boss expects me to pull rabbits out of hats every day, I can see the Magician at work and, if I need it, ask her to share her secrets for juggling so many balls in the air at one time.

Appreciating archetypal difference is extremely useful in dealing with very difficult people. For example, if your mother-in-law drives you crazy because she engages in nonstop complaining, you may see in her the negative aspects of the Orphan (self-pity) and the Altruist (giving beyond her means and then getting bitter about it). You may not be able to change her behavior completely, but you can do active listening to show her you hear her pain and also thank her profusely every time she does something for you. If she feels heard enough, she just might make small talk.

Similarly, if your boss criticizes you nonstop, that may be evidence of the Warrior's worry that someone may let the team down. He will stay on your case until he is satisfied that you are smart enough and tough enough to handle things on your own. This can be particularly annoying if you are a woman or a man of color and the boss is male and white. It will feel like racism or sexism (which to a lesser or greater degree it is). However, if you call it, he may see you as the enemy and go after you. Therefore, it is helpful to anticipate his concerns and let him know you are totally on top of the situation. Think of him as a coach and let him know when you've "got it," so he can go on to worry about some other perceived threat to your organization's success.

Eight: Understanding the archetypal basis for the ways in which people see the world cannot only make you smarter, but also help you see beyond the unconscious bias scholars and journalists often bring to their work. Until recently, historians wrote primarily about military and political events—events important to the Warrior archetype. We can see a similar Warrior bias in journalists who provide political coverage focusing on the "horse race" rather than the policy issues at stake. Some politicians seeking to communicate truths outside the Warrior paradigm have experienced such frustration that they try to circumvent the news media and go directly to the people by means of public events and Internet communications. Often, it seems as if scholars and journalists are consciously trying to suppress information. However, the truth is more banal. They are being true to what they see—and what they can see is controlled by the lens of the Warrior archetype. To the Warrior, the overarching questions are who is winning and what tactics are they employing to do so. It therefore makes perfect sense that the Warrior-possessed media focus on these questions.

The more archetypes that are activated in your life, the more truth you are able to understand. As you get better at decoding an archetypal bias, you can make inferences that move beyond scholarly and media biases to figure out what really is happening in the world. Scholars and journalists who expand their own archetypal horizons can create a force working against the regressive undertow that currently distorts events and holds back the expansion of consciousness evidenced in the population in general.

Experts in leadership development understand how important it is that our organizational leaders see the world clearly, so currently they counsel paradigm vigilance (that is, questioning our basic assumptions about how we see the world). A good practice to ensure that you are seeing all sides of an issue is to identify the archetypes that have been speaking through the arguments you have considered and discover the other archetypal positions that might be of help.

If we fail to understand the archetypal bases of many so-called truths, it is easy for any of us to mistake our projections for reality and, in the process, devalue people who see the realities we miss. Then, it is as if we are caught in a maze, moving in circles, while others forge ahead.

Archetypes exist in us whether we recognize them or not. If we do not notice them, they can take us over, substituting their own limited reality for the more infinitely variable and interesting possibilities that actually exist in the world. That historians wrote exclusively about politics and battles at one time does not mean that other rather colorful and exciting things didn't happen. The relatively new focus on social history restores a record of what life was like for people who were neither in the government nor fighting wars. The results are exciting.

The same is true with our lives. One wonderful by-product of identifying the archetypes active in our lives is that we no longer mistake an archetypal perspective for reality. Thus, we are clearer in our thinking and more open in our understanding of the world as it is—beyond how we may be predisposed to see it. As Shakespeare's Hamlet puts it, "There are more things in heaven and earth, Horatio, than are dreamt of in your philosophy."

LAST THOUGHTS

The chapters that follow describe the archetypal stages and tasks essential to the hero's journey. As you read them, you may notice which archetypes have been most active in your life up to now, where you see signs of these archetypes in the people and in the events around you, and which archetype or archetypes might help you to attain greater freedom and fulfillment than you now possess. Some readers might prefer to take a break at this point to complete the Heroic Myth Self-Tests (Appendix A). If you do so, you may wish to read first those chapters that describe the archetypes most active in your life and later pick up the chapters that are less relevant to your present situation.

However, some readers have shared with me that the chapters on archetypes they were at first disinterested in—or even averse to—proved to be most helpful in advancing their journeys. Especially for experienced journeyers, it often is the untried and even unloved aspects of ourselves that hold the greatest power to liberate us.

While this book serves as a map to help orient you to your journey and to recognize your commonality with heroes in all times and places, remember that each one of us also is unique. Because no map can show you the part of your journey that is most you, it is essential that you trust totally your own process. As Don Juan explains to Carlos Castaneda in *A Separate Reality*, whatever path you choose, it leads nowhere. It is no disgrace to try a single path as many times as you need, for there is only one test of a true path—that it brings you joy. The only way out is through, and the only person who knows what is right for you—is you.

CHAPTER 2

Surviving Difficulty:
From the Innocent to the Orphan

> Heaven lies about us in our infancy!
> Shades of the prison-house begin to close
> > Upon the growing Boy
> At length the man perceives it die away,
> And fade into the light of common day.
>
> —William Wordsworth, *Ode: Intimations of Immortality*
> *from Recollections of Early Childhood*

The hero experiences, and learns from, adversity.

Have you ever felt like a motherless child? Have you been abandoned, betrayed, neglected, or abused? Do you sometimes wonder why so many difficult things happen to you? Do you sometimes even let yourself down by failing to live up to your own dreams and aspirations?

Or have you been very fortunate, experienced little difficulty, yet your life feels a bit flat? Do you have a sense that you could have more vitality, more depth, or more passion in your life? Have you noticed that sometimes people who seem less privileged have more vitality, soul, or intensity? Perhaps you had no role models for vibrant, heroic living.

Either way, this chapter is for you.

Many of us are encouraged by parents, teachers, friends, and insurance companies to try, throughout life, to remain as safe and secure as possible. Self-help books, correctly pointing out difficulties that result from dysfunctional households, imply that life works only when we come from healthy, moral, and stable families. The accompanying inference is that you have less chance of making a difference if you did not have every advantage growing up.[1]

Literature and myth, attuned as they are to the truth of the human soul and spirit, give us a very different message. Few if any heroes come from ideal circumstances—and when they do, they leave them. The classic tragic hero, Oedipus, was left by his father on a hillside to die when he was a newborn. David Copperfield lived in an oppressive orphanage. King Arthur, an illegitimate son of royalty, was raised by foster parents in ignorance of his true parentage. Cinderella had a wicked stepmother who treated her like a servant.

In Hinduism, Krishna was saved from his uncle, the king, who would have killed him, because his parents exchanged him for the daughter of a herdsman. He was raised by stepparents in relative poverty. The Buddha was born to royal overprotective parents, but his true journey did not begin until he left the castle to pursue life among the unprotected, unprivileged masses. In Greek myth, Demeter, the goddess of agriculture, did not experience her full power until her daughter was abducted and taken to the underworld. Then, for the first time, Demeter felt excruciating pain and humiliating powerlessness, after which she founded the Eleusinian mysteries to teach the secrets of life and death to humanity.

If you have had an experience where something intimate was exposed or where you stood unprotected, abandoned, betrayed, or victimized, do not despair. Instead, understand it as a mythic event calling you to the quest.

FROM INNOCENT TO ORPHAN:
THE FORTUNATE FALL

Many cultures have myths recounting a golden age to which people yearn to return. In the Judeo-Christian tradition, it is the story of Adam and Eve's expulsion from the Garden of Eden. At first, Adam and Eve lived blissfully in the garden. God took care of their every need, but warned them not to eat of the Tree of Knowledge of Good and Evil. The serpent tempted Eve and she ate an apple from that tree. When she offered it to Adam, he also ate. As a result, they were ushered out of paradise. After that, Adam had to make a living by the sweat of his brow, and Eve had to suffer in childbirth. Once they were immortal, but now they knew they would die. The biblical promise, however, is that someday humankind will reenter paradise. This happens not only through the expiation of suffering and hard work but also, paradoxically, through knowledge. First we must fall from innocence so that later we can return to it at a more sophisticated and less childish level.

The story of Adam and Eve clearly has archetypal elements. Not only do similar stories exist in most cultures and religions, but in our own culture, even people who are not practicing Jews or Christians have an experience like the Fall. It is a developmental stage in growing up. For many, it comes in the form of disillusionment with their parents. For example, all little children idolize their parents. But what if a parent abuses you, either sexually, emotionally, or physically? What if you are neglected and ignored? What if your parents are never home, or when they are home, they numb out with alcohol, drugs, or television? For you, the fall from childlike innocence is extreme and painful.

For some whose parents who are better balanced and healthier, the initial fall is milder. For me, it occurred when my father lost a business and became very depressed, distant, and, on occasion, harsh. I realized, to my dismay, that my parents did not know how to teach me a way to thrive in the world. They did not know how to do this for themselves either, of course. In a world that changes rapidly, it is a rare set of parents who actually can groom the next generation for what is to come.

Growing up always includes the dawning realization that parents are not perfect. The Innocent feels entitled to the perfect mother and father and feels terribly cheated when that is not the case. Inevitably, we will have friends who disappoint us, lie to us, and talk behind our backs. We will see teachers and other authority figures abuse power. We also will realize that everyone is not treated equally in the world or with due respect and that, beyond social injustice, horrible tragedies happen to some individuals in their everyday lives. People are maimed, experience chronic illnesses of all types, or die. They lose their great love, or their faith in love, or their mind.

There is a certain level of danger inherent in the hero's journey that awakens our souls. The ego desperately wants safety. The soul wants to live. The truth is, we cannot lead a real life without risk. We do not develop depth without pain.

Many people have told me that all their life decisions have had the single goal of keeping safe. Inside, they feel empty because they are not living their lives fully. Then something happens. They are diagnosed with cancer, their child dies, their spouse leaves, or that seemingly secure job is eliminated—and suddenly they realize that they cannot escape life. As they become more conscious, they often conclude that nothing they feared was actually as painful as the inner despair they experienced when they were holding back from living their lives.

When we try to avoid the journey, it captures us.

EXPERIENCING THE FALL IN EVERYDAY LIFE

Not all of us experience the Orphan archetype with the same intensity. Some people simply encounter less difficulty in their lives than others. One way to tell whether you have just moved through these stages in a light and easy way or are stuck somewhere along the path is to examine how you feel about others who express characteristics of the Orphan. Those who have taken this part of the journey generally have a genuine sense of empathy for people who are in trouble or in pain. If you find yourself being angry or blaming toward those who have been victimized in some way, who are poor or otherwise in distress, it is likely that you are repressing your own inner Orphan and the powerful gifts inside.

Conversely, if you frequently feel powerless and do not know where to turn, it may be important to seek help going through the Orphan phase of the journey. Ideally, none of us should have to experience our pain alone. Indeed, it is part of the gift of the Orphan to accept that we all are wounded and we all are partial. Therefore, we need each other—not only because we want comfort and support, but also because each of us has a piece of the puzzle and no one has all the answers. Particularly if your life has been very difficult or if you come from a dysfunctional family, it may be essential to get the help of a professional and/or a support group as you go through this part of the journey.

Too many people today are arrested at the more primitive manifestations of the Orphan archetype because they are unable to acknowledge to themselves and to others how and when they feel powerless, or lack skills, or need assistance. The more depriving our lives have been, the more likely we are to expect others to take advantage of our plight and cause further oppression. At best, this can help us to avoid further abuse. At worst, it keeps us from asking for the aid we need. Moreover, if we have consistently received the message that we are sick, bad, crazy, stupid, or ugly, we learn to believe that we do not deserve the best and the most of life.

We also are thrown out of innocence whenever people and institutions we have taken for granted refuse to serve as our security blankets. Both men and women, in childlike innocence, tend to assume that their spouse or partner either wants or should want to do the things that make them comfortable. Women often unconsciously assume that husbands are there to lift heavy boxes, fix the car, and make money. Men often assume that wives are there to provide nurturance, cook, arrange the social life, and care for the children. A woman may feel betrayed if her husband declares his own needs, decides to drop out, and quits a well-paying job or leaves for a woman who makes him happier—especially if she has sacrificed her own needs to be the traditional wife. A man may feel equally outraged when his wife decides she wants to devote herself to a demanding job or leave her husband to find herself, and the outrage is intensified when either spouse has ignored genuine needs to provide for the family.

Of course, marriage as an institution is designed to provide some security and continuity in life. It is painful for all when a marriage fails. Yet in the world today a radical change has been occurring. In the old system, it fundamentally did not matter if you were happy or not. The point was to do your duty. If you did so, marriages and families would be stable and people would have safety and security. Now, the very idea that we have a right to happiness leads people to feel their marital unhappiness and refuse to be numb. Experiencing deep dissatisfaction of the kind that can occur in marriages lacking foundational trust and love may motivate you to leave or to risk an honest look at yourself and your spouse and to work for change. The result, however, is that marriages do not (if they ever did) provide automatic, long-term security.

The same paradigm exists in the workplace. In earlier times, change often was very slow. Your role in society was determined by your sex, race, and class. Professions ran in families, which is why family names were often based on occupations. If your last name is Carpenter, your ancestors likely were carpenters. More recently, people found a company that provided security and expected to stay with it for their entire career, the assumption being that loyalty was rewarded with security. Or they started a family business to provide long-term independence and stability.

We have to know that this urge for security is basic to the Innocent. One way many people today are experiencing the Fall in life is recognizing that organizations do not provide the kind of security we expect from them. Even if we start our own business, the economy is changing so quickly that we cannot be certain the company will survive over time. Attempts to provide a safety net for people also are shaky. Social Security is at risk; limits have been set on welfare; and health insurance often is contingent on keeping one's job.

The Fall actually comes in waves throughout life. We can feel very grown-up and on our own, and then something happens. The following are a few examples people have shared with me recently:

- You have worked for a company for twenty years. You are competent, loyal, and hardworking—and they lay you off anyway.
- You have put your husband through graduate school, raised the children, bolstered his success—and, without warning, he leaves you for a trophy wife.
- You stayed at a job you hated to support your wife and children. You thought she appreciated your protecting her from the harsh "real world." Then she says you are boring and leaves you to find herself.
- You are a young person who has worked hard in school and done what your parents and teachers expected of you, assuming that would set you up for a good career, a home, and a family. Suddenly, you realize that jobs are scarce, housing prices are

out of sight, and it is unlikely you ever will be as well off as your parents are.

- You spent years in school preparing to be a physician or psychologist. You expected respect and a good life. Suddenly, managed care is limiting your pay, and a clerk in his or her twenties calls you by your first name and tells you what treatments you can and cannot provide to your patients or clients.

- You spent years in a religious or spiritual tradition that you thought would keep you safe. You believed that if you prayed, or meditated, or visioned just right, you would have what you needed. Then, suddenly, you lost your health or your money, or your religious leader was caught using power to gain sexual favors or money. Now your faith is undermined.

- You sacrificed all your life for your family. Now you are old and lonely and vulnerable and you want your children to take you in and care for you. Yet they are caught up in their work and family and have little time for you.

- You always have tried to be a very good person. Events occur that cause you to see that you have seriously compromised your principles. Suddenly, you do not trust yourself anymore. If you, who have tried to be so good, cannot be trusted entirely, you wonder, then who *is* trustworthy?

Sometimes, no matter how realistic we think we are, it is hard to keep up with the blows life deals us. Yet this is what growing up—at every stage of life—is all about.

SURVIVING IN A FALLEN WORLD

The Orphan is a disappointed idealist, and the higher the ideals about the world, the worse reality appears. Feeling like an orphan after the Fall is an exceptionally difficult mode. The world appears dangerous; villains and pitfalls are everywhere. Like a damsel in distress, the Orphan must cope with a hostile environment without appropriate strength or skills. It seems to be a dog-eat-dog world, where people are either victims or victimizers. Even villainous behavior may be justified as simply realistic, because the operative rule is "Do unto others before they do unto you." The dominant emotion of this worldview is fear and its basic motivation is survival.

This stage is so painful that people often escape from it by using various opiates: drugs, alcohol, work, consumerism, mindless pleasure. Or they may misuse relationships, work, or religion as a means to dull the pain and provide a spurious sense of safety. Ironically, such addictions have the side effect of increasing our sense of powerlessness and negativity; in the case of drugs and alcohol, they even foster distrust and paranoia.

We defend such escapes, when we resort to them, as reasonable strategies for coping with the human condition: "Of course I take a few drinks (pills, etc.) every day. It's a tough life. How else would I get through it?" And we believe it is not realistic to expect much of life. An employee might complain that work is drudgery. "I hate my job, but I have to feed my kids. It's just the way things are." A woman might simply assume that men "are just no good" and stay in a relationship in which she is emotionally or even physically battered because "he is better than most men." A man might complain that his wife nags, but then shrug it off with "that's just how it is with women."

The archetype of the Orphan is a tricky place to be. The Orphan's task is to move out of innocence and denial and learn that suffering, pain, scarcity, and death are an inevitable part of life. The anger and pain this engenders will be proportional to one's initial illusions. This Fall leads to realism, because the job of the Orphan is to develop realistic expectations about life. When people give up their original childlike expectations, they are likely to go to the other extreme and expect too little from life.

The Orphan's story is about a felt powerlessness, yet the Orphan's yearning for a return to a primal kind of innocence remains. This desire is childlike, whatever our age. We wish to have every need met by an all-loving mother or father figure. When others do not meet our needs, we may feel abandoned. The Orphan wants to live in a garden, safe and cared for, but instead feels dumped out into the wilderness, prey to villains and monsters. The Orphan's dilemma is about looking for people to care for us, about forgoing autonomy and independence to secure that care; it's even about trying to be the all-loving parent—to our lovers, our children, our clients, our constituents—anything to prove that that protection is or can be there.

After the Fall comes the long and sometimes slow climb back to trust and hope. The Orphan eventually must learn enough self-reliance to hold out against temptations to stay in negative or dehumanizing conditions. Most often, that cannot be done until we embark on a search for someone to take care of us. "Maybe there is no one, now, who will watch over me, but perhaps I can find someone." Some women look for a Big Daddy; some men look for the perfect nurturing wife; many look for the great political leader, the movement, the cause, or the million-dollar deal that will make everything all right. Virtually everyone fantasizes about winning the lottery.

REFUSING THE FALL

In a very challenging economic climate, employees may place all their faith in a CEO, expecting him or her to save them. Sometimes, when market conditions or other factors are unfavorable, there simply is nothing the CEO can do. However, I have seen employees respond like an angry lynch mob determined to take revenge on their former "savior." In similar ways, the media sets up our political leaders by first portraying them as larger than life, then tearing them down.

Some people who have been victimized have learned to use their pain manipulatively—to get others to feel sorry for them or to feel guilty and hence to do what they want. Members of oppressed groups can play on other people's liberal guilt and thus gain a sense of control. Using their pain as a vehicle for manipulation, they can divert themselves with making others uncomfortable and remain oblivious to the fact that their own situation is not improving.

We also see an epidemic of rage expressed in frivolous lawsuits. Rather than accept that a loved one really was mortally ill, some people sue the doctor. Rather than recognize culpability when they get fired, some people gear up to sue their employer. One such woman had taken legal action against every employer she listed in her professional résumé! Every time someone called her to task for nonperformance, she sued them. (While many lawsuits are necessary and justified, I am talking here about the kind that people engage in to distract themselves from having to face the hard facts of life.)

The successful resolution of the Orphan dilemma often depends on getting over the child's sense of entitlement. If I believe I was entitled to a happy childhood and I did not have one, I can spend the rest of my life feeling cheated and never get on with living. If I believe I have a right to a perfect life, any hardship can leave me bitter and unhappy.

THE PSEUDO-HERO

The experience of the Fall is hurting and yearning for rescue and discovering that no one either will or can do anything about it. We can respond to this with anger, or we can face our real vulnerability. It is, of course, embarrassing for most adults to feel so fragile—even for a short while. After all, we are supposed to be mature, independent, and self-sufficient, so most people who are in this place cannot acknowledge it, even to themselves. Usually, they are "just fine," but in fact they feel very lost and empty, even desperate. The roles they play often are varieties of the archetypes that inform the next stages of the journey; however, they may get form right, but not the substance.

If they are attracted by the role of the Altruist, they will be unable—no matter how hard they work at it—to sacrifice truly out of love and care for others, and their sacrifice will not be transformative. If they sacrifice for their children, the children then must pay and pay and pay—by being appropriately grateful, by living the life the parents wish *they* had lived, in short, by sacrificing their own lives in return. It is this pseudo-sacrifice, which really is a form of manipulation, that has given sacrifice a bad name.

Virtually everyone these days seems to understand how manipulative the sacrificing mother can be, but another, equally pernicious version is the man who works at a job he hates, says he does it for his wife and children, and then makes them pay by deferring to him, protecting him from criticism or anger, and making him feel safe and secure in his castle. Such a man nearly always requires his wife to sacrifice her own journey in his drama of martyrdom. In these two cases and in others, the underlying message is: "I've sacrificed for you, so don't leave me; stay with me, feed my illusions, help me feel safe and secure."

Codependence is also a defense against feeling the Orphan's feelings. Rather than deal with our own pain, we focus on rescuing others. In the process, we are likely to stay in a relationship in which neither person can ever really grow up and be successful. Here the underlying message is: "Give my life meaning by allowing me to care for you."

Instead of the pseudo-Altruist role, Innocents refusing the Fall may act out the shadow side of the Warrior, becoming the victimizer: looting, raping, battering, exploiting, polluting, using others. This is the classic stance of "I take whatever I want because I am strong and I can." Or they may become workaholics, using work to distract them from the vulnerability they are afraid to face. In Jungian psychology, the shadow is formed by repression.

If we do not express the positive side of an archetype, it can take us over, but in its negative form.

With recent cultural permission to "follow our bliss" and find ourselves, we also find the emergence of the pseudo-Wanderer, whose narcissistic self-involvement revolves around one self-improvement project after another—each promising a return to paradise.

Paradoxically, the real heroic response of the Orphan experiencing the Fall is to feel our own pain, disappointment, and loss—that is, to accept being an Orphan. This requires real grieving and an honest admission that we need others in our life. It ultimately is more heroic to risk acknowledging that "I am in pain and I do not know what to do" than to bluff and/or take our disappointment out on others.

Some years ago, I was on staff at a workshop with a psychotherapist who did deep cathartic work with participants. We cried, beat on pillows, and told the stories of the ways we had been disappointed, used, and victimized and how we felt needy and powerless. This was empowering because we lost our fear of going into our pain or rage. It did not need to seem so big anymore. We also learned that we did not have to repress our pain or act out that rage on others. Expressing it in safe surroundings was enough.[2]

Like many other helping professionals, I discovered subsequently that people, particularly those with abusive backgrounds, do not necessarily have to relive every trauma they have experienced. Doing so is just too painful. It is enough to get beyond denial to express the pain they still feel. Then it is possible to experience their genuine feelings now, in the moment, without holding their breath for fear of lapsing back into intolerable feelings of terror, sadness, or despair. Reliving everything can retraumatize people. In such instances, being able to remind oneself that "that was then and this is now" can allow the journey to proceed and other inner allies to surface.[3]

Gaining such skills for dealing with past traumas allows the Orphan stage of any experience of the Fall to be intense, manageable, and relatively short! Some people, I have noticed, tend to want to linger here, acting out their anger or using their victimization as an excuse not to take on the normal responsibilities of adult life. It is important to keep balance in the psyche. The Fall, which is the subject of this chapter, is never all that is going on. Some people need to be reminded that the Orphan is just one archetype among many. We move on to other stages of the journey when we develop a genuine, grounded, and realistic sense of hope.

BALANCING WARINESS WITH HOPE

The growing-up process ultimately requires the development of "street smarts." What we need to grow up with is not so much warnings about how bad the world is, but practical advice and experience in dealing with a fallen world. If we are lucky, our parents, teachers, and friends helped us to:

- recognize the difference between tempters and guides;
- distinguish between safe and unsafe environments;
- develop an appropriate balance between skepticism and openness;
- know how to ask for help in ways that increase the likelihood that it will be forthcoming;
- recognize the appropriate balance of give and take in personal and business relationships;
- learn from our mistakes without blaming ourselves for making them;
- expect to be treated well and have enough empathy for others to reciprocate in kind; and
- avoid traumatizing situations, or recover from them quickly if they occur.

Many of us, however, did not have such favorable upbringings. Some of us come from very dysfunctional or even abusive families; some come from overly protective families that failed to prepare us for the world; and some had parents who simply were not that capable of realism themselves. In such cases, once we do acknowledge our pain, keeping hope alive can be a real challenge.

Samuel Beckett's existential drama *Waiting for Godot*[4] touches audiences because something about it is quintessentially human. Estragon and Vladimir are waiting by the roadside for Godot (God, or whatever it is we hope will rescue us) to come. So little happens, their life is so devoid of interest, that it is excruciating to watch them. As night falls each day, a boy appears and tells them that Godot cannot make it but surely will come tomorrow. Only two days are enacted in the play, but it is clear that in between these two days they have been waiting a very long time. Toward the conclusion of the play, Vladimir says, "We'll hang ourselves tomorrow. . . . Unless Godot comes." When Estragon asks, "And if he comes?" Vladimir answers, "We'll be saved." Finally, Estragon and Vladimir decide to leave, but do not move.

Sitting in the audience, one wants to scream, "Get a life! Get a job! Find a girlfriend! Do anything, but do not just keep waiting for rescue that will never come!" Nonetheless, this play moves us precisely because Vladimir and Estragon cling to hope even when their lives are empty and rescue seems unlikely. Hope keeps people alive in concentration camps as well as in any number of abusive or dehumanizing situations. Most of us have no idea how many people spend their lives with so little sense of joy or meaning that they fight off suicide every day.

Once people overcome denial and face the reality of their lives, the next danger is despair. Warriors might be utterly frustrated that Orphans do not take their lives into their own hands, but many of us are not ready to do so. What keeps people alive when they have little to live for is simply the hope of rescue. It is no use telling those who feel powerless to grow up and take responsibility for their lives if they do not believe they are capable of it! First they must be provided with some hope that they *will* be cared for.

The stories, then, that the culture has evolved for the Orphan are rags-to-riches plots and very conventional love stories. The subtheme of these plots is that suffering will be redemptive and will bring back the absent parent. In Charles Dickens's novels, an orphan suffers poverty and mistreatment until finally it is discovered that he is the long lost heir to a huge fortune. Reunited with his father, he will be cared for forever. In the classic version of the romantic love story (for instance, Samuel Richardson's *Pamela, or Virtue Rewarded*), the heroine suffers greatly—sometimes from poverty, but almost always from assaults on her virtue. If she manages not to lose her virginity, she is rewarded with marriage to a rich man, a Sugar Daddy who very clearly is a father substitute. The happy ending promises that she will be cared for the rest of her life. The romantic love myth and the rags-to-riches plot are often intertwined. In the traditional romantic love plot, the heroine finds not only true love, but also someone to support her.

The title character of F. Scott Fitzgerald's *The Great Gatsby* is motivated to make a fortune so that he may win the affections of Daisy, the rich and beautiful golden girl. In this characteristically modern novel, Daisy does not return his affections, he is murdered, and virtually no one attends his funeral. Yet what is compelling in the novel is the quality of hope that sustains him and that Fitzgerald suggests is endemic to the American dreams.

It is the hope that love or riches (or both) might be possible that frequently gets people to embark upon a quest. The "savior" can be a lover *or* it can be a business venture, a job, or professional training that might allow us to make enough money to purchase a sense of total security and control over our lives. The promise is that never again will we have to experience that terrible sense of powerlessness, of having needs—deep-seated survival needs—and being unable to meet them. Ideally, the journey itself provides experiences that can foster a sense of realism about life and its possibilities, that helps many avoid Gatsby's tragic fate.

When the Orphan archetype is active in our lives, we desperately want teachers who know all the answers; as patients, we want doctors or therapists to be all-wise and all-knowing and to "make it all better"; as lovers, we want to find the perfect mate and have a relationship that makes us happy without having to work at it. In our theology, we want to believe that if we are good, God will take care of us; if we meditate enough, we will have peace; or if we follow the rules, we will be safe. In our politics, we hope for a great leader, a compelling movement, a dynamic political party that will take care of our country's problems. As consumers, we are attracted by products that promise the quick fix: use this detergent and you will be a good mother; drive this car and gorgeous women will climb all over you; try this diet and men will find you irresistible.

Thus, at this stage, we can be deeply distressed if anyone criticizes a therapist, a case worker, a religion, or a political movement that provides our hedge against despair. It also is helpful to remember that no matter how sophisticated our thinking may be in other parts of our lives, in the part that wants rescue we will be at a fairly rudimentary level of cognitive development marked by absolutism and dualistic thinking.

The truth is, when we feel the most helpless, it can be very comforting to find some authority, program of action, or theory and put all our faith in it. It even helps to try a new diet or exercise plan, not only because good health makes us happier, but also because anything that focuses positive intention reinforces our faith in life.

When we feel entirely out of control, the simple decision to put faith and trust in another's hands can be liberating—especially if we place our trust in someone who warrants it. Furthermore, the daily discipline to be faithful to that decision is life affirming at this stage of the journey.

When we cast other people in the roles of saviors, however, difficulties do arise. Someone we believe to be larger than life inevitably will let us down. For example, our rescuer may not be wise enough or ethical enough to deserve our trust. Some people who set themselves up as rescuers do so not so much to help as to feel important and powerful. Moreover, when the Orphan archetype is active in one's life, it is natural to distrust oneself. In fact, Orphans generally believe deep down that their dilemma is their own fault. That means they often will put up with abuse, especially if they are told it is for their own good.

The reality is, people who take on rescuing roles really are Orphans too, on the inside. Playing the part of savior is a way of pretending that it is others, not themselves, who are troubled. You can recognize people like this because very quickly they begin to undermine your self-esteem, so that you will remain dependent on them. Typically, they play on your fears: without this religion, this form of therapy, this political movement, you will be lost in sin, hopelessly sick, or overrun by communists (or fascists or chaos).

Some men who initially seem dedicated to rescue eventually convince wives and girlfriends that no one else ever will love them and that they never could make it in the world on their own. Some women similarly convince husbands and boyfriends that they are so disgusting and impossible that no one else would put up with them. In such relationships, emotional abuse frequently escalates into violence.

In the ethics of care it is important to make certain that the rescuer is not using another to avoid his or her own pain. Supervision, support groups, and similar mechanisms that allow others to be privy to what is going on between the helper and the person being helped are critical in stopping such dysfunctional patterns.

No persons should be counseling others unless they (1) have been seriously engaged in doing their own work over time and (2) admit to being peers on the journey and share their own vulnerabilities. In fact, it is particularly helpful when dealing with Orphan issues to do so in peer groups or with the support of friends who also share their own vulnerabilities and pains. This decreases the chance that we will project the role of savior onto anyone and allows us to learn that everyone has strengths and weaknesses. Thus, it moves us out of seeing people dualistically—as those who have everything together and those who do not.

To move beyond the Orphan state of the journey, one first must fully *be* in it, and that means confronting one's own pain, despair, and cynicism. It also means mourning the loss of Eden, letting oneself know that there is no safety, that God (at least the childish notion of a "Daddy God") is dead. Of course, Orphans cannot do this all at once. Denial is a much underrated survival mechanism. We can face our pain only in proportion to our hope. Furthermore, denial generally protects us from feeling more pain at any given time than we can handle. In fact, for those of us who see ourselves as strong, together people, it often is only in retrospect that we realize how bad we really felt.

A QUESTION OF BLAME

The Orphan's dilemma is that she or he cannot resolve problems without assigning blame. Sometimes it works to believe that our suffering is our own fault, if it prompts us to change our lives in positive ways. Many of the world's religions foster this belief, telling us that "the wages of sin is death," that God destroys immoral civilizations and cities, or that our suffering is an example of karmic justice for our behavior in former lives.

The logic is simple: if it is our fault, then maybe we can do something about it. Otherwise, our suffering just seems capricious, and then where are we? Without hope! Some years ago I was talking to a six-year-old boy whose parents had just separated. He looked at me with big, serious eyes and said, "If they had just told me what was wrong, I know I could have done something about it." Later, I realized that this child felt that, in some nameless way, he was responsible for the failure of his parents' marriage. Believing that our suffering is our own fault is *not* helpful if it fails to give us a handle on how to do something about the situation. In such a case, it leads us to conclude that our pain is justified, so we stay in it longer than necessary.

Women, racial minorities, gays, the elderly—members of these groups will do nothing about discrimination if they consciously or unconsciously believe they are inferior and hence deserve unequal treatment. None of us can hold out against the pressure to work inhumanly long hours if we consciously or unconsciously believe we are inadequate, that we *should* be able to take the stress.

Once I taught an advanced college course that was not meeting the needs of one of the students, largely because it was too much of a stretch for her. About halfway through the semester, the student became hostile, so I asked her to meet with me. Because the course was designed to foster responsibility in students, its format changed significantly during the semester in response to their stated concerns. My hope in talking to this student was to get her to realize that at any time the course could have been different had she simply asked for what she wanted.

I learned an immense amount during our conversation. For one thing, I learned that some people ask for what they want by complaining. They know no other way. In this case, I simply had not understood the student's form of communication. I also learned about "fault." The student explained her anger by saying that at first she thought it was her "fault" that she was not learning, but then she realized it was my "fault"—that I was not teaching the class well. As we talked, I felt more and more frustrated. Finally, I realized that for her the situation *had* to be someone's fault—and better mine than hers. It could not be just a bad fit between a teaching method and one student.

I had wanted to teach her responsibility for her life—a responsibility that could lead her to drop the class or ask for what she needed. What I did not yet understand—and the reason I had not been able to help her—was that because she equated responsibility with fault and blame, my saying "you are responsible for your learning" could be heard only as an accusation that she was to blame for not understanding. She was not yet capable of taking such responsibility. She quite simply needed more help from me.

What *can* make movement happen for those who are immobilized by insecurity or self-recrimination? Love, hope, and the message that their suffering indeed is not their fault and that someone else who is not so powerless and lost and needy will help them. After exploring this process for a while, I have come to believe that a variety of contents for this message are useful for different people or for the same people in different situations. It is the *process* here that is important. For example, those in the Orphan mode can be helped by forms of religion that identify a cause outside the person for the difficulty—an evil force that can be blamed for people's ills and a savior (or a dogma or practice) that can change their lives. All liberation movements also begin here: unions, the women's movement, the men's movement, various civil rights movements, all must tell people that their oppression is not their fault. They also hold out the hope that collective effort can make a difference. Similarly, twelve-step programs begin the process of recovery by explaining that addiction is an illness, thus taking the onus off the individual addict. Moreover, even though individuals are not strong enough to conquer their addiction, a higher power, the group, and the program can save them.

In therapy, analysis, or friendship, you can encourage people to tell their stories in a way that helps them see that their pain comes from somewhere outside the self, that it is a result of early childhood trauma, social conditions, their parents, etc.—in short, that it is not their fault. Further, this approach establishes that they will have help in dealing with and moving beyond their pain.

Self-blame not only is crippling because it makes it impossible for Orphans to trust themselves; it also is counterproductive because it fosters free-floating projection. To feel less bad about themselves, Orphans often will project blame onto others: the people close to them (lovers, friends, mates, parents, employers, or teachers), God, or the culture as a whole. As a result, they heighten the sense that they are living in an unsafe world. Even worse, to the extent that they blame those around them for all the suffering in their lives, they alienate others and make their own lives more isolated and hopeless.

Accordingly, as people are able to fix the blame firmly in one location, they free themselves from the general process of blaming the world. Further, as they identify ways to deal with that root cause, to establish that they do not have to be at the mercy of evil, of their illness, of patriarchy, capitalism, etc., they can begin to believe it is possible to take responsibility for their own lives.

If you tend to blame yourself for your pain, temporarily relying on someone outside—a higher power, a therapist, an analyst, a group, a movement, a church—can help you move beyond the dualism of dependence/independence and gradually gain the skills to take charge of your life. You do not have to do it all yourself, nor do you need to wait passively for rescue or accept mistreatment from anyone. There is no shame in asking for help when you need it. All really well-adjusted people do so.

You also can protect yourself from being used or conned in such situations simply by noticing whether the expert you have chosen helps you make decisions or tries to make them for you. Good interventions (by this I mean any action a therapist takes that helps you) will strengthen and empower you, not take your journey out of your hands.

Putting yourself in the therapist's, priest's, or guru's hands or placing your trust in a program (for instance, a twelve-step program) can provide the security to start moving and get your life in order. Later, however, you will look back and realize that if the intervention worked, it was because you were supported to make the decisions that fit for who you are. Remember Glinda, the good witch in *The Wizard of Oz*, who tells Dorothy at the end of her journey that she could have gone home any time she wanted to? Dorothy asks why she did not tell her that before, and Glinda explains that Dorothy would not have believed her. First she had to convince Dorothy that there was a great and powerful wizard who could fix things for her. In journeying to find him, Dorothy developed and experienced her competence. Later, she realized that she was able to kill the Wicked Witch herself, and it was her own power that would get her home. Until she had experienced these things, however, she would have felt too powerless to proceed except under the illusion that she was about to be rescued.

By linking the examples of religions, twelve-step programs, political liberation movements, and analysis or therapy, in no way do I intend a lack of respect for the integrity and worth of each, nor do I suggest that they are merely interchangeable. Rather, I submit that each uses a process that works by aiding someone in the transition from despair to hope, from feeling powerless to claiming some sense of self-worth and agency.

The essential tools for empowering Orphans are: (1) love—an individual or a group who shows care and concern; (2) an opportunity to tell and retell their story in a way that overcomes denial (recounting how painful it was before they were saved, stopped drinking, became liberated, left their family of origin, etc.); (3) an analysis that moves the locus of the blame outside the individual, that says the fault lies elsewhere; and (4) a program of action to help them take responsibility for their own lives.

In many religions, in twelve-step programs, in therapy or analysis, and in political consciousness-raising groups, people may allow themselves to begin to feel their pain. Although their lives may have been exceedingly difficult, often they are so scared of their pain that they block it. In the safety of the group, they may process that pain in a way that frees them from it. They also may borrow courage from the therapist, the analyst, the religious leader, or the group to allow themselves to feel the full horror of their lives. Or if their lives have been simply ordinary, they may need permission to understand that they have a right to their own pain, even though it has not been as great as that of others they know.

Years ago, for example, my own pain was rough and glaring, but I denied it because it was not as great as that of many other people. It was quite a breakthrough for me to acknowledge that I had pain even though I came from a relatively happy, middle-class family. As I came to recognize and legitimize my own pain, I could overcome my denial and act to change my life. I could not make my life better until I acknowledged where things were not working for me.

Obviously, like any good thing, this step of the process can be abused. People can begin to love the attention they get from having troubles. They can start to compete to see who has had it worst—a kind of reverse status! People who bond around shared pain, illness, or victimization can feel threatened by those who start thriving and try to hold them back.

It also is my experience that when I have a hard time letting go of pain or anger about some past injustice or trauma, likely some more subtle form of it is still going on. For example, if you are angry because a former husband treated you disrespectfully and you just cannot let it go, look to your current relationships. Is there somewhere you are being treated similarly—even in a less obvious way? As we develop better boundaries and more effective ways of being treated well, it is surprising how fast we stop resonating to things that have hurt us in the past.

The point, of course, is not to get hooked on suffering but to become free to learn about joy, effectiveness, productivity, abundance, and liberation. You listen to your own and to others' painful memories not to stay there, but to open the door to growth and change. Once you have processed much of the pain, it is best to get on with life, even as you continue to tell your story. One key way is to focus on helping others, especially those who have had similar difficulties. Seeing how common such problems are fosters realism, while the act of helping moves you out of self-involvement into concern for the world. At this point, you are ready to proceed with the journey.

People who have had reasonably normal lives as well as those who have had professional and/or group support over time can often do some or all of their psychological work themselves. In such cases, it is helpful to find a way to express your own truth. Some people write their stories in journals. Julia Cameron, in *The Artist's Way*, suggests beginning every day by writing morning pages, which simply record whatever is up for you at that moment.[5] More visually oriented people may paint, others write music. Some may feel a compelling need to work, sculpt, paint, or compose because they are finding their true vocation. They may also feel an equal compulsion because it is their means of working through denial by telling their story in a fashion that they themselves can hear. For people who express their wisdom with their hands, the story may never be told in a way more verbal people can understand, but it may be encoded in the pattern of a quilt, in a weaving, in the shape of a piece of pottery. What matters most is that you can see or hear your own truth and as a result can act in your own behalf to live the life most uniquely your own.

If you do not have a group with which to work through difficult issues, it is appropriate to ask your spouse, a friend, a parent, or someone else you trust to be an empathetic listener whenever you experience pain. You can ask this person to let you rant and rave and even blame others, so that you can reach a catharsis before you settle down to determine what you actually might think or do once those strong feelings have been released. Rather than trying to solve your problems, their role is just to be there supporting and comforting you so you do not suffer alone.

SELF-HELP AND CULTURAL TRANSFORMATION

The journey discussed in this book is going on simultaneously in individuals and the larger culture. Today there are support groups and twelve-step programs for almost everything. Just a few years ago, people were embarrassed if they had to see a psychologist; now they discuss their therapists over lunch with their friends and colleagues. We have seen a proliferation of self-help books that have avid readers. Ours is, in some ways, a culture that wants to get well, and one increasingly open to spiritual as well as scientific means for getting there.

Until recently, it was primarily liberal movements—civil rights, women's and men's, gay rights, peace, environmental—that emphasized the personal side of political liberation. Now people from all parts of the political spectrum are doing so. Virtually everyone today understands that the culture is experiencing a paradigm shift of major proportions—and that such a change requires a shift in consciousness. They may not use archetypal language to describe what is happening, but they understand that a wide variety of professional and self-help interventions are supporting people in taking responsibility for their own lives.

For a time, business was the last bastion of the old hierarchical order. Now, however, many bosses are learning that they have to influence rather than compel their employees. Flatter, more egalitarian structures are replacing hierarchies even in the corporate world. These changes require greater responsibility from ordinary workers and in that way propel us on our journeys.

Much of modern philosophy and literature helps us to overcome a belief that a deity will rescue us from ourselves and to let go of our childlike innocence. The legacy of the belief that suffering is somehow our just punishment for being sinful or bad has been so debilitating that much of our art and philosophy have focused on dispelling this idea. Nineteenth- and early-twentieth-century naturalism and modern existentialism brought these themes home to us powerfully. Central to these traditions is the declaration that God is dead, nature is inert, or at least uncaring, and life has no inherent meaning. Suffering does not happen to us for a reason or because God is displeased with us; it happens simply by chance—inhuman, uncaring chance. Nothing that happens means anything beyond itself.

These philosophically nihilistic beliefs, and the art and literature they inspire, operate as a kind of collective therapy to help us overcome our denial. They tell the human story in a way that focuses on our pain—on meaninglessness, loss, alienation, the difficulty of human connection—and on a sense that the economic world has become a machine and we are mere cogs in it, that life has lost grace and meaning, and that basically no one will take care of us. They counter the denial that keeps us in innocence and tell us we are not to blame for our pain.

Finally, in the best cases, modern literature and philosophy force us to confront the urgency of action. They push us to stop looking for rescuers and to grow up and take responsibility for our lives and our future. It may be that we as humans have created the current threat to the planet—in the form of nuclear holocaust or environmental degradation—to force ourselves into maturity.

Doing so requires increased cognitive complexity and the capacity to differentiate between suffering that is harmful and should be alleviated and suffering that is an inevitable part of growth and change. The intensity of the pain the Orphan experiences after the Fall is partially the result of simple-minded either/or thinking. It is only the belief that there should be a Daddy God caring for us and protecting us that makes the contemporary confrontation with the notion that "God is dead" so painful. Who said life was going to be Edenic, anyway? Where did we get the notion that someone was supposed to take care of us? When we give up the idea that a deity protects us, we can accept some degree of suffering and sacrifice as essential to life without defining suffering as what life *is*. God is not so much dead; rather, spiritually, we no longer are children. It is time to grow up.

Beyond the dualism that sees "life as suffering" or "life as Eden" is an awareness of pain and suffering as part of life's flow. Indeed, pain and loss are transformative personally, not as a constant mode of life, but as part of an ongoing process whereby we give up what no longer serves us or those we love and move into the unknown. Our pain, our suffering, would be too great were our psychological growth concentrated in one brief period. We give things up little by little. That's the psychological reason for denial—it keeps us from having to confront all our problems at once!

Our denial structures work to protect us from knowledge of the extent of our suffering precisely because we are not equipped to deal with all of it simultaneously. Each time we become aware that we are suffering, it is a signal that we are ready to move on and make changes in our lives. Our task, then, is to explore the suffering, to be aware of it, to claim fully that we indeed are hurting. In this way, suffering can be a gift. It captures our attention and indicates that it is time for us to move on, to learn new behaviors, to try new challenges.

Suffering may be a gift in other ways as well. Particularly later on in the quest, our problem may not be so much a sense of powerlessness as an inflated sense of power, a belief that we have it all together, that we are better, more competent, worthier than others.

Suffering is the leveler that reminds us of our common mortality, that none of us is exempt from the difficulties of human existence.

Some people who have suffered tragedies have an almost transcendent freedom, for they have faced "the worst" and survived it. They know they can face anything. Life does not have to be just so, it does not have to be Eden, for them to love it. As Christ taught us, even death by crucifixion is followed by resurrection. Similarly, in *Death: The Final Stage of Growth*, Elisabeth Kübler-Ross recounts the peace and freedom felt by people who have been declared clinically dead and come back to life—how their experiences of love and light freed them from the fear of death that so interferes with most of our lives.[6]

How we deal with death, of course, is tied in with how we respond to all the little deaths in our lives—the loss of friends, family, lovers, of particularly special times and places, of jobs or opportunities, hopes and dreams, systems of belief. Interestingly, it often seems unnecessary to suffer in large ways if we learn the small, daily ways of giving to others and letting go of the present to meet the unknown. Some people need to face "the worst" to learn this lesson. Others do not. The dailiness of giving and letting go provides them with the skills they need to cope when a loved one dies or they find themselves critically ill.

Some people block out these little deaths. They leave without saying good-bye. They graduate from high school or college and neither celebrate nor mourn the life that will be no more. They pretend that birthdays are just like any other day. It is as if there will not be a loss if they do not acknowledge it. Such people always must pick a fight to get out of a relationship or pretend it never meant anything to them. Those who block all their endings become so constipated emotionally that they have no room to let anything else in. They begin to feel uncomfortable and numb.

Others who have gained more wisdom know that sometimes they must leave a relationship, a place, or a job because it is time to grow, to move on. They know that growing older holds new opportunities, but it also means the end of youth. Such people can celebrate the future and their new area of growth while fully acknowledging what it has meant to them to be with that person, in that job or school, or in that location. They can take time also to be thankful for what has been and to mourn its loss. This thanksgiving and mourning empties them out and makes way for the new. Having felt those feelings, they are ready for the excitement of new growth.

This is the meaning of the concept of the "fortunate Fall" and the ultimate gift of the archetype of the Orphan. We are propelled out of dependency and into our journeys. On the road, we learn through experience that pain need not be meaningless affliction; it can provide ample motivation for learning, bonding, and growth.

GETTING ACQUAINTED WITH THE ORPHAN ARCHETYPE

To familiarize yourself with the Orphan archetype, make a collage out of Orphan-like pictures from magazines; make lists of songs, movies, and books that express the Orphan; collect pictures of yourself, relatives, colleagues, and friends in an Orphan mode. Practice noticing when you are thinking or acting like an Orphan.

Orphan Exercises

Step One: Develop the habit every day of letting yourself feel your feelings. When you feel lonely, mistreated, or bad in any way, reach out and share with others what you are feeling. You may not think you know how to do this, but start with the basics: "mad," "sad," "glad," "scared," and "love." Your repertoire of feelings will develop as you practice this step. Let yourself be vulnerable. Ask others for their support and support them in kind.

Step Two: Develop an awareness of your body so that you release emotions stored there. Massage, body work, yoga, and many kinds of exercise that encourage physical awareness can be helpful.

Step Three: When you experience severe pain, frustration, or loss, take some time alone or with trusted friends to feel your feelings fully. Let out your tears, your rage, your fear by simply breathing in and then expressing whatever sounds or movements come. It is essential not to judge this process. Just allow your feelings and let them go. After they are expressed fully, find a way to restore yourself—take a ritual bath, lie on the earth and bathe in the sun or moon, eat your favorite meal. In the process, share what you experienced in your journal or with your friend. Then affirm that you are safe and loved!

CHAPTER 3

Finding Yourself: The Wanderer

I fear me this—is Loneliness—
The Maker of the soul
Its Caverns and its Corridors
Illuminate—or seal—

—Emily Dickinson, *318*

The hero rides out to face the unknown.

Does your life seem confining? Are you tired of giving up parts of yourself in order to survive or fit in? Do you feel alienated, lonely, bored, or misunderstood? Does some part of you crave more adventure? Or are you being thrown out of a comfortable situation, so that you have to face the unknown? If any one of these applies to you, you are being called by the Wanderer.

The archetype of the Wanderer is exemplified by stories of the knight, the cowboy, and the explorer who set off alone to see the world. During their travels they find a treasure that symbolically represents the gift of their true selves. Consciously taking one's journey, setting out to confront the unknown, marks the beginning of life lived at a new level. For one thing, the Wanderer makes the radical assertion that life is not primarily suffering; it is an *adventure*.

Human life began in Africa in a hospitable climate. It was, in a way, Eden. People could survive simply by gathering the plentiful fruit and vegetables mother earth provided. Yet, Homo sapiens is inherently curious. So group after group set out to see the world. As they traveled, they encountered harsh, cold, and difficult climates where their survival depended upon adapting. And yet they kept going until eventually they populated almost the entire globe. Later, Europeans traveled to the New World, Easterners in the United States caravaned west to the frontier, and today we are exploring space, the new frontier. The Wanderer archetype is endemic to our species. Without it, we are not quite human.

Today, the world is settled. We have few geographical frontiers left to explore, but there are frontiers of the human heart and mind. Many of us are being thrown out of our jobs or marriages; we are leaving school or our current career seeking something better, or we are moving into positions of authority that require us to tap into resources we did not know we had. The fact that our whole society is experiencing massive change and all fields of study and endeavor are in the throes of a paradigm shift means we must learn to adapt, just as our ancestors did when they began to wander throughout the world.

We often are aware of the Wanderers who externalize their journeys and either literally travel or experiment widely with new behaviors. But there also are heroes whose external behavior seems conventional enough, yet whose explorations of their inner world are profound. Emily Dickinson was one. In the latter years of her life, she hardly ever ventured even downstairs, yet no one who reads her poetry can miss the uniqueness, importance, or intense vitality of her quest.

Wanderers may be self-made men or women of business, workplace iconoclasts, or countercultural dropouts living on the edge of society, but they all define themselves in direct opposition to a conformist norm. In philosophy, politics, health, and education, they are likely to distrust orthodox solutions, choosing instead to be very radical or just idiosyncratic. In fitness, they are likely to choose solitary exercise like long-distance running or swimming. As learners, they question the answers given by authorities and search out their own truths. Wanderers' identities come from being outsiders. They are decidedly not team players. In their spiritual life, they may experience doubt, especially if they have been taught that God rewards a measure of conformity and traditional morality, qualities likely to be at variance with the needs of their developing, experimenting psyches. Yet the dark night of the soul they experience often leads to a more mature and adequate faith.

The Wanderer archetype emerges in most people in adolescence as we rebel against old-fogy parents and in mid-life when we resist expectations that we be totally responsible performance machines. In such critical life passages, the Wanderer pressures us to think about who we are and what we want and to stand up to those who think they know best what we should do.

CAPTIVITY

If the Orphan's story starts in paradise, the Wanderer's begins in captivity. In fairy tales, the prospective Wanderer may be entrapped in a tower or cave and is usually the captive of a witch, an ogre, a dragon, or some other fearsome beast. Often the captor is a symbol of the status quo, of conformity and false identity imposed by prevailing cultural roles. [Or the hero—especially if she is female—may be enchanted by a mirror, as is Alfred Lord Tennyson's Lady of Shalott (from the poem of the same name). Such an image, interpreted psychologically, suggests she is preoccupied with her appearance and with pleasing, rather than with what she sees and what pleases her.] Often the hero is told that the cage is Eden and that leaving inevitably will require a fall from grace—that is, the cage is as good as it gets. The first job of the Wanderer is to develop true sight: to declare or acknowledge that the cage is a cage and the captor is a villain. This is especially hard to do because the hero may not only be frightened of the quest but disapprove of it, and these feelings and judgments are likely to be reinforced by those of others. To the Altruist, the urge to the quest may seem selfish and therefore wrong, because it involves turning one's back on care and duty in the pursuit of self-discovery and self-actualization. For the Warrior, it may seem escapist and weak. If Wanderers choose to go on their journey, they may even feel guilty, for the act of claiming one's identity and developing an ego classically is portrayed as an insult to the gods. Think, for example, of Eve eating the apple or Prometheus stealing fire. To the Orphan, the quest sounds unspeakably dangerous!

Because we often are afraid of major changes in others as well as ourselves, we may discourage budding heroes from embarking on their quests. We want them to stay the way they are. For one thing, we may be afraid of losing our lovers, spouses, friends, even parents, if they seem to be changing too much. We may be particularly threatened if someone who has lived to please or serve us all of a sudden declines to do so!

The pressure to conform, to do one's duty, to do what others want, is strong for both men and women, but it is stronger for women because their role has been defined in terms of nurturance and duty. Often women forbear taking their journeys because they fear it will hurt their husbands, fathers, mothers, children, or friends; yet women daily hurt others when they do *not* do so. Similarly, many men are trapped in their protector role and do not dare take their journeys because of a sense of responsibility not only to their children but to the wives who appear to be fragile and incapable of taking care of themselves. Both men and women tend to retard their journeys for fear their new interests may jeopardize their jobs. If they change, they fear that they may not fit in.

The nice thing about Wanderers taking their journey is that it has a ripple effect, allowing loved ones and colleagues to take theirs as well. Perhaps at first others will be threatened and angry; but sooner or later, they will have to either leave or come along. If they leave, Wanderers may experience aloneness for a while, but sooner or later, if Wanderers so desire, they will develop better relationships, ones that are more genuinely satisfying because they are based on respect for that journey. Of course, when Wanderers step outside consensus reality and begin to see the world and themselves with their own eyes, they always face the fear that the punishment for doing so will be perpetual isolation or, in a more extreme sense, a friendless death in poverty. In spite of that fear—which speaks to the heart of the infantile terror that we cannot survive if we do not please others (parents first, teachers, bosses, sometimes even mates)—Wanderers make the decision to leave the world of the known for the unknown.

However much people have learned about giving and letting go, their sacrifices will be for nothing unless they also learn who they are. It is not helpful to tell people to transcend their ego until they have developed one. It is not useful to tell people to transcend desire until they have allowed themselves to fully go for what they want.

I maintain that not everyone knows what he or she desires. Certainly, narcissistic Orphans seem to live entirely by desire: "I want this! I want that!" But their desires are not really true, educated desires at all. Mainly they are forms of addiction, masking a primal emptiness and hunger for the real. Narcissists do not yet have a genuine sense of identity and consequently feel an emptiness. Their wants are programmed by the culture—they say "I want a cigarette" or "I want a new convertible." They think that getting these things will help them feel good. Even strategies for personal growth may not emerge out of a true self, but out of a compulsion to satisfy addictive cravings: "I want to lose ten pounds so I can attract more men and have a better sex life," "I want to go to college so I can make lots of money, have a great stereo system, and be the envy of my friends."

When people have not developed much sense of a separate, autonomous self, they basically are run by what they think to be the opinions of others. At my husband's twenty-fifth high-school reunion, one woman confided to me that a number of people she knew who had been invited said they did not want to come because they looked too fat or too old and/or they were not successful enough! Clearly, these people had not developed, even in their forties, a sense of themselves apart from such external considerations.

One of the major addictions in our culture is to romance. This works because the culture has made sex and love artificially scarce commodities, leading people to spend endless hours trying to manipulate the world so they will get enough. We are taught that we need to conform to certain images of feminine and masculine behavior to be loved and to be thought of as sexually appealing. Yet, as long as we play roles rather than take our journeys, we never feel loved for ourselves and we never experience the power of truly intimate sexual connection. Thus, we may have lots of lovers but still feel empty, needy, and wanting something more.

If that were not enough, our economic and educational systems capitalize on this shortage of love. We are taught to work hard so we can have things that will make us loved, respected, or admired. This includes buying nice clothes and cars, finding attractive places to live, having the money to purchase good health and dental care, and perhaps even to join a health club—all this to attract a mate. It certainly is a powerful way to motivate a workforce. This strategy, however, ultimately does not work in the best interest of people.

For one thing, those who are driven by their addictions in this way do not have the time or the inclination to develop a sense of self. Instead, they settle for stylish pseudo-independence, buying monogrammed towels, briefcases, or the individualized dolls of the month, using products that are pitched to appeal to their urge to be different and fashionably iconoclastic. Pseudo-Wanderers, even in their urge to wander, get channeled into conforming to whatever is considered to be the "in" way to be. Without a self, it really is not possible to either give much love or take it in. In the latter case, when people play a role to get love or respect—and hide who they really are (which may well be a mass of neediness)—they never really feel loved for themselves. It is the role that feels loved.

Further, even their loving may ultimately be harmful to other people, for it is likely to be compulsive, proprietary, controlling, and dependent. Because their sense of identity comes from having (as in possessing) that child, that boyfriend, that girlfriend, they need that person to be a certain way. They need that person to stay around even if his or her own journey calls. Such role-players may need others to act in certain ways to make themselves look good. They also may abridge their own growth so as not to threaten a relationship, or out of fear that if they do not sacrifice their good to the other's, some harm will come to that loved one.

The Orphan and the Altruist at their first levels of understanding, and sometimes even at the second, believe that to have love, they must compromise who they are. At some level, they believe that if they were fully to be themselves, they would end up alone, friendless, and poor.

Many women do not like the Wanderer stage. As Carol Gilligan points out in *In a Different Voice: Psychological Theory and Women's Development*, while men fear intimacy, women fear aloneness.[1] I see here two different responses to the same belief system. In our culture, we tend to believe we can have intimacy *or* we can have autonomy and selfhood. So women tend to choose intimacy and men choose independence. The irony is that in choosing this way, neither really gets what she or he wants. For one thing, people really want both. For another, it is not possible to truly get one without the other.

If we choose intimacy instead of independence, we cannot be fully *ourselves* in a relationship, because we have too much invested in keeping it; we play it "safe," play a role, and wonder why we feel so alone. If, on the other hand, we choose independence, our need for intimacy does not go away. Indeed, because it is repressed and therefore unacknowledged and unexamined, it manifests itself in compulsive and uncontrolled urges and activities. Most men or women who believe in "I-don't-need-anyone" stoicism are dreadfully lonely. Many—while maintaining the illusion of self-sufficiency—are absolutely terrified of abandonment.

Men in this state infantilize women, so that women (they believe) will not have the confidence to leave them. They want to keep their wives, if not barefoot and pregnant, at least without the skills and confidence needed to have a career that could support them well. Similarly, at work they define their secretary's role as part mother, part wife, so they always will be taken care of. Finally, they are so dependent upon the regard of their male colleagues, bosses, and oftentimes even their subordinates that they will violate their own sense of ethics rather than face the possibility of not being seen as manly.

Such men are particularly vulnerable to charges of being "soft." Thus, they would never, for instance, say that they do not want to dispose of chemical waste in the cheapest way, for then they might be accused of some idealistic concern for the environment. They can be controlled—even to the point of acting immorally—by the fear that they will seem to care—about the earth, about women, about other people. Women who have adopted this macho ethic act the same way, with the complicating factor that they also seek to gain male approval by acting like "one of the boys."

Accurate generalizations about sex differences are enormously important in helping us understand one another, but often they can make men and women seem more distinct and different than they are. Although the fear of aloneness is primary for many women, next to that is a corresponding fear of intimacy. So, too, men who are most conscious and obvious about their fear of intimacy also fear aloneness. As long as the problem is defined, as it is in our culture, as an either/or situation in which one can be autonomous and independent *or* one can have love and belong, we all will fear both.

We do not move out of this dualistic formulation of the dilemma until we resolve it on its own terms. Wanderers confront the fear that they will be unable to survive alone and decide that whatever the cost in loneliness, isolation, even social ostracism, they will be themselves. It is critical to do both at some time in one's life. Women tend to be so afraid of aloneness that they stay overlong in the Altruist mode; and of course this fear is accentuated by the cultural notion that to be alone and female is to be a failure (clearly you could not get a man). To wish to be alone is either unthinkable or not nurturing, and hence unfeminine.

Men, on the other hand, are so enamored of independence that they get stuck there, since independence in our culture is practically a synonym for masculinity. Furthermore, their independence has an undercurrent of sadness to it, especially if they have sacrificed their need for love to their desire to be separate and whole. This explains why Daniel Levinson, in his study of male development, *The Seasons of a Man's Life*, found that many high-achieving males could not even describe their wives![2]

After Betty Friedan's *The Feminine Mystique* appeared in 1969, many women concluded that liberation came from having a career. This is partly true, because women are freer to make their own choices if they have an independent income and are more fulfilled if they have a way of to achieve something that is socially valued. Today, however, many women are incredibly disillusioned. To succeed, they have become as career-minded as many men have, with the result that achievement has replaced relationship as the center of their lives.

Whenever we deny our need for other people, we block them out, at least partially. In doing so, we become or remain (at least in the area in which we are doing the blocking) narcissistic. The result of blocking our yearning for connection, then, is loneliness.

ALIENATION AND ESCAPE

When the Wanderer archetype emerges in our life, we will feel cut off, even if we are never truly alone. We have many ways of finding solitude. One is actually to live alone, travel alone, spend our time alone. Relatively few people adopt this course for any extended period of time. Other ways have the advantage of masking our aloneness, sometimes even to ourselves. One is to discount what we feel, what we want, and to give others what we think they want: to be what *we* think they want us to be. Another is to treat people as objects for the gratification of our own desires. This requires that we allow ourselves no real awareness of their separate human identity. Actually, anytime someone acts in one-up/one-down roles with another person, that will be a solitary interaction.

Still another way to be alone, as we have seen with traditional sex roles, is always to act a part—the perfect woman or man, mother or father, boss or employee—i.e., to *be* our roles. Or we can continue living with our family if we don't get along with them; we can stay in a bad marriage; we can live with roommates with whom we have little in common. If we really are serious about being alone, we can decide that everyone is out to get us or to get something from us.

Lest I sound unduly negative here, let me hasten to add that, in fact, all these strategies demonstrate how imaginative we are in making sure that we take our journeys. The very emptiness and vulnerability that result from such fearful approaches to life motivate many of us to take the action necessary to discover or create a self. Certainly, many people manage to be alienated and lonely all their lives without ever growing or changing, but others use these times to be "secret heroes," thinking new thoughts and imagining new alternatives while on the surface they go about their normal lives as usual. A woman I know looks back on an eleven-year, extremely conventional and superficial marriage as a safe haven, a cocoon in which she hid while she prepared to soar. But when she was in the marriage, she did not know this. In fact, it was the intensification of her sense of emptiness in the traditional female role and loneliness in the marital relationship that was, by its very unpleasantness, her call to the quest. For many, *alienation within captivity is the initial stage of wandering*, followed by a conscious choice to embark on the journey.

The archetypal American hero leaves the small town and embraces his journey; the beat hero and later the hippie hit the open road; the Western hero rides off into the sunset. The contemporary woman leaves her parents, husband, or lover and takes off too. So prevalent is this expression of the Wanderer archetype that Erica Jong wrote in the 1960s, in *How to Save Your Own Life*, that "Leaving one's husband is the only, the cosmic theme."[3] Today, leaving your job is the most common wanderer theme. Yet the individual who does not leave the small town, or the spouse who does not leave the limiting marriage, or the worker who stays with the corporation is often no less alone than the Wanderer. Towns, marriages, and organizations are all going through radical changes today. If we stay, we have to evolve to stay relevant and doing so inevitably raises issues of identity.

When it is time to take the journey, Wanderers will feel alone whether or not they are married, have children and friends, or hold a prestigious job. They cannot avoid this experience. All their attempts to do so simply repress their awareness of where they are, so that they are slower to learn lessons and thus stay lonely longer. And, although some people take off on the quest with a high sense of adventure, many experience it as thrust upon them by their feeling of alienation or claustrophobia, by the death of a loved one, or by abandonment or betrayal.

Furthermore, it is unlikely that any of our attempts to break through to persons at this stage and be truly intimate with them will work. They will continue to set up barriers to intimacy because their developmental task is to confront being alone. Very few people, moreover, are conscious enough of their own patterns of growth to tell you that honestly. Most will say, "Sure I want to be close," but then they sabotage intimacy. The only thing that really speeds them up is to become conscious that they are, in fact, alone.

Abandonment actually is quite facilitative at this stage. When Wanderers do not let another in, whether it is parent, lover, therapist, analyst, or teacher, it is important for that helper to pull away so that Wanderers can experience fully the aloneness they have created for their own growth. Otherwise, they will be diverted from recognizing their loneliness by fighting off the assaults of others against their walls. Some people simply will not grow until they are abandoned. Charlotte Brontë's Lucy Snow (in *Villette*) is such a one. She willingly gives her life over to serving almost anyone. Every time Lucy settles in to do so, however, Brontë kills the person off, leaving Lucy with no excuse not to choose to live her own life.

As women opted for expanded opportunities, many men realized for the first time that power does not necessarily bring freedom. Indeed, anytime we become invested in being one up, we already are locked into a prison, as any man knows who has been taught that only sissies cry. Nothing can make you feel more alone than never being able to share your pain with another.

The hero's journey requires us to find our uniqueness. We simply cannot do that without enough solitude to find out who we are. Most of us need some time alone every day just to stay clear. Furthermore, all the strategies we use to avoid this task—searches for Mr. or Ms. Right, the perfect job that will give us our identity, etc.—do help us, in the end, to learn what we need to learn. They give us practice in desire and assertion. A woman initially may go to college to get an MRS degree and end up taking herself seriously. A man may become increasingly sophisticated in strategies to score and in the process learn that men, like women, can be expressive with their feelings. Pretty soon he is so enamored with being open and honest, he forgets all about the scorecard and opens up to loving.

Even when our desires are programmed by the culture, they ultimately can help us grow, especially if we are attentive to feedback. For example, if one of my desires is a cigarette every five minutes, I need to begin to be attentive to the warnings on the package and that developing cough. We get educated partly by throwing ourselves into things and finding out what really pays off in a sense of fulfillment and what does not. Sometimes we can save ourselves long detours by thinking and feeling a course through before we actually try it: "Well, I could go after that guy, but if I succeed, it likely would break up my marriage. Actually, I want my marriage more than I want that fling." Or "I'm really nuts about this guy and want to become involved with him whatever the consequences. Besides, this might be the crisis that will get my husband to go into marriage counseling with me." Or "I see that I am attracted to other men. Perhaps that means that something is wrong with my marriage. Maybe I should explore that first." Or "I really am not monogamous. Jim and I will have to confront that someday. Why not now?" Or "I don't approve of adultery. Can I face myself if I do this?"

Of course, life does not always follow our scripts. We get feedback from what really happens; this sharpens our reality principle so that we can think things through more intelligently the next time. The point is, we live out some options and we imagine our way through others. In either case, we learn what we want, what we believe in, what our values are. We will never know who we are and what we want if we just stay in our old ruts. This is why we must wander a bit to grow.

This process of listening to our own desires and acting to fulfill them is fundamental to building an identity. We come into this world with a self, but it is more a potential than a fully developed identity.

I would add that we probably cannot build a self *without* playing roles. Our first sense of pride comes from playing roles well, and our choice of which roles to play is a rudimentary stab at choosing an identity. For example, a woman may choose to play the dumb blonde, the competent, reliable type, the fearless, devil-may-care adventurer, or the motherly, nurturing type. She also decides whether or not to try to be a good student and whether to try to please her parents or be a rebel. She chooses whether to be a career woman or a homemaker, whether to study art, science, or whatever. Even not choosing still is choosing by default. As she decides among all these roles and tries them on for size, she begins to get some notion of who she is.

If she plays the roles well, she may begin to gain enough confidence to ask more fundamental questions about who she is apart from such roles. Or she may have such high standards that she feels inadequate in everything she does, in which case she may sink into a serious depression. Even then, if a therapist or friend is sensitive to the basic nature of the situation, the crisis can be used to help her find a sense of herself outside the parts she plays. At some point, if we are to continue to grow, we begin to differentiate ourselves from the roles we play. Often, we do this when roles that felt good initially now feel empty. In practice, this usually means that we have stopped making choices and asserting what we want. For example, a woman sees that everything she now does was preordained by the roles she chose last year, ten years ago, maybe even thirty years ago. Moreover, she may come to understand that maybe even those choices were so influenced by expectations of the culture or by her family or friends that they were not free at all. Maybe she got married, quit her job, and had kids just because everyone else did.

Actually, when she made those choices, she was not very experienced and not very clear about what she really wanted. Making them helped her become someone capable of better ones. However, expectations that she choose who she is at twenty-one and act that out for the rest of her life militate against her freedom to make new life choices. Ultimately, of course, that is easy enough to redress. She can decide that the culture, other people, or voices in her own head are wrong to give her a "life sentence" for prior bad decisions, and she can start making new ones. But even then her situation remains complicated. Perhaps she decides she does not want to be a wife because she married before she ever experimented with life and gained a sense of competence in the world. And if she is a mother, the odds are great that she will continue that responsibility whether or not she now feels ready for parenthood.

Paradoxically, it is in resolving what sometimes seems an intolerable opposition between parental or professional responsibilities and personal exploration that people often find out more fully who they are. They come to know themselves moment by moment by the decisions they make, trying to reconcile their care for others with their responsibility to themselves. Maturity comes with that curious mixture of taking responsibility for our prior choices while being as imaginative as possible in finding ways to continue our journeys.

Wanderers do not learn their lessons all at once. Like all the archetypes, they learn an initial lesson and then circle back. The first time they take independent action may be as a child, expressing an opinion unpopular with friends or teachers. They may be very influenced by the archetype as they pull away from parents and explore what it means to be an adult and not a child anymore. They may experience it many more times as adults when they follow their heart or convictions and risk the loss of marriage, job, friendship, or popularity with friends. This is a lifelong process that sometimes requires more than mere risking. Sometimes we have to lose one good to gain another.

Wanderers' first choices for themselves, like those of Altruists and Warriors, are crude and clumsy. Usually they have gone along with someone else, against their own wishes, for so long that their resentment is deep by the time they act in their own interest. The result is that they choose themselves in the midst of a veritable explosion of rage. Or they may put off making a hard decision in their conscious mind; their unconscious mind then takes over and makes them break some rule that gets them thrown out, as Eve was expelled from the garden, instead of choosing actively to explore the new world.

When people have grown up in an environment that glorifies martyrdom, being good, and making others happy, their desire for autonomy and independence will be interpreted, even by themselves, as wrong. Their first forays into wandering, accordingly, will consist of seemingly uncontrollable acting out. They will be noticeably bad! Maybe they will hang out in bars, take drugs, become promiscuous, even steal, and seem always to be hurting and letting down those they love. They do so, of course, because the price of that love is being good, and being good tends to mean, in such circles, forgoing one's quest in order to please others. Unfortunately, this pattern can be catastrophic, because those caught in it become increasingly convinced of their worthlessness. They can be helped if they are encouraged to see that, even though their loved ones might respond by feeling threatened and expressing disapproval, they do, nevertheless, have a responsibility to take their journeys and find out who they are.

Illness is another pattern that may emerge when we do not wander when we need to. We may become sick as an unconscious way to stop the cycle we are in. However, as we become more practiced at staying with ourselves, we find that we no longer have bumpy crises in which we have to leave situations dramatically to save ourselves, or in which we have to almost kill ourselves to recognize that we need to change. Indeed, the Wanderer ultimately teaches us to be ourselves—to be true to ourselves fully in every moment. This takes enormous discipline and requires that we stay in touch with our body, heart, mind, and soul all the time in every interaction. As long as we do this, big explosions need not occur.

FLEEING THE CAPTOR

At the first level of wandering, subtlety is not the issue. The big question is whether one will act at all. While the pivotal person for Orphans is the rescuer, the transformative person or concept for Wanderers is the villain or captor. In fact, it is the identification of the villain as a real threat that motivates the journey. Once they identify a person, institution, or belief system as the cause of their misery, Wanderers can avoid or flee the cause.

This is the stage of separation. Feminists who identify men as oppressors, people of color who see whites as the enemy, workers who hate their jobs and blame the companies or their bosses, working class and poor people who conclude that capitalists never can be trusted—all strive to live as separately from the oppressing groups as possible. To the extent that the identities of the oppressed are, or seem to be, defined by internalized values of the oppressors, this self-imposed isolation provides time and space for the formation of a separate group identity. Women, for instance, ask themselves the question, "What does it mean to be female apart from stereotypes about femininity?" In the workplace, Wanderers struggle to differentiate themselves by resisting the pressure to be defined by the attitudes of their team or organization.

In the Wanderer stage, men or women who feel trapped in their marriages initially might be able to justify divorce only if it can be established that their spouse is villainous. The only way they can leave their jobs is to convince themselves that their workplace is dysfunctional or their boss abusive.

In classic hero myths, the young hero is motivated to go on his solitary journey because the kingdom has become a wasteland. The cause for this desolation and alienation is the old king; maybe he is impotent or has committed a crime. In more realistic stories, it is because he has become a tyrant. The aspiring hero goes off into the unknown and confronts a dragon, finds a treasure (the grail, a sacred fish), and comes back bringing with him what is needed to provide new life for the kingdom.

At the return from the journey, the hero in such legends often is proclaimed king or queen. Then everyone does what the new ruler says. Over time, the new ruler inevitably becomes attached to his or her own way of seeing the world, thus retarding social progress. The next young challenger comes along and sees the resulting deadness, but instead of interpreting the problem as one inherent in the system, declares that the old ruler is the villain. The cycle begins again.

The Orphan wants to be taken care of and the Altruist will deal with the situation by giving more and more to shore up the king and/or to help make the kingdom work better. But the part of each of us that is a Wanderer sooner or later will experience our "kings" and "queens"—the people we serve or who we thought would save us—as villains and tyrants. Our job, then, is to leave them, actually or simply by distancing enough to claim ourselves. What is critical in either case is to stop postponing our journey for them.

Psychotherapy quite often encourages the Wanderer archetype. When clients are unhappy, the psychotherapist helps them see that their suffering results from the failures of their mothers (the bad queen) and/or their fathers (the bad king). The client is encouraged to make new and different decisions and to take his or her own journey. Such approaches, of course, work best if the client is stuck in Orphan or otherwise needs to awaken his or her inner Wanderer.

If the Wanderer archetype already is activated in the client, it does not matter whether they really need to flee—they will think they do. A friend of mine was complaining to me about a woman who comes to her for marital counseling. In spite of the fact that the woman's husband was a very sweet fellow who was willing to do just about anything to keep her and make her happy, this woman persisted in seeing him as a villain. The counselor was most irritated at her because, according to the counselor, the woman had a perfect opportunity for an extremely happy marriage. What my friend did not see was that her client could not have a happy marriage because as yet she was incapable of taking her own journey while staying with him. As long as they were together, she would compromise, try to please him, and in any number of ways do things that aborted her own quest. No matter how wonderful her husband was, he was a captor to her and she needed to take some time away until she had developed sufficient boundaries so that she could be with him and be herself at the same time.

This is, of course, the same reason teenagers decide their parents are uptight, or oppressive, or that they just do not understand. Very few people feel justified in leaving anyone or anything—a parent, a child, a lover, a mentor, a job, a way of life—without coming to the conclusion that *what they are leaving is bad.* It is inconceivable just to want to leave because one needs to grow. The realization that one's rescuer always becomes an oppressor if one does not move on when it is time to do so comes later, if at all. As a rule of thumb, if someone else suddenly becomes hostile to you, or if ways of behaving that used to please this person do not anymore, it is useful to recognize that unless you have changed radically, the other person probably is changing and your relationship no longer fits. Your old friend or lover probably will need some distance from you. If you do not allow the distance, the other person will pick fights and make you the villain to enforce it.

However, if you do allow separateness and decide to give the other person room to grow, it is very likely that eventually you will be rewarded with a new, deeper, and more honest relationship, or at worst with the knowledge that in letting go you did a good thing—for both of you. Even if you are terrified of being left, want to control those you love, and hence try to make them abort their journeys, it is best to pause, go back, face your fear and loneliness, process them, *and let go.*

For most of us, opposition is critical to the formation of identity. It is the pressure in the culture in general and in our families, schools, and communities to conform to a particular mode of behavior that forces us to confront our differences and thus sharpen our sense of identity. When fitting in doesn't work for us—and sooner or later we will find ourselves somewhere where it does not—we will face the crisis of having to choose either to become chameleons or to take the risk of dissociating ourselves from others.

In the workplace today, advocates for major organizational shifts often find themselves locked into conflict with people protecting their turf and the status quo. Everyone, moreover, fears embarking upon the unknown. For this reason, many organizations teeter on the brink of change until financial difficulties absolutely mandate fast-track transformation. When people finally recognize that they must change or the organization will go under, the resistance lessens enough for transformation to occur. Taking the risk to walk into the unknown forces us onto our "road of trials," which is the initiation into heroism. Most of us experience this initiation often in our lives—every time we are pulled between our desire to stay within the known, safe world and our seemingly conflicting need to grow and risk confronting the unknown. It is this tension that accounts for the pain attendant upon growing up and leaving home experienced by teenagers or young adults; the difficulty of the mid-life crisis that challenges us to leave behind a sense of identity based on a role, achievement, or relationship to others in favor of facing deep psychological and spiritual questions about who we are; the psychological dislocation that happens when our workplaces change rapidly even for the most spiritual and trusting; and the fear of approaching death.

THE ROAD OF TRIALS

Jean Auel's best-selling novel *Clan of the Cave Bear* portrays the Wanderer's dilemma. Ayla, one of the first *Homo sapiens*, is swimming one day when an earthquake kills her whole tribe. She is only five. Wandering alone for days, she finally is picked up by Iza, the medicine woman of the Clan. The Clan, we learn, is human, but of a different sub-species than *Homo sapiens*. These people have phenomenal memories, but are not very good at abstract thinking or problem solving. They also have absolutely rigid, patriarchal sex role patterns. Deviation on critical points is punishable by death, but the patterns by now are so genetically encoded that no one in the Clan even thinks of deviation anymore.[4]

The tension between the desire for growth, for mastery, for pushing the limits of one's capacity to achieve versus one's desire to please and fit in is a quintessential Wanderer situation. Ayla's story is illustrative. She is strikingly different from the people around her, and they fear her difference. So does she, because it threatens her survival, which is dependent—when she is a child— upon pleasing the Clan. To find herself, she must leave the people she most loves so that she can stop compromising to please them.

The most important difference Ayla feels is her capacity for androgyny. She is capable of performing both male and female tasks, and she is curious enough to want to learn everything she can. She resolves her dilemma by conforming when she is with the Clan, but when she is alone, she secretly teaches herself to hunt. When Ayla's ability to hunt inevitably is discovered, her punishment is to be declared dead. Usually, Clan members who are pronounced dead actually die, so strong is their belief in the declaration. But there is a provision in Clan mythology that, if a person comes back from the dead after a certain number of "moons," he or she can be accepted back into the tribe. That means Ayla has to survive on her own for a long time—and in winter. "On her own" means dealing with not only physical survival but also the emotional crisis of learning to trust her own sense of reality as opposed to that of the Clan—they say she is dead; she thinks (but is not sure) she is alive.

When she comes back, she *is* accepted. She very much wants to be part of the Clan again, for she has been dreadfully lonely, yet the experience of making it on her own has made her even more confident and therefore less malleable and more independent of Clan mores. When Ayla has a child, she runs off so that it will not be put to death as a mutant. Ayla figures out that the child is not deformed. The baby is half Clan and half Other (their term for *Homo sapiens*) and so looks very different from other Clan babies. Even though this situation is resolved through a combination of Ayla's cleverness and the leader's compassion, the clash between the more and more independent and adventurous Ayla and the increasingly disoriented Clan is growing. No resolution seems possible, however, because she so loves them, and they her. Almost no one wants to sever this relationship—except one person.

Enter the villain: Broud, the one Clan member who has truly hated Ayla (because he has been envious of the attention she has received), is put in charge. His first action is to declare Ayla dead once again. She goes off to find the Others, people like herself, not knowing whether she ever will. In Auel's sequel, *Valley of the Horses*, we learn that Ayla ends up spending three years—including three hard winters—away from human society, kept company only by a cave lion and a horse.

Having left the Clan and, with them, her child, she nevertheless takes with her the belief that the cost of being alone is giving up critical pieces of who she is. She can have love at the price of conformity or be alone for the rest of her life. Clan members, for instance, do not laugh or cry. Alone in her valley, Ayla debates what of herself she is willing to give up to be less lonely. She decides she would be willing to give up hunting but not laughing. It never occurs to her that she could find a community in which she could be *fully* herself. Even when a man of her own kind finds her and falls in love with her—a man who simply assumes that everyone laughs and cries and who prefers and admires women who hunt well—she cannot believe it and keeps acting as if he were a sexist Clan male.

The point here is that originally the threat was real. Ayla was totally dependent for her physical and emotional survival on the Clan. She did need to compromise to remain within the tribe. She learned major lessons both by disciplining herself to please them—especially in doing it for the love of her parent figures, Creb and Iza—and by defying custom as much as she thought she could get away with. One can see here the passage of childhood into adolescence—the dual lessons of obedience and rebellion. Yet Ayla, like most of us, transfers these lessons to situations in which they no longer are relevant.[5]

The belief that we have to compromise critical parts of ourselves to fit in makes visible and real to us both our need for love and our equally strong need to explore who we are. The tension between these incredibly strong and apparently conflicting impulses leads us first to give up important pieces of ourselves to conform, and in that way to learn how much love and belonging mean to us, and finally, radically, to choose ourselves and our journeys as even more important to us than care of others or perhaps even our own survival.

Because the culture has overglorified the harsh, solitary journey of the classic hero and because society so needs people who can work collaboratively, we have become disenchanted with the traditional heroic ideal of the Wanderer. Like that of Altruistic martyrdom, the problem of the Wanderer is not with the archetype itself, but rather with a confusion about what the archetype means for people. Just as martyrdom is destructive when suffering is justified for its own sake, solitude can be an escape from community—and hence destructive—if it, too, seems like a value in itself. For instance, if maturity is equated with independence—and independence is defined as not needing anyone else—it can stop an individual's growth.

However, making an absolute choice for ourselves and our own integrity, even if it means being alone and unloved, is the prerequisite for heroism and ultimately for being able to love other people while remaining autonomous. It is essential for creating the proper boundaries so that we can see the difference between ourselves and others—so that we will not have to objectify them to know ourselves and what we want. Only then is it possible to both empathize with and honor another, yet still do what we need to do for ourselves.

Boundaries also are essential for finding our own vocations. Part of being human is being a creator, bringing into being things that were not here before. That's what it means to say we were created in God's image. Ayla, in her solitary valley, made and invented tools; she tamed a horse and a cave lion; she experimented with new medicinal recipes and new ways to dress and wear her hair. Only the discovery that she could survive alone freed her to be as creative and competent as she was able to be. By exploring her potential in this way, she not only created things and experiences outside herself, she discovered herself as someone to be proud of.

Work helps us to find our identity, first because it is the way people survive—by toil. When we learn we can support ourselves, we do not have to be dependent on other people. Beyond that, when we find work—whether paid or avocational—that expresses our souls, we find ourselves by what we bring into being. The Wanderer's quest, then, also is about choice, productivity, creativity. Once we know we can survive on our own, doing our real work, we can be independent of people and organizations without compromising anything essential to who we are.

No matter how much people want to feel loved, appreciated, and a part of things, they will be lonely until they make a commitment to themselves, a commitment that is so total that they will give up community and love, if necessary, to be fully who they are. Perhaps this is why some of the most secure people I know—and the people with the clearest sense of their own identity—have taken great risks. In this list I would put several friends: a woman who knew in her soul she must be an artist and left a marriage to a wealthy man to pursue her art; a man in mid-life who left a secure job to start his own business developing a product he had invented; and a number of men and women who risked social ostracism and/or losing their jobs by making public their love for someone of the same sex. I also would include a woman who left a high-status job as a scientist to enter the ministry, not even sure that any church in her denomination would accept a woman minister.

Not every Wanderer makes decisions so dramatic, but every one of us—if we are to grow past a certain point—needs to make an absolute commitment to ourselves. Like the Altruist, we do so in stages. We begin angry that we have to make such hard choices. At first we act like Orphans, kicking and screaming that someone else is supposed to be caring for us! Or we complain that no one loves us for who we really are, that we would like to do such and such, but no jobs are available in that field. In short, we express dissatisfaction that life is hard, and we take that secure job that is not what we really want to do or stay in relationships that seem safe, even if they are not very satisfying to us.

Then, one day, we accept loneliness and a sense of an existential void, sometimes felt in the solar plexus, as just the way things are: "We all walk alone," we may say, "each and every one of us." Fully accepting and feeling anything always sends us into another place. It is only struggling against our growth that locks us in. In this case, accepting loneliness leads to rebellion: those quiet or public experiments in acting on what you really want, loving who you really love, doing the work you care about, finding out who you are. Then the sense of enjoyment that Ayla discovers in her own company, in which solitude becomes something quite different from loneliness, creeps in. The more we are ourselves, the less alone we feel. We are never really alone when we have ourselves.

EMBRACING YOUR OWN LIFE

Thus, the Wanderer's journey helps us free ourselves from worrying what others will think and lets us embrace fully our own natures and our own journeys. One of the best examples of a hero who comes to understand this is Sissy Hankshaw in Tom Robbins's novel *Even Cowgirls Get the Blues*. Sissy was born with oversized thumbs. Virtually everyone sees her as handicapped, but she resists this way of looking at things. As a young teenager, she stands before the mirror and realizes that she is beautiful. If she were to have plastic surgery to reduce the size of her thumbs, she could lead a "normal life." While she contemplates this alternative, her thumbs begin to twitch and urge her to "live life at some other level if she dared." Instead of having plastic surgery, Sissy goes on to become the world's greatest hitchhiker. She is so good, she motivates cars on the other side of a four-lane highway to pick her up. In fact, she takes hitchhiking to the level of a Zen experience. Like everyone else, however, Sissy has her moments of self-doubt, and during one she marries and gives up her "career." When she frees her husband's pet bird, however, he takes her to a psychiatric clinic. One of the psychiatrists (the namesake of the author) understands her. He explains to his colleague, Dr. Goldman, a Freudian psychologist, his enthusiasm for Sissy by telling him how impressive it is that she has become the best hitchhiker in the world. She truly has found the life she was meant for. Dr. Goldman, missing the point entirely, asks if he means she has transcended her affliction. Dr. Robbins says no. He explains that transcendence smacks of hierarchy, the class system, of a way of thinking that cannot see Sissy's innate value. He continues:

> The trick is not to transcend but to *transform* them. Not to degrade them or deny them—and that's what transcendence amounts to—but to reveal them more fully, to heighten their reality, to search for their latent significance. I fail to detect a single healthy impulse in the cowardly attempt to transcend the physical world. On the other hand, to transform a physical entity by changing the climate around it through the manner in which one regards it is a marvelous undertaking, creative and courageous.[6]

Sissy so changes Dr. Robbins's life that he "calls in well" and never returns to the clinic.

In this view, all people are heroic, and all are essential to human evolution. Our task is merely to affirm completely who we are. We do not have to spend all or even any of our time trying to prove that we are okay. That is why the "black is beautiful" campaign is so critical to African Americans, and the gay pride movement is essential to lesbians and gays. That is why affirming femaleness is so transformative for women, and that is why good mental, emotional, and physical health for everyone requires learning to love oneself fully and unconditionally. People who have taken the Wanderer's journey are great assets to workplaces and communities. They serve as scouts, bringing new ideas back and they are not afraid to tell it like it is; they insist on doing the work and community service that reflects their purpose and feeds their passion.

COMMUNITY

Thus, the movement into isolation and loneliness ultimately leads back to community: Sissy finds the cowgirls. Ayla finds people of her own kind. Your typical iconoclast finds his or her perfect workplace, plays an active role within the community, and settles down. The archetypal Wanderer, then, moves from dependence to independence to an autonomy defined in the context of interdependence. Many who have learned to embrace their independence and even aloneness find later that they miss human connection. They have become capable of experiencing intimacy at a new level because they have developed a strong enough sense of self that they are not afraid of being swallowed up in the other. To their surprise, they often find, just when they are ready, that people and communities exist that love them for exactly who they are.

As they resolve the conflict between love and autonomy by choosing themselves without denying their yearning for connection, the seemingly impossible conflict dissolves. In this new way of seeing the world, the *reward* for being fully and wholly ourselves is love, respect, and community. But for most of us, the full enjoyment of this reward does not come until we gain the Warrior's ability to assert our own wishes in the relationship, the Altruist's capacity to give and to commit to others, and the Innocent's knowledge that there is no scarcity, that we can have all the love we need as our birthright. We do not have to *pay* for it by forfeiting our lives.

GETTING ACQUAINTED WITH THE WANDERER ARCHETYPE

To familiarize yourself with the Wanderer archetype, make a collage out of Wanderer-like pictures from magazines; make lists of songs, movies, and books that express the Wanderer; collect pictures of yourself, relatives, colleagues, and friends in a Wanderer mode. Practice noticing when you are thinking or acting like a Wanderer.

Wanderer Exercises

Step One: Pay attention to the habits, experiences, activities, situations, and ideas that do not fit for you. They may be wrong, unhealthy, or limiting, or they may be fine for others but are not for you.

Step Two: When you can, walk away from everything that is not right for you. If you cannot actually leave, then mentally distance, keeping your inner freedom. Begin imagining alternatives, envisioning the options that would be more appropriate for you.

Step Three: As you say no to what is not right for you, allow your heart and your curiosity to push you to explore other possibilities. Look for experiences and ideas that feel congruent with who you are and what you want to know at this time in your life. Look for the people, places, and activities that resonate with your true essence and commit to them.

CHAPTER 4

Proving Your Worth: The Warrior

Lives of great men all remind us
We can make our lives sublime,
And, departing, leave behind us
Footprints on the sands of time. . . .

Let us, then, be up and doing,
With a heart for any fate;
Still achieving, still pursuing,
Learn to labour and to wait.

—Henry Wadsworth Longfellow, *A Psalm of Life*

The hero slays the dragon.

Do you have high standards? Do you push yourself to achieve? Do you defend yourself, or others, from harm, insult, or attack? Is achievement important to you? Do you strive to be the best you can be? Do you work harder and longer than may be good for you?

Getting acquainted at parties, people usually ask, "What do you do?" Even children are asked routinely, "What do you want to be when you grow up?" The Warrior wants to place people by their job and how successful they are. We care enormously in our culture about our careers, for work (or school) is the area of our lives in which we prove our worth. Often, we cannot stop working because we do not feel we are of any value when we are not being productive.

All this began in hunting and gathering times. Imagine yourself living at a subsistence level. You are hungry. If you do not find food soon, you and the people counting on you will die. The pressure is intense and you feel a gnawing in your stomach. If you are a man, you hunt with other men. If you are a woman, you and the other women gather nuts, vegetables, anything edible. In either case, if you are successful, not only do you get to eat, you gain the respect of others. If, over time, you are unsuccessful, you die.

When you have enough food to have spare time, you invent new designs for weapons, baskets to carry what you gather, and containers for cooking and storing. Both you and others know that developing skill is essential. Therefore, you work hard to be the best hunter or gatherer you can be. The better you become, the more respect you get from others. Indeed, in a tribal economy, everyone depends on the competence of everyone else. We may talk about "quality" in the modern world, but in the primitive world it meant everything. To do a task in an unskilled or sloppy manner endangered the health and safety of everyone. Your precision and skill, then, was a mark of who you were inside.

We can relate to what life was like for hunters and gatherers if we remember that there are many kinds of hunger in human life besides hunger for food. We are hungry not only for food, but also for love, for sex, for power, for adventure, sometimes even for meaning.

Hunters and gatherers provide the deep background for the Warrior and Altruist archetypes, which, in turn, define why men and women often seem so different. Male culture is derived from the Warrior tradition (hunter) and female culture from the Altruist tradition (gatherer). Within these ancient gender roles, men organized to kill prey, which evolved into killing threatening or competing hunters, clans, or tribes. Women organized to care for children and each other as they wandered over the plains or through the brush in search of food. Both archetypes provide ways to get your needs met. The Warrior helps you be fierce, fight, and win. The Altruist helps you develop reciprocity within community: everyone contributes, everyone receives, and thus everyone has enough.

In the modern world, the Warrior archetype is as essential to women as it is to men, since we all need to make our way in a competitive economy. Moreover, the Warrior archetype protects the boundaries, so anyone without access to their Warrior is at risk of abuse, neglect, or being undervalued. The Warrior also is important because it helps all of us to stay connected to our primal desires. It helps us know what we want and then go forward to get it. If you think of the hunter history of the Warrior, how the archetype developed, you can see why the Warrior is so focused on competence and achievement: incompetence in the hunt or in crafting weapons literally could get you killed.

The ability to support yourself is fundamental to adult life. Our equivalent of the "hunt" is landing a job. Then in that job we must demonstrate excellence. The widespread use of phrases like "make a killing" and "wiping out" or "killing" the competition reveal the deep archetypal structure of much of the contemporary workplace. Moreover, the loss of employment threatens self-worth, as well as one's ability to feed one's family. It can feel like dying.

There is pride that comes from excellence in whatever you do, no matter how humble your work, and there also is pride in coming home with a check so you can support yourself and your family. For the Warrior, self-esteem actually intensifies if success involves some real struggle. Listening one evening to a family discussion of how much stress young people have to endure, my husband's grandfather, a successful immigrant businessman, silenced us by interjecting, "You want to know about stress? Stress is coming to a new country, not speaking a word of the language, and getting on a subway to go to a strange part of town, knowing you must come home with a job or your wife and children will not eat. That's stress." People who have had it very easy often lack the self-esteem that comes from having to do something difficult, unpleasant, or risky.

Until we gain this ability to provide for ourselves, we have not really proven ourselves in the world. However, we can get stuck in the journey because social pressure, advertising, and the context of a materialistic culture keep upping the stakes. We think that proving ourselves means always making more and more money to buy more and more things. After a while, our efforts become divorced from the satisfaction of any genuine human drive or need, and then we get bored. Hunting a bison with a spear or facing off an invading band to protect those you love requires intensity. But what if you work in a bureaucracy, pushing paper with no real sense that your work makes a difference, no sense that making a mistake might have serious consequences? This, of course, is why the Warrior invents savage organizational politics—to keep the adrenaline flowing.

Moreover, advertising creates a secondary level of perceived need by connecting a product with a primal human desire. For example, advertising implicitly promises that if you wear this cologne or aftershave, you will find love (or at least sex). If you buy this convenience food, you will be a good parent. If you purchase this car, you will know freedom. If these products help you find love, care for your children, or go where you want to go, such advertising can be in the service of genuine human satisfaction. However, often the products themselves cannot deliver any long-term satisfaction. When your entire focus is on earning enough for a bigger television or some other product, it is entirely possible to be full of anxiety while simultaneously being bored out of your mind.

Chris Saade, a colleague of mine with a charming Lebanese accent, electrifies audiences when he leans in, shakes his fist, and challenges them to let themselves know what they "desire" (a word that, when Chris says it, has three long, drawn-out syllables, "de... si... er... "). When he does this, I see people in the audience who look back at him in fear. They do not want to know what they truly yearn for, because if they do, they might have to change their lives. Yet many seemingly successful people today are finding out the truth in the saying, "You can never get enough of what you do not want." We can have money, status, even apparent freedom, yet be miserable because we do not tap into our real hungers and yearnings.

As with many of the archetypes, the Warrior can bring great gifts, but it also can demean if we get caught up in its form and forget what we are striving to achieve or gain. If we have the courage to ask primal questions of ourselves, about what we desire at a gut level, the Warrior archetype can help us find the focus, skill, and drive to fulfill that desire.

ALL I WANT IS A LITTLE RESPECT!

Basic to Warrior energy is a sense of pride and dignity. The cowboy, insulted by the outlaw, meets him at high noon to settle the score. What is at stake is one's honor. To the Warrior, it is shameful to allow yourself to be disrespected. It also is dishonorable to allow someone else—especially someone weaker or defenseless—to be mistreated.

In the Camelot stories, the knights were expected to rescue anyone in distress. Unless they were saving someone, moreover, they did not fight anyone they did not respect, for to do so was considered disgraceful. In addition, they were sworn, when fighting, to fight fair. This included not harming an unarmed person. Taking advantage of someone in no position to defend himself showed that you were not a true knight.

The nobility inherent in the Warrior tradition is very important today. Warriors in business love to beat a worthy competitor, which means the company that gives you a good fight. The same is true in athletics. The best contests are between teams that are very close in ability. Over time, Warriors who do not fight fair lose their self-respect and the respect of others. Indeed, they may become villains, even in their own eyes.

The Warrior, then, also is about internal discipline. This means that your inner Warrior helps you say no to temptation, cheating, laziness, or debauchery. It holds the boundaries against the more negative aspects of our sensory desires. Think of the seven deadly sins: sloth, gluttony, avarice, lust, wrath, pride, and envy.

In most Warrior archetype plots, the hero goes through a series of life-threatening adventures. The more difficult the situation, the more fascinating the story. But the hero never gives up. Instead, he or she demonstrates strength, courage, and ingenuity in finding a way to triumph over seemingly impossible odds.

STANDING YOUR GROUND

If we think about the journey of the Orphan seeking rescue, we can appreciate the great advance that happens when people stop identifying with the victim to be rescued and begin identifying with the Warrior rescuer. How much more powerful one feels! Developmentally, the Warrior helps people take control of their lives and empowers them to help others as well as themselves. When you have access to your inner Warrior, you will do whatever you need to prevail.

The Warrior is the detective hunting down the criminal, the comic-book superhero fighting against evil (for truth, justice, and the American way), the soldier going off to war. The archetype also is expressed in competitive sports, the corporate jungle, political campaigns, liberation movements, labor unions, and power struggles between co-workers, friends, and lovers.

The structure of the human brain shows evidence of our evolutionary history; parts of it are identifiable today as similar to the brains of our reptilian and mammalian ancestors. The Warrior archetype overlays the aggressive and territorial tendencies we share with reptiles with distinctly human traits in meeting basic needs for safety, food, and sex; added are objectives like learning and receiving an education, attaining career success, and, basically, striving for a distinctly human (versus reptilian) fulfilled and satisfied existence. Any aggressive means of achieving these goals, however, has a reptilian side to it.

The Warrior also helps us overcome the natural instinct to survive at any cost. To be fully human is to know that it sometimes is necessary to endure suffering or die for a cause. Scholar Joseph Campbell noted sacred Warrior traditions in a number of cultures where the strongest fighters sometimes were tortured to death. Their ability to endure pain without flinching demonstrated the highest Warrior virtues—courage, fortitude, and endurance. People with a Warrior spirit who go to see a psychotherapist can be dumbfounded that they are encouraged not only to feel, but to share their feelings. Orphans need to learn to feel their feelings so they can move through them and let them go. Warriors strive to channel their feelings as a resource for their power, enabling them to perform the action best suited for achieving the goal, whether it be peace of mind, financial success, or desired familial bonds.

The Warrior provides hope that good can and will triumph over evil, but even more fundamentally, the story tells us, when people have the courage to fight for themselves, they can affect their destinies. Any ending in which good does not triumph, therefore, seems fundamentally disempowering because we take it to mean that we are powerless and because, in undermining the major belief system of the culture, it reinforces cynicism, alienation, and despair. When the hero does triumph over the villain, however, it reinforces our faith that it is possible not only to identify the dragon but to slay the beast: we can take charge of our lives, eliminate our problems, and make a better world. In doing so, we rescue the damsel in distress who is the Orphan in all of us. The Warrior says to the Orphan within: "You do not always have to look for someone outside yourself to save you; I can take care of you."

The Warrior teaches us to claim our power and assert our identity in the world. This power can be physical, psychological, intellectual, or spiritual. On the physical level, the archetype presides over the assertion that we have a right to be alive. Warrior consciousness includes self-defense, a willingness and an ability to fight when we are being attacked. On the psychological level, it has to do with the creation of healthy boundaries, so that we know where we end and other people begin, and an ability to assert ourselves.

Intellectually, the Warrior helps us learn discrimination, to see which path, which ideas, which values are more useful and life-enhancing than others. On the spiritual level, it means learning to differentiate among theologies: to know which bring more life and which kill or maim the life force within us. The Warrior also helps us to speak out and to fight for what nourishes our minds, our hearts, and our souls, and to vanquish those things that sap and deplete the human spirit by speaking the truth about them and refusing to accept them or to allow them into our lives.

The development of warrioring capabilities is essential to a full life, and it is a necessary complement to the virtues associated with the Altruist. Initially, Altruists see themselves as sacrificing for others, while Warriors, at the relatively primitive level, assume that they need to slay others to protect themselves. Their willingness to do so is an important expression of commitment to themselves and their own self-worth; it is the fundamental assertion that they have a right to be here and to be treated with dignity and respect.

Historically, women, racial minorities, and the working class all have been culturally defined as inferior; as such, their role has been to serve. To the degree that these groups have internalized such ideas, much of their giving and serving is linked unconsciously to their belief that they do not have a right to be here unless they do serve—i.e., that they do not have a right to exist for their own sake. Many women can conceive of doing things just because they want to only after they have satisfied the needs and wishes of their children, their husbands, their bosses, their friends, and on and on. Because those demands never can be met entirely, anything they do for themselves is accompanied by guilt—even if what they are doing is attending to their basic health needs, like going out for a jog. As a result, they can feel profoundly orphaned.

Today, many groups that previously were cast in supporting roles have begun to identify themselves as Warriors—partly because of their eagerness to compete in the corporate jungle and partly because of their crusader impulse to fight for equal rights. However, successfully presenting yourself as a Warrior can be complicated by societal fear of assertion in women and in men of color. For example, women frequently mask their Warrior qualities under a maternal or seductive affect because women who are as directly assertive as their male colleagues often are dismissed as bitches or seen as unnatural and unfeminine. Similarly, some African-American males have complained to me that they feel they must pull their punches; they act coolly competent, affable, and/or very warm and caring so as not to awaken the terror with which many Caucasians appear to regard angry black men.

If we begin from a cultural one-down position, our Warrior energy focuses on gaining recognition as an equal. However, more typically, the Warrior's impulse is more competitive—to prove we are "the best." This can be a powerful economic motivation, as the competitive urge pushes people to give their all so as to succeed. In medieval times, Warriors jousted to determine who was the best fighter. You also can think of figures like John Henry, the steel-driving man, dying in the process of proving he could lay more railroad track in less time than the newfangled machine brought in to replace him.

The real Warrior stands by a fair contest. However, many pseudo-Warriors are happy to rig it. Pseudo-Warriors include men who find their sense of self-worth primarily by asserting their superiority over women, upper-class men and women who assume an innate superiority over working-class people, or whites who feel superior to people with darker skin. Though the rules are stacked in their favor, these groups can believe that they are better simply because they wound up on top; they may be oblivious to the advantages that put them there. In such cases, the high-level Warrior's commitment to the principle of justice gives way to the lesser principle of "might makes right."

When adolescents feel demeaned and have no outlet for their Warrior energies, they form gangs and take their aggression out on one another. Or they begin abusing drugs and alcohol, laying waste to their own bodies. The Warrior archetype always is present in teenage boys and girls, since their developmental task is to begin proving themselves in the world. Ideally, they will have opportunities to excel in some competitive activity, such as athletics, scholarship, or creative endeavors. They also need meaningful ways to contribute to the larger society, such as community service projects through church or school or opportunities to engage in useful entrepreneurial activities.

An adolescent boy feels oppressed by a father who seems strict and overbearing. The son complains that his father runs his life, evaluates his every move, and thinks he himself is always right. As the son's Warrior starts to develop, he argues with his father and sometimes even defies him. Eventually, however, his Warrior becomes more like an inner father. The son develops his own standards, imposes his own discipline on himself, and begins to achieve in academic and athletic endeavors. He then notices that his own father relaxes and does not have to control his every move. And when the son does disagree with the father, he says so calmly, sparking a dialogue, not a fight.

If the father had not noticed and appreciated the growth of the boy's Warrior, he could have caused it to go underground by continuing his control over him after the boy was developed enough to show self-control. The boy might then begin to act out in self-destructive ways. If the father is Warrior-possessed, he may feel a compulsive need to compete, win, and be right—all the time. One man recognized he was in trouble in this area when he discovered he could not even allow his daughter to beat him at checkers! The perils of the Warrior archetype are strongest for men because they have been so socialized to live out Warrior energy. Some men today recognize that the pressure to live up to the Warrior image of the stoic performance machine carries too great a cost. They may seem very privileged because of their success in the corporate world, but they are dying at their desks in record numbers. Typically, we take it for granted that men die early—and often of heart attacks. Rarely do we recognize that early death is a peril of possession by the Warrior archetype.

A WARRIOR CULTURE

Warriors change their worlds by concentrated effort. Whether in families, schools, workplaces, friendships, communities, or the culture as a whole, this archetype informs people's attempts to change their environments to suit their own needs and to conform to their values.

However, people who move into warrioring before finding their own identities act out the form of the slaying-the-dragon plot, but without the meaning. They may win, but the victory is hollow. They do not know what they really want, so they cannot get it. Without the Altruist, the Warrior competes merely to gain personal advantage instead of to protect or help others. Indeed, the Warrior is a heroic archetype only when its courage and focus are employed for the greater good.

Whether it is an empty ritual, deeply satisfying, or seen as needing redefinition for changing times, the hero/villain/victim myth has informed, and to some degree still informs, our culture's basic secular belief system. The ritual that underlies the Warrior myth is found, of course, in war, but it also is played out culturally in our sports, business practices, religions—even in our economic (e.g., capitalist), scientific (e.g., Darwinian selection), and educational theories (e.g., bell-shaped curve). In the realm of sports, we have seen over the centuries a progression from gladiatorial contests, in which the loser actually was killed, to football, baseball, basketball, and soccer, in which the antagonist simply is defeated.

In politics, too, we find an interesting progression. In the most primitive mode, the hero kills the old king (the tyrant) and—at least theoretically—saves the victimized populace. Variations on this process continue in the modern era in many parts of the world, where change still is brought about by a bloody coup or by revolution. In our country, we have found a way to avoid such bloodshed through the democratic process. The old king is neither ritually dismembered, as in some primitive cultures, nor killed in his sleep, nor tried and executed for his crimes. But, as we are reminded each election year, the rhetoric based upon these ancient practices remains in use.

The challenger—whether in electoral or intraorganizational politics—explains how he or she will save the country or the organization and how the incumbent is responsible for all its ills. The incumbent, of course, retaliates by describing how he or she has, in fact, made major improvements in the country/state/organization and how the opposition would ruin things if it were in power. The language is revealing. We talk about defeating the opposition at the polls. With a big enough margin of victory, we may even exult: "We slaughtered them!" Such warlike rhetoric, of course, also is basic to business, in which the object is to defeat the competition.

Although the person defeated in sports, politics, or business no longer is regarded as a villain *per se*, the persistence of this idea is evident in the way defeat still brings shame on the loser—a response more appropriate to a recognition that one is bad than simply that one has lost a contest. We all know stories from economic depressions about tycoons who suddenly lost their money and committed suicide because they could not face not being on top. In the downsizing epidemic in the early 1990s, many people became depressed when they lost their jobs because they felt like losers! Even when they did nothing to cause the layoff, many still felt ashamed when they were let go.

We can see that the hold of the Warrior is beginning to loosen somewhat in our political world. Twenty years ago, presidential hopeful Edmund Muskie lost any chance of winning when he teared up on television, thus appearing lack the requisite toughness for the job. In 1992 the American people elected Bill Clinton, a candidate who avoided the draft and shamelessly tears up on television. After Clinton soundly defeated Bob Dole in the 1996 election, Dole won a substantial measure of public affection by joking about his loss in speeches and TV ads! Neither Clinton nor Dole, or course, would get away with such behavior if they were seen as even slightly wimpy.

Even when the Warrior is well balanced with other archetypes, Warriors must be tough-minded and realistic if they hope to change the world. They need to be able to look their adversary in the eye and say, "You are a dragon and I am going to slay you." Or "I do not care how you feel, I want to win and that means I have to defeat you." In the workplace, particularly, Warriors test co-workers to see if they are tough enough. This hazing can be unnerving to those with less Warrior in their psyches. However, its purpose is to make certain that the team is solid, with no wimps who will let the others down. A man on a management team with me once explained that the workplace is like a battlefield. "I need to know that you will not get scared and bolt when the going gets tough. I need to know you can stand the heat."

In *The Golden Bough*, Sir James George Frazer relates a myth that, to me, describes the plight of executives who are in Warrior-possessed organizations. The king of the woods cannot let down his guard for a moment even to sleep because someone might kill him to become the new king. Frazer writes: "Surely no crowned head ever lay uneasier, or was visited by more evil dreams than his. For year in, year out, in summer and winter, in fair weather and in foul, he had to keep his lonely watch, and whenever he snatched a troubled slumber it was at the peril of his life. The least relaxation of his vigilance, the smallest abatement of his strength of limb or skill of fence, put him in jeopardy; gray hairs might seal his death-warrant."[1] For our leaders to live long and healthy lives, it is important that both they and their environments balance the Warrior with other archetypes.

ACHIEVING ARCHETYPAL BALANCE

When any archetype is balanced with the others, it tends to be expressed in its higher, more integrated and positive form. When the Warrior archetype is integrated into a balanced consciousness, it is less about greed than about love. We can think of the archetypes in this book as layers of an onion. As we go deeper, we gain access to more and more archetypes. Warriors who have access only to their Orphan and Wanderer can be ruthless. However, Warriors with developed Altruist archetypes fight in the service of others. If the Innocent and Magician archetypes also are awakened, their struggles are informed equally by spirituality. Soldiers may fight for their loved ones, their country, their religious convictions, and to make the world a better place. Political leaders, social activists, and concerned volunteers struggle to improve the lives of those around them. In *Shambhala: The Sacred Path of the Warrior*, Chogyam Trungpa argues that "The essence of warriorship, the essence of human bravery, is refusing to give up on anyone or anything."[2] It is here that one can see how the lessons of sacrifice and the lessons of mastery work together. Gaining a more sophisticated level of skill at one allows the development of a more sophisticated level of skill at the other.

The harmful side effects of warrioring come in its more primitive forms. When freed from dualism and absolutism, warrioring becomes a healthy, positive human process: taking action to protect oneself and those one loves from harm. Whether it is killing the predatory animal, heading off the invading band, or identifying acid rain or nuclear proliferation as a threat to humankind, we need Warriors to take strong action to protect us all.

The levels Warriors experience, then, also are related to how well they have learned to confront fear. At the early stages—those in which the only answer seems to be a literal slaying of the enemy—fear is rampant. One can imagine a cold war general who could not imagine enough weapons to counter the Communist threat. His world was defined by a vision of perpetual threat in which the villain is imagined to be totally irrational and bent on destroying all that the general is or holds dear. The only possibility he sees is to kill or be killed. The symbolic contest in politics, business, sports, or school is mild by comparison, but its fears are real as well: the fear of defeat, of not being the best, of being inadequate, inferior, a loser.

At the next level, the enemy is seen not as someone to slay or defeat, but as someone to convert to your side. The villain is redefined as a victim to be saved. Whether we are talking of crusading Christianity, Marxism, feminism, or pull-yourself-up-by-your-bootstraps capitalism, Warriors take the truth that enabled them to develop some sense of hope and meaning in their lives and use it to go out and convert the world. Analogously, in private life, Warriors undertake Pygmalion projects to improve loved ones and friends.

It is difficult to accept human difference when you are yearning to build an ideal, humane world. One of the central ways Altruists try to make the world better is to give up parts of themselves that do not seem to fit what others want. Warriors, in contrast, change other people. But in both cases, *sameness* is seen as a prerequisite to the creation of a loving community. Either we change ourselves or we get rid of or transform *others!*

The truth is that utopian movements tend to become autocratic when the psychological development of individuals within them, or within the larger society, has not evolved to the stage necessary to support a new social system. For example, contemporary organizational theory encourages flatter structures, fewer middle managers, more worker autonomy, and even self-organizing teams. For these strategies to be successful, the people implementing them at minimum must have some access not only to a higher, less absolute level of Warrior but also to their respective Orphan, Wanderer, and Altruist archetypes.

Although warrioring, by itself, will not produce utopia, it does teach a very important process that contributes to building a better world for each of us. What do Warriors learn? First, to trust their own truths and act on them with absolute conviction in the face of danger. To do so, however, they must take control of, and responsibility for, their own lives. Orphans see themselves as victims, and Wanderers as outsiders. By defining themselves as having no power in the culture, they do not have to take any responsibility for it. To identify yourself as a Warrior is to say, "I am responsible for what happens here" and "I must do what I can to make this a better world for myself and for others." It also requires you to claim your authority. Warriors learn to trust their own judgment about what is harmful and, perhaps most important, they develop the courage to fight for what they want or believe in, even when doing so requires great risk—the loss of a job, a mate, friends, social regard, or even their very lives.

BEYOND SLAYING THE DRAGON

Over time, the Warrior archetype has evolved. Gladiatorial contests have been replaced by football. Imperialism has been replaced by corporate takeovers where the blood on the floor is figurative, not real. The woman who a few years ago would have lambasted a man for a sexist remark now says in a fairly bored and disinterested way, "Oh, come off it." The stronger and more confident Warriors become, the less they must use violence, the more gentle they can be—with themselves and others. Finally, they need not define the other as villain, opponent, or even a potential convert; rather, the other becomes another possible hero, like themselves.

Accordingly, Warrior plots evolve from hero/villain/victim to hero/hero/hero. That the Warrior's truth now is simply one among many does not preclude commitment—to ideals, people, causes, or beliefs. Even in a relativistic world, Warriors embrace their beliefs and understandings with their whole hearts. It is, therefore, a high-level achievement in the Warrior process for a seemingly antithetical truth to be greeted not as an enemy, but as a potential friend: "Here's my truth. I will explain it to you as fully as I can, and you can explain yours to me." The task of the hero, then, is to *bridge*, not to slay or convert.

In the first and second editions of this book, I wrote about my fantasy of the end of the cold war. I had a vision of representatives from the Soviet Union sitting down with those of the United States. The Soviet representatives would begin by explaining that they feel they have done a good job of providing economic equity for their people, but they are concerned that it has been at the cost of political repression and a certain dullness to life. The U.S. ambassadors would reply by saying that they, too, feel only partly successful. The United States has much personal freedom and lots of excitement and variety, but great extremes of wealth and humiliating poverty remain. The two powers would proceed to put their heads together, sharing their own piece of the truth, and try to come up with a plan that would combine the best of both systems. Since then, of course, the cold war has ended and the USSR no longer exists.

I come from the generation that crouched under school desks in anticipation of a nuclear attack. Perhaps it is too soon to recognize the thawing out of human feeling that comes from knowing that that kind of threat is unlikely today. Still, the cold war helped all of us learn to live our lives in the face of the knowledge that our world might end—at any time. The developmental gift that comes from confronting one's own most frightening dragons—whether one slays them or merely stands up to them and begins a dialogue—is *courage* and a corresponding freedom from bondage to one's fears. At best, the Warrior ultimately learns to make friends with fear by long acquaintance. Instead of being immobilized by it, coming on like Attila the Hun, becoming locked into a paranoid, simplistic mode of addressing problems or even repressing it, the hero comes to see that fear can be an invitation to growth.

One of my favorite examples of a hero who develops such a positive relationship with her fear comes from Susan Griffin's *Women and Nature.* Griffin writes of "an old woman who was wicked in her honesty" who would ask questions of her mirror. When she asks why she is afraid of the dark, her mirror tells her, "Because you have reason to fear. You are small and you might be devoured." The woman determines to become too large to be devoured. However, once she does so, she discovers that she is afraid to be so big, and the mirror explains, "There is no disputing who you are. And it is not easy for you to hide." The woman then stops hiding. During her next attack of fear, the mirror tells her that she is afraid "because . . . no one else sees what you see, no one else can tell you if what you see is true." So she decides to trust herself.

Many years later, she realizes she is afraid of birthdays, and her mirror tells her, "There is something you have always wanted to do which you have been afraid of doing and you know time is running out." The woman goes immediately away from her mirror to "seize the time." Eventually, she and her mirror become friends and the mirror weeps for her in compassion when her fears are real. Finally, her reflection asks her, "What do you still fear?" And the old woman answers, "I still fear death. I still fear change." And her mirror agrees. "Yes, they are frightening. Death is a closed door, . . . and change is a door hanging open." "Yes, but fear is a key," laughed the wicked old woman, "and we still have our fears." She smiled.[3]

FROM DUALISM TO COMPLEXITY

Once we receive the gift of an archetype, it loosens its hold on us. When we become less frightened, our thinking can relax and become open to complexity; it then becomes clear how limited the hero/villain/victim formulation of reality is. Tom Robbins's *Even Cowgirls Get the Blues* illustrates this. The cowgirls of the Rubber Rose Ranch have taken on the "shoot-out at the O.K. Corral" mentality of the Wild West. They are preparing to shoot it out with the G-men who have been sent by the U.S. government ostensibly to rescue the whooping cranes that are vacationing on the ranch. In reality, however, the G-men plan to kill the birds. The cowgirls see themselves as defending the birds (and with them, nature) against the assaults of patriarchal civilization. At the last moment, the leader of the cowgirls has a vision from the Great Goddess herself, who tells her they should run away.

For one thing, there is no way they can defeat the G-men—the contest is too uneven. But at the same time, she also calls into question the whole concept of villains and heroes. The enemy of women, she explains, is not men, just as the enemy of blacks is not whites. The enemy is "the tyranny of the dull mind."[4]

The motivation to think more complexly and imaginatively in solving conflict comes from a variety of sources. Sometimes the challenge is forced upon us when we experience the villain as too big to fight. Perhaps this is why women have not taken particularly to combat: men are physically stronger! In the face of the incredible military advantage enjoyed by the British, Gandhi came up with a more complex and successful approach to liberating India than the typical call to arms. Defeating them in combat was not feasible, but he could win his "war" for independence by being a moral force that even the British were forced to respect. In the United States, Martin Luther King Jr. used a similar approach. Rather than seeing whites as the enemy, he called on them to join forces with blacks against the common enemy of racism. In demonstrating courageous nonviolence, he and the civil rights movement took the moral high road.

CELEBRATING EXCELLENCE

When we move out of the Warrior's dualistic emphasis on defeating the enemy, we open the door to redirecting that combative energy into a clear and direct focus on accomplishing our goals.

The high-level contemporary Warrior is less intent on competing with others than on competing with his or her self. We know that with children, self-esteem, at least in part, comes from genuine accomplishment. Whether one excels at school or sports as a child or later in the arts, sciences, or some form of business, we think well of ourselves to the degree that we are genuinely good at what we do. We all share a natural human tendency to want to improve. Thus, we can measure our competence against ourselves more than against that of others. Or we can focus primarily on achieving the results we want (straight A's, a successful business, bettering our previous time in running any given distance), with only peripheral attention to people or situations that may keep us from getting there.

The paradigm shift occurring in consciousness, politics, and the workplace calls for a greater sense of equality between and among people. In the face of this, we do not have to be better than anyone else to enjoy our own sense of competence. Moreover, social prosperity does not come from one group besting another. In fact, we can see what happens in countries that have incredible disparities of wealth: everyone suffers. The general standard of living declines, drug use and crime go up, and the social winners feel like prisoners in their own homes because the streets no longer are safe. We also have seen in the failure of communism what happens when the human need to achieve and aspire is suppressed in favor of equality defined as the lowest common denominator.

However, when everyone is well educated and encouraged to become the best he or she can be, economic prosperity increases, the quality of life improves, and drug use and crime decline. When running for president in 1992, Bill Clinton argued: "We do not have a person to waste." In his book *Frames of Mind*, Harvard professor Howard Gardner claims that the old paradigm of the "smart ones" and the "dumb ones" is anachronistic. He identifies eight basic kinds of intelligence; none of us has them all. Thus, we literally need each other to reach a complete understanding of the world.[5]

Archetypes evolve as we do. The evolution of the Warrior from hunter to fighter to achiever creates the potential for unprecedented individual and mass prosperity. People today can tap into the intense aliveness of this archetype without being pulled into its historically oppressive downside.

The Warrior helps us to set goals and then design a plan for achieving them. If you get a sense of satisfaction from writing a "to do" list and checking off what you have done, your inner Warrior is activated, especially if that list reflects what you truly want to accomplish. For several years, a colleague and I met regularly over breakfast to set our goals and support one another in staying with them. Both of us were aware that much of our time had been spent following other people's agendas, not our own. The accountability built into our "goals breakfasts" transformed our lives. We had formed an ad hoc Warrior team for the purpose of mutual enhancement. Within a year, each of us became much happier and livelier as we sought more consistently to live out our dreams and not simply respond to the needs and demands of others.

We see the same ethic today in the business world, where the ability to be a good team member frequently is valued more than being the solo star. Work teams often have goals that translate into objectives for each member. Success depends on everyone achieving his or her best, rather than on some people beating out others.

Increasingly, we are coming to understand that for organizations, quality is the key to sustainability over time. This realization translates into systems in which every worker strives for a high-quality performance every day. When we devalue other archetypal stages, an exclusive focus on quality can lead to workaholic over-achievement and chronic burnout. However, if we balance the Warrior with other archetypes, we can achieve true excellence, which fosters high morale. In *Care of the Soul*, Jungian analyst Thomas Moore maintains that our souls find great satisfaction anytime we do our best.[6] Such accomplishment can occur at work or at home. It may bring in income or it may be done for its own sake or as a gift to others. In either case, a quality product or service mirrors our souls and, in this way, reflects back to us our genuine worth. Therefore, you can find no better route to high self-esteem than a commitment to excellence in everything you do.

Imagine a world in which every person believed that he or she mattered and could make a contribution that helps us all. Imagine that at home, at school, and in recreational activities, each child's gifts were recognized and developed. Then, if each child also learned to tap into the inner Warrior, everyone would grow into a productive and responsible adult. In such a world, it would be possible to attain prosperity beyond any previously imagined, while simultaneously building a more just and humane society.

THE ACHIEVEMENT OF HUMILITY

The Achilles' heel of the Warrior is arrogance. The classic tragic hero (who is a Warrior) falls from power because of "hubris," that is, pride. Therefore, it is essential for the hero to learn humility. In one of my favorite Camelot stories, King Arthur allows himself to be seduced by wine, women, and song. He awakens in prison not knowing that Excalibur, the sword that ensured his invulnerability, has been stolen and replaced by a powerless replica. Arthur is told he can be released from prison if he fights a great antagonist (who now has Excalibur). In the duel, Arthur is getting the worst of it until he remembers that his power comes from the divine. When he prays, the Lady of the Lake, who had given him his sword originally, appears and magically sends Excalibur back to him through the air.

In a more modern version of this archetypal plot, Tom Brown Jr. writes in *The Search* about going into the forest for a year with only the clothes on his back and a knife. He was prepared for this solitary venture by Stalking Wolf, a Native American teacher, who taught him to be a tracker. Brown managed not only to survive a very hard, cold winter, but to enjoy (at least most of) the time.

The most paradoxically rewarding experience came near the end of his sojourn, when he went on a long fast. After twelve days, he was about to start eating again, but something strange happened. None of his skills served him. For seven more days, every animal he tried to stalk eluded him, and he feared he would starve to death. He grew very weak and began to have fainting spells. Then he had a clear chance to kill a small animal, but his hand stopped and would not move. At that point, he gave up and just surrendered to a mystic sense of trust in the universe and oneness that brings him exquisite joy. In the next instant, a deer almost walks up to him. He kills, cooks, and eats it in a feast of thanksgiving.

This moment of letting go is not always so transcendent. Sometimes it is motivated by a business reversal, a heart attack, the loss of a loved one, or a tragic event, and we can do nothing but accept it. Sometimes it is only maturity and the knowledge that none of the Warrior's skills is effective against death that force the Warrior to "give in" to greater life.

Warriors become burned out because they live life as a struggle against others and against parts of themselves that they regard as unworthy. I have seen many men and women finally realize how the struggle to be one up ultimately was killing them—their souls and their hearts, and sometimes their bodies as well.

Warriors who once felt such justifiable pride and exuberance over attaining the ability to take charge of their lives and make things happen years later begin to feel exhausted and drained. The transformation for many occurs when they start looking at all the strategies they are using just to keep going: addiction to caffeine, uppers, or alcohol or simply mobilizing their fear of failure to keep them racing onward and upward. In the latter case, a healthy desire to achieve has become obsessive and addictive. What they must do then is admit their ordinary human vulnerability and their need for love, for other people, and for spiritual and physical sustenance and nurturance.

Warriors first develop confidence by proving their superiority to others, because they have taken more control over their own lives than most and can make things happen while others seem to wait passively for things to happen to them. One of the gifts, then, when control fails is the dawning recognition that fundamentally we are not that different from one another. We are all in the same boat, and we are all, ultimately, interdependent: we need other people; we need the earth; we need God.

When Warriors give over control—as Tom Brown does in *The Search*—they move beyond the one-up/one-down view of life. The only reason to want to be one up is a belief that it is not fine to be just ordinary. Previously, not being special or different was equated with the Orphan's powerlessness, and therefore seemed contemptible to Warriors. In recognizing oneness with the earth and interdependence with other people, they come to honor humanness in those who are in control of their lives as well as those who have given over control or had it wrested from them. When heroes give up the need to be "better than," they stop having to prove themselves all the time and can, at least occasionally, just *be*.

The first few times Warriors try to assert their own wishes, they inevitably engage in overkill and therefore do not get very good results. However, at the next stage, they learn to be more subtle and politic and get what they want more often. Ultimately, however, Warriors must give over control of the outcome and assert themselves as part of the dance of life. The process of assertion then becomes its own reward, because it makes them more themselves.

It is then that miracles begin to happen. Often, after they have let go of their attachment to a particular outcome, when they have put themselves and their desires out there with no attendant wish to manipulate people or make people satisfy them, Warriors discover that the results are better than they dared hope. It is at this point that Buddhist notions of nonattachment and Judeo-Christian mystic beliefs about transcending ego begin to make sense and to be useful to the hero.

Symbolically, it is important that at the end of the old heroic myth, after he has confronted his fear by slaying the dragon, the

Warrior comes home and marries. The reward for his battle is that he becomes, finally, a lover. Without the skills of assertion and boundary setting, no real peer love relationship is possible—only one in which one person simply conquers and the other appeases. These skills allow for the creation of a positive relationship with another human being, with institutions, and with the world in general. Ultimately, they make it possible to love and savor life itself.

Many of the great lovers in literature begin by quarreling with one another—for example, Shakespeare's Beatrice and Benedict (*Much Ado About Nothing*) and Jane Austen's Darcy and Elizabeth (*Pride and Prejudice*). Each has the strength, self-respect, and facility for assertion that allows them to negotiate a mutually satisfactory relationship. Healthy intimacy demands the daily, hourly assertion of who you are and what you want and a willingness to look at how conflicting desires can come together to create a mutually enriching life.

So, too, in business. You have only part of the equation if you invent a better mousetrap but cannot market it. Being good at your work is only one step toward job satisfaction. The next is to create a sense of human community where employees, customers, and other stakeholders feel seen and appreciated.

GETTING ACQUAINTED WITH THE WARRIOR ARCHETYPE

To familiarize yourself with the Warrior archetype, make a collage out of Warrior-like pictures from magazines; make lists of songs, movies, and books that express the Warrior; collect pictures of yourself, relatives, colleagues, and friends in a Warrior mode. Practice noticing when you are thinking or acting like a Warrior.

Warrior Exercises

Step One: Breathe deep into your belly and ask yourself what you really desire. This is deeper and more primal than what you "want," but it does not have to be just basic urges either. To what degree is your present life fulfilling these desires?

Step Two: What are your values? What principles do you feel committed to standing up for? To what degree are you currently living up to your ethical standards?

Step Three: Define your goals for the next few years. Then identify what you need to do—and by when—to accomplish them. Create a system of accountability so you can keep track of your progress. (If you get new information that would suggest you alter your plan, do so.)

Step Four: What is happening in your life that seems to you to be going wrong? What might you do about it? Design and implement a plan of action to remedy this wrong.

CHAPTER 5

Showing Generosity: The Altruist

> If I speak in the tongues of men and of angels, but have not love, I
> am a noisy gong or a clanging cymbal. And if I have prophetic pow-
> ers, and understand all mysteries and all knowledge, and if I have all
> faith, so as to remove mountains, but have not love, I am nothing. If
> I give away all I have, and if I deliver my body to be burned, but have
> not love, I gain nothing. . . . So faith, hope, love abide, these three;
> but the greatest of these is love.
>
> —1 Corinthians 13:1–3, 13

The hero commits to something greater than his or her self.

What do you love enough to die for? Your child? Your spouse or
partner? Your parents? Would you give your life if it would ensure
world peace, or end hunger, or preserve freedom? Short of dying,
what do you sacrifice to make this world a better place? Are you as
interested in the effect of your work on the world as you are in how
much money or status it brings you? What do you value? What do
you want to give to the world? What do you want your legacy to be?

Heroes from time immemorial have lived for something greater
than themselves. They may live for their country, for history, for
family, for principle, for love, or for God. The motivations differ,
but by definition, heroes have a transcendent function, bringing
renewed life not only to themselves but to the world. We are living
in a time of immense challenge and opportunity. The choices we

make today as individuals collectively create the world we all will inhabit tomorrow. Progress is not automatic. Rather, it results from the aggregate decisions of individuals who consider not only their own good, but the greater good of society, humankind, and the planet.

The Altruist archetype* overlays the mammalian brain with distinctly human features, just the way the Warrior archetype does with the reptilian brain. Mammals not only suckle their young, they also like to cuddle up with each other, and they form lasting bonds. When predators attack mammalian herds, the old, the weak, and the ailing will go to the outside of the pack, sacrificing themselves for the good of the others. Our mammalian heritage gives us the capacity for love and devotion and an instinct to sacrifice ourselves when necessary. The Altruist archetype helps us to bring these virtues to consciousness, so that we can choose not only whom we love but also if and when we are willing to sacrifice ourselves for others.

---

* In the first two editions of this book, I referred to the archetype of care and sacrifice as the Martyr. In writing this edition, I concluded that the word "martyr" has taken on such a pejorative connotation that I had to use another name to help people connect with the part of each of us that lives for something beyond ourselves. However, even with this change of terminology, the archetype still asks us to give not only what is easy, but what sometimes is very difficult. Indeed, there are times that demand that we give something up or that we give to others what we could have kept to ourselves. Also, life follows a natural progression. For example, people who are very successful in business may focus on proving themselves and amassing wealth early in their lives, and later turn to charitable pursuits. In addition, life has a built-in balance, even early on, if you have a family. You may be a fiercely competitive Warrior at work, but at home you may sacrifice your desires willingly in order to be supportive of your spouse, partner, or children.

The term "martyr" used to command great respect. It referred to someone who was willing to die or to sacrifice something of value for principle, for love, or to help others. Ironically, sacrifice has gone out of fashion. At a time when the homeless line our streets, children and the elderly are too often neglected, and the gap between the rich and the poor continues to expand, too few of us seem willing to give generously through our taxes, donations to private charities, or gifts of our own time, to correct these inequities. Contemporary self-help literature often lumps the most noble acts of caring under the rubric of codependence (which has to do with giving inappropriately to those who will use your help to continue an addictive practice). This leaves many with the bizarre idea that always thinking of yourself first is healthy, while caring for others is inherently a sign that you are sick.

When the Altruist archetype emerges in our lives, it helps us connect with the full range of our mammalian and human ancestry. As with other archetypes, the expression of the Altruist evolves from very concrete to more abstract. In primitive societies, human sacrifices were offered to curry favor with the gods. More advanced cultures revered great heroes and religious saints and martyrs who were willing to die for their country or their faith. In our own time, it is expressed in our willingness to forgo individual achievement to be a good team player, to sacrifice for our children, and to give to the less fortunate.

ALTRUISM AND ECSTASY

In ancient civilizations, not only did the deities offer models of martyrdom, their deaths and resurrection were linked with eroticism. For instance, the Greek god Dionysus was seen as irresistible to women. In the Dionysian rites, followers would crowd around him (like groupies following rock stars), grabbing whatever part they could touch. Eventually, they would reach such heights of passionate intensity that they would tear him apart in a frenzy of ecstasy, but he would always return, reborn in the new year.

The Greek Eleusinian mysteries explained the origin of the seasons through the myth of Demeter, the grain goddess, and her daughter, Persephone. Persephone was kidnapped by Hades, the lord of the underworld, who was smitten with love (or at least lust) for her. Demeter was so saddened by Persephone's abduction that she sat crying instead of making the crops grow. As famine spread throughout the land, Zeus intervened and had Demeter's beloved daughter returned to her. When he did so, the crops and flowers flourished once again. Yet because Persephone had eaten a pomegranate seed while in the underworld, she had to return there for a portion of each year; that portion of the year the earth experiences as winter.

Basic to every fertility religion is the knowledge that death and sacrifice are prerequisites to rebirth. This is a basic law of the natural and spiritual worlds. The mysteries of Demeter and Persephone likely originated with the development of agriculture. For thousands of years, people gathered at Eleusis and elsewhere to learn the processes of agriculture, sex, birth, and death. In agriculture, the seed is planted in the ground; for a time nothing appears to be happening, until finally it sprouts. With sex, the egg is fertilized by the sperm and planted in the womb, where it gestates for nine months until the baby is born. When we die, we are buried in the earth, and it looks like we are gone forever. However, the priestesses of Eleusis would explain that, as surely as the seed produces the grain and sex leads to babies, death is followed by rebirth and new life.

While the Orphan seeks rescue from suffering and loss, the Altruist accepts them as potentially transformational. Our major modern religions also extol the transformative quality of sacrifice. As Carol Ochs argues in *Behind the Sex of God*, the central stories of Judaism and Christianity—Abraham's willingness to sacrifice Isaac and God the Father's willingness to sacrifice Christ—dramatize the healing power of martyrdom. If one's love for one's child is great, offering up that child is the ultimate sacrifice, greater even than sacrificing oneself.[1] Taken metaphorically, the willingness to sacrifice one's "child" may represent a step beyond the narcissistic egocentricity of the Orphan that requires us to learn to give and care not only when it is easy, but also when it is difficult, when it feels as if giving is at one's own expense.

Similarly, Buddhist practice teaches us to find happiness by letting go of our desires. Paradoxically, we can find satisfaction not through getting what we want, but by sacrificing ego attachment for the greater good of transcendent bliss.

Sacrifice and martyrdom may be unfashionable in a pleasure-seeking world, but hardly a soul does not believe in them in some form. At their base is a recognition that "I am not the only person in the world." Sometimes we choose to do something not so much because we want to, but because it will be good for someone else or because we believe it to be right. Some sacrifice is necessary if we wish to interact lovingly with other people. And, although it may not make us feel ecstatic, we all know the sense of joy and self-esteem that results when we act to help others. Scientific research even suggests that doing so strengthens our immune systems.[2]

ACCEPTANCE OF MORTALITY

Understanding that death is basic to nature also is part of accepting the sacrificial aspect of life. The leaves fall off the tree every autumn, making spring blossoms possible. All animal life, including humans, lives by eating other life forms. As much as we try to deny it, humans are part of the food chain. We eat plants and animals and excrete substances that fertilize the soil so that more plants can grow. Every life breath depends upon our symbiotic relationship with plants, with whom we exchange oxygen and carbon dioxide. In death, our bodies decay and fertilize the soil. This is the wisdom that fertility religions teach us.

Our lives are our contribution to the universe. We can give this gift freely and lovingly, or we can hold back as if it were possible by refusing life to avoid death. But no one can. How much worse to die never having lived! The final lesson of the Altruist is to choose to give the gift of one's life for the giving's sake, knowing that life is its own reward and remembering that all the little deaths, the losses in our lives always bring with them transformation and new life, that actual deaths are not final but merely a more dramatic passage into the unknown.

Until we are willing to give ourselves over to life, we always will be possessed by death. We may reject sacrifice philosophically, but we will find inevitably that we martyr ourselves to our wandering, our warrioring, even our magic making. I believe that human beings have an innate need to sacrifice for something beyond themselves. As I write, my twenty-one-year-old daughter is cooped up in an editing room, working inhumanly long hours to finish an educational video designed to help young drug users stay alive. She could never work that hard out of ambition, but she can out of love.

In organizational settings, I meet so many people whose work is motivated by an incredible sense of wanting to make a difference to the world; these people could be making much more money and/or having more recreational time, but instead are committed to work they think matters. Because they know what they do helps people, they endure interminably boring meetings, brain-numbing paperwork, and long hours.

In his management classic *Deep Change*, Robert Quinn argues that today's heroic organizational leaders must care more about contributing to the world than about their own climb up the corporate ladder. What the world needs now, he says, is visionary leadership. Working with a management team in the process of developing a vision statement, he asks them if they would be willing to die for this vision. (Of course, he does not mean literally die. He means lose their jobs.) Success, in this new paradigm, is not based on how much money you make, but on your ability to contribute to the world. His point is that the paradigm shift occurring in our economic and social life requires leadership that puts the good of the organization and the wider community ahead of personal gain.[3]

Most of us know that in our private lives, the establishment of a healthy family requires a willingness to put your immediate desires aside for the sake of others. Any parent who stays up all night with a sick child knows that however exhausted they feel the next day, they would not have failed to be there for that child. Anyone involved in a serious, committed love relationship knows that you just have to let go of the need to always get your own way for that relationship to work. Most couples go through a Warrior period, in which both parties, in a battle of wills, try to remake the other in their own image. When this Pygmalion project fails, as it almost always does, it becomes possible to stop being two warring individuals and to establish a sense of "us" as a couple. When this happens, we make choices not necessarily because they are best for "me," but because they are good for "us."

Many self-destructive and addictive tendencies in our "me-first" world can be traced to our failure to honor in ourselves the human need to sacrifice for something greater than ourselves. If we do not sacrifice consciously for something we believe in, we will be possessed by the martyr's shadow—behaviors that threaten to take our lives but bring no redemption.

Sacrifice can be fulfilling when it is fueled by genuine passion. For example, chivalric literature extols the suffering of the knight who does whatever is necessary to prove his love for his mistress. Eventually, his efforts pay off, not only in winning her favor, but also in developing discipline, courage, and honor. Such knights also find fulfillment in swearing absolute loyalty to the king, dying, if need be, for their country.

Many people take jobs that do not pay well and offer little chance for promotion. They may work in day-care facilities, in homes for the aged, in community organizations, or in other places that make a great difference in the lives of those they serve. Few of us may know who they are, but they daily make the world a better place. Although the rewards may not translate into material wealth or power, if they know they truly are helping others, they rightly feel that their lives have meaning and value.

The resonance of the Altruist archetype in today's world was demonstrated by the outpouring of grief after the death of England's Princess Diana. Diana could have spent all of her time being a playgirl. Instead, she spent countless hours at what she considered "her work," publicly lending support to those organizations caring for people in need. And people loved her for it. In particular, they responded to her early concern for AIDS patients and her personal campaign to publicize the ongoing harm to civilians, many of them children, caused by land mines.

The heroes with whom people identify today are not larger than life. They are struggling with the same ordinary dilemmas we all face. People loved Princess Diana because she let them in, sharing with the world her struggles with bulimia and her disappointment in what seemed like every girl's fantasy (to marry the prince). In this way, she was appreciated as a fellow human, with sorrows as well as strengths. Heroes do not wait to help the world until they have it all together. The hero brings life to a dying culture, in part, by being both caring and real. All of us can do this by living our lives fully. Our capacity to do so is related psychologically to our willingness to give what it requires of us: to love as fully as we can, even though we know that doing so opens us up to pain and sorrow; to live our vocational purpose, to do our work, even though we risk failure, poverty, or receiving little or no appreciation; and ultimately to die, for that is the price we pay for having lived.

WHY SACRIFICE HAS A BAD NAME

Although widely practiced in both its positive and negative variations, sacrifice has gotten a bad name because in the past it has too often been prescribed, not chosen. If you have been socialized by your parents, by the church/synagogue, or by your schooling to sacrifice the essence of your individuality to be "good," there is no way you can give freely. Before learning to give appropriately, it is necessary to say no to gratuitous, role-defined sacrifice.

Sacrifice cannot be redemptive if it is required! Men have been expected to compete in a marketplace metaphorically envisioned as a "jungle" and to fight when necessary to protect home and hearth. Women were taught to create a home environment marked by care and gentleness. The existence of such a private sanctuary from the storm was dependent upon women's sacrifices—not only the necessary sacrifices required by raising children, but more than that. Because men had opted out of the world of care for the world of conquest, women were expected to supply the care for both parties. In practice, this meant that women had to sacrifice their creative expression and their achievement urge in order to care for others. This arrangement has been crippling to women because, instead of sacrifice being just one developmental task, it has defined their lives. Furthermore, the mythos of love and sacrifice has been used to *keep* women in traditional and limited roles.

While men have not been expected to forego personal achievement for care, the culture has assigned them the role of the provider, which means they have had to take on dangerous or tedious work, if it was required to put food on the table. Furthermore, the Warrior archetype, in which the masculine role has been cast, also feeds into the Altruist archetype, with its demand that individuals be willing not only to fight to win, but if necessary to die for their cause. Moreover, stoic Warriors sacrifice everything else to become performance machines. I sometimes think that men who die from heart attacks induced by work-related stress can be seen as dying from hearts broken by believing that no one cares how they feel as long as they make money for the company and the family.

If you think about the stereotypes of the American mom or the Jewish mother, you can see how the traditional selfless female role can distort a woman's full humanity rather than bringing out her innate nobility. Its results are bitterness, manipulation, and guilt-inducing behavior. You also can see that when men are forced into the provider role with no permission to consider their own deeper desires or concerns, they can develop a macho sense of entitlement, which comes down to wanting tribute to make up for not quite having a real life. When people are forced by role expectations to give up their lives for someone else, they inevitably will require that the other person pay. We see this with bitter wives who berate their husbands; mothers and fathers who lay guilt trips on their children; and men in demeaning jobs who come home and order their families around.

More often than not, sacrifice is not rewarded. The wife may sacrifice career (or career advancement) or simply doing what she loves to help her husband or children, yet find she is taken increasingly for granted. She also may internalize this negative self-valuation, introducing herself socially as "I'm just a housewife." A husband may work as a trash collector to support his family and find they are ashamed of what he does, even though he is doing it entirely for them. An employee may give up his weekends and evenings to the company and be downsized anyway. People in caregiving professions like teaching or nursing pay a price in income (unless they invoke the Warrior and form a union). Indeed, often people watching others sacrifice themselves to do for others assume they have no self-esteem and treat them accordingly.

Good-hearted people organize government and charitable programs to help those in poverty. Most beneficiaries use such programs appropriately to get back on their feet. In doing so, they honor the sacrifices made on their behalf. Of course, some always find a way to use the system for personal profit, seeing the "bleeding hearts" who support these programs as chumps. Others misuse their subsidies to underwrite addictive and self-destructive behaviors. To the degree that the altruistic intent in establishing such programs is not balanced by realism and tough-mindedness, individuals and whole societies may turn away from giving entirely or so carefully monitor recipients that their dignity is undermined. Pseudo-Altruists use the inevitable chiselers as an excuse to retreat from social responsibility, while more high-minded individuals employ their intelligence to fine-tune their ability to make a "tough-love" difference for those in need.

GRATUITOUS SACRIFICE STOPS HERE

The decision to care, even at the cost of self-sacrifice, is a choice for life and against despair. It also is the dominant spiritual lesson people have been working on for thousands of years and, as we have seen, it is the essence of Christianity and Judaism, modern existential thought, as well as much of progressive politics. Heroes in all times and places always have been those individuals who lived for something beyond themselves.

I was talking recently with a friend about this book, and he said that to him the hero is someone who has endured life's trials and tribulations. When pressed, he explained that he actually meant something more than that. Heroes, he continued, not only endure hardships, they maintain their love of life, their courage, and their capacity to care for others. No matter how much suffering they experience, they do not pass it on. They absorb it and declare: "Suffering stops here!"

In the primitive Altruist's morality, it is appropriate for mothers to sacrifice personal growth and fulfillment for their children. Their daughters will sacrifice for their children in turn. Fathers and sons are expected to give their lives willingly, if called, for their country. Everyone sacrifices themselves to God or, more precisely, they sacrifice in the service of good those parts of themselves that they regard as wrong or sinful. Nothing much is going on but sacrifice. It has become an end in itself; hence, it does nothing to improve the world. Indeed, it usually adds to the world's cumulative pain.

At a higher level, consciousness kicks in, and with it the transformative power of personal choice. In Joseph Heller's novel *Catch–22*, Yossarian, the central character, recognizes that the social system in which he lives (the army during World War II) is defined entirely by suffering, with every victim victimizing some-one else: "Someone had to do something sometime. Every victim was a culprit, every culprit a victim, and somebody had to stand up sometime to try to break the lousy chain of inherited habit that was imperiling them all."[4] Although he has been told he is flying bombing missions to save home and country, he discovers his covert mission was simply to preserve international business. So he stops flying. Yossarian knows that he cannot necessarily be free, since the army can court-martial him. However, instead of the meaningless affliction of flying more missions, his refusal can have some positive effect. At the very least, he is living by his own values and has regained his integrity. At most, his example may prompt others to refuse to fly more bombing missions, too. Then the chain of suffering may be broken.

Yossarian comes to understand that the sacrifices he has been forced to make are actively destructive to himself and others. As long as he keeps flying bombing missions, he complies with the forces on both sides that are killing people needlessly. The choice to say no also requires sacrifice—perhaps he will have to give up an honorable discharge and hence lose respect and career oppor-tunities back home; yet, this sacrifice *is* transformative because it is an appropriate and courageous response to the actual needs of his specific situation.

How can you tell whether you are giving appropriately? When you are, it feels compatible with your identity, an outgrowth of who you are. Ultimately, we know who we are by what we would die for. Great martyrs like Martin Luther King Jr. and Yitzhak Rabin, for instance, so believed in themselves and their cause that they knowingly risked death rather than endure the soul-harming living death of being less than they could be. So, too, for Mother Teresa. She worked with the homeless and dying because that was her calling. For many of us, making decisions about when and how much to sacrifice helps us learn who we are.

THE DIGNITY OF RECEIVING

Giving cannot be transformative unless it is received. If someone gives to us and we refuse the gift, no harm necessarily is done, but no great good is accomplished either. If someone gives to us and we use what they give to enable our addictions or other bad behavior, actual harm results. If we develop an attitude of entitlement, we may receive an enormous amount, but never notice. The result may be that others stop giving to us because their gifts seem so invisible and devalued.

Once we define ourselves as the giver in a particular situation or relationship, we may not notice how much we also receive. This is particularly true for parents. I remember once when my daughter, Shanna, was only about four or five. I came home from a particularly intense day at work, made her a quick bite to eat, and rushed to get her and her friend to their gymnastics class. The class was too far from home to come back, so I waited, hungry and tired, for an hour and a half, bit my tongue while she fooled around after practice, rushed us home, got her bathed and dressed for bed, and read a story. I still had not had time to eat or change out of my business clothes.

When she then asked me to sing her to sleep, I said rather crossly, "I'm tired. You have to think of me sometimes, too." As she turned over to go to sleep, she reached out, touched my cheek with her little hand, and said, "Mom, I always think of you." There was such love in her voice that I felt fully seen and loved by her. At her touch, my energy returned. Certainly that was as great a gift as my making her dinner and taking her to her lesson. But had I been attached to the idea of being the all-giving mother, I could not have let in her love in the simple, honest way she gave it to me. How great it feels when a child throws open her arms to greet you, jumping up and down with happiness, shouting "Mommy's home!" or "Daddy's home!"

Raising Shanna, I have reconnected with the girl in me, learned to play again, and experienced daily delight and love. When I fully let that in, I know that she has brought at least as much to me as I have shared with her. Very few of our relationships really have to be one way. Therapists learn from their clients; teachers learn from their students; ministers learn from their congregations. When the energy is not flowing both ways, something is wrong. If the giving and receiving happen with no blocking, then both receive more than they give—because the process intensifies and enriches the energy exchanged. Learning to give or to sacrifice appropriately surely is as hard as learning to play baseball. Our first attempts always are very clumsy. People may misinterpret our giving and think we want something in return. Or, like the mother who abandons her career or the father who works in a field he hates in order to support his family, we overdo it. But with practice comes improvement; our giving and receiving take on the effortlessness shown by real pros playing catch. It all seems easy—throwing and catching and letting go again.

For some people, giving is painful because they feel they have to control or manipulate everything if the ball is ever to come back to them. And if they think that—after having thrown the ball to first base, they have to get it back from first base—they may be sorely disappointed. But sooner or later—from third base or left field—the ball returns.

The more we give in this kind of free way, the more we get, because nature abhors a vacuum; it fills us up. That is, it does so unless we have misunderstood sacrifice and see the state of emptying out as a static good rather than only a stage in the process. Then we get what we asked for—emptiness, depletion.

When we learn both to take and to give, we can move into a flow of giving and receiving that is love's essence—reciprocity. In this way, the flow of energy does not go just one way, but both. I give to you and you to me and we both receive the energy fully. Christ said to "love your neighbor as yourself." Sacrifice, however, has been misinterpreted as loving your neighbor *instead* of yourself.

For love to be transformative, it must be let in. That is why Christ asked his disciples at the Last Supper to eat the bread and drink the wine "in remembrance of me." It also is why the Hebrews were enjoined to eat special Passover foods to celebrate the Exodus from Egypt. Eating is a powerful symbol for taking a gift in, for nothing is truly a gift until it is received. Conscious receiving raises the difficult issue of choice and of taking responsibility for having chosen to let in one thing and not another. Yes, I will marry you, but not you. Yes, I will work with you, but not you.

Sometimes we are unable to receive gifts because we are afraid that in receiving them, we will obligate ourselves to pay the giver back. This kind of contractual giving may be a form of manipulation. We can use our intuition and turn down gifts that have inappropriate strings attached, but we also should be aware that sometimes we simply project our fears onto the giver.

Communication in relationships vastly improves when we make our expectations explicit to our loved ones. Almost everyone gives what they would like to receive, without realizing that the other person may want something very different. I once was in a relationship with a man who felt I did not really love him because I did not do little things for him like sew buttons on his shirt. When he told me this, I got angry because I thought he was being a male chauvinist. Later, I realized that it was not so much that he wanted me to be conventionally female, but that his idea of how you show love was doing little things like that for one another. Because my idea of how to show love is to say, "I love you" and share the secrets of your heart, I felt unloved by him—not recognizing that he showed his love for me by returning my overdue library books! To stay together, we would have had to learn each other's giving vocabulary. The same is true at work.

COMMITMENT, BALANCE, AND
THE ENNOBLED LIFE

For many, even the thought of making a major commitment to someone else raises major fears. For example, it might be nice to marry this person, but what if I find someone later whom I like better? Or what if he leaves me? What if he is unsuccessful? What if she turns out like her mother? What if she gets cancer and I have to take care of her? To commit is to risk the unknown, but even more than that it requires sacrificing the idea of the perfect mate to love a real, flawed human being. When we do so honestly and freely, out of clear preference, the result can be transformative. If the commitment is reciprocal, it can make for a magic relationship of closeness and joy. If it is not, it still can be personally transformative, because through it we learn the skill of loving fully and not holding back from that experience. And we learn we can survive the loss of what we love most.

So, too, with life. Commitment to living this life means giving up rigid ideas about what the world should be and loving what it is. That, of course, does not mean that we do not work to make the world a better place or to improve our relationships. It means that we can give up the pose of being disappointed idealists and let ourselves know what a blessing it is to be alive. We allow ourselves to let it all in. It also means giving up the notion of scarcity—that there is not enough to go around and that I am not enough, you are not enough, and the world is not enough. In accepting life, we can believe that plenty of love, goods, and room are available to make us happy.

In our technological age, we can have cell phones, car phones, fax machines, and electronic mail wherever we go. As a result, we can continue working long after we theoretically "go home." People of conscience also want to spend quality time with their spouses or partners, children, parents, and friends, and they commit time to self-improvement, introspection, worship, and values clarification—not to mention getting requisite exercise and doing community service.

Many of us today are afflicted by "life greed." In the late 1980s and into the 1990s, it was fashionable to learn the Warrior skill of envisioning what you want and going for it. This was good, in part, because many of us discovered we could have and be more than we thought possible. However, during this same period, the gap between the haves and have-nots grew exponentially. Some people realized their wildest dreams, while others lost their homes and were living on the streets. The Altruist calls on us to care not only for our own families, but for our communities, not just for those who look and act like us, but for those who do not.

Life for the relatively advantaged has became more and more hectic, even as it seemed possible to have and be anything. Today, the Altruist archetype helps us to sacrifice our perfectionism, recognizing that we are unlikely to have perfect children, keep an immaculate home, write the great American novel, *and* climb the corporate ladder, at least not all at once. It can also help us spend less time on achievement and more time caring for others, less effort on keeping up with the Joneses and more on visiting with them to create real community or working with them to solve social problems.

In a Warrior culture, personal achievement can seem to mean, and be, everything in life. However, what do we gain if some of us have more and more gadgets while others go hungry? Mindfulness and conscious choice help immeasurably in finding an appropriate balance between personal ambition and generosity. Ultimately, we know more about who we are by the choices we make. For example, a parent who decides to pull back from career advancement to attend to a troubled teenager may feel some envy years later when colleagues have surpassed him in achievement.

Yet, if he remembers that he made that decision himself and takes a moment to celebrate the benefit to the child, he can end up feeling ennobled, rather than cheated by life.

LOVE THY NEIGHBOR AS THYSELF

After slaying the dragon, the archetypal hero generally finds and falls in love with the woman (or man) of his (her) dreams. Genuine altruism results from love. Our first great loves are our parents, then relatives and friends. At some time, we may develop a crush on a teacher or other older adult. Later, as we grow up, we experience romantic love. Then we may have children of our own. When we really love someone, giving to that person is a great pleasure. It does not necessarily feel like a sacrifice. Notice how pleased little children are when they do anything that makes their parents happy. Notice also how pleased parents are if they can help their children thrive and grow. When making love with someone very special, we get as much delight in bringing our partner pleasure as in experiencing our own.

You may become part of a work team in which you all strongly believe in your mission. Perhaps the team goes through a difficult time. Instead of fighting, you hang tough together. A bond is created that can last forever. If you need to work late or pitch in to do something that really is not your job, you do not care. You are happy to help out.

During natural disasters, people usually put competitiveness aside and simply help one another, as people of the same nation often do in time of war. They are aware of a common bond and a need for one another, and also a sense of the fragility of human life. Typically, when people are asked what they would do if a nuclear bomb was about to be dropped on their city, they reply that they would call someone to tell them that they love them. Moreover, when we share difficult experiences with people, it is natural to let down our defenses and get more intimate, even telling things about ourselves that ordinarily would be too private to share.

The most authentic expression of altruism comes from love. And when we really love someone, we do not feel separate. In a Warrior culture, the emphasis is on proving ourselves; therefore, how much money, approval, and attention we get depends on how we measure up in comparison with others. In an Altruist culture, people merit money, approval, and attention simply because we care about them. They do not have to be specially gifted or work terribly hard. They just have to be themselves.

In her pioneering sociological study *The Female World*, Jessie Bernard described the difference between the historically private world of women and the public world of men. The private world operates in keeping with the Altruist archetype and the public world by the standards of the Warrior archetype. So Bernard and others maintain that our economic theories are based solely on the male experience in the male world. Therefore, we assume that people make economic and career decisions out of self-interest; working hard to make more money and gain greater status and power. It is not that this analysis is wrong, only that it is incomplete.

Women, Bernard notes, have lived by very different rules. In the home and in communities, women's work was not paid and held no possibility of advancement. Even if women worked in the wage economy, their earnings were low and opportunities to increase their pay and status minimal. Therefore, women worked for love and duty, rather than for personal advantage. In this female world, you gave to people not to achieve more, but because you loved them or could see that they needed your help.[5]

In *The Chalice and the Blade*, Riane Eisler traces the origin of these two coexisting worlds to the time when warrior bands conquered agrarian, goddess-worshiping peoples. She calls them

partnership and dominance societies, noting the relatively egalitarian nature of one and the hierarchical nature of the other.[6]

The legacy of the female has been undervalued and generally
ignored by scholars and theorists until recently. Sometimes it is
hard to notice what is happening when it is not studied in school
or covered by the media. Yet many women (and some men) still
live by the precepts of an Altruist culture. I am thinking of two
women, both of whom have been very important to me and to my
understanding of the Altruist approach to life. One enormously
talented woman spent many years traveling with her husband,
forgoing the opportunity to develop her own career. Yet, everywhere she went, she simply did what people needed—she counseled them, gave them massages and nutritional advice, decorated
their houses, painted murals on their walls, and made them meals.
She just gave what she could as a way to contribute to the hosts
she visited on her rounds. Sometimes she got paid, and sometimes
she did not. But she always had what she needed. This way of living seemed natural to her. The only problem arose when others
saw her as less accomplished than some of her contemporaries
because she was not following an identifiable career track.

The other woman works tirelessly to help people of color,
women, and individuals with disabilities. Whenever anyone needs
help, she is there. In her case, she often works for rather low-paying
nonprofit organizations, and she volunteers on the side and enjoys
(in her free time) doing favors for people and buying them presents
(which almost always are handmade, so she also is supporting struggling artists). She is not codependent, and she is not doing all this
out of some deep-seated neurosis. She does it freely, out of love.

Both of these women live by the rules of the female world. Of
course, men always have been a part of this more altruistic realm,
even while participating in the public world of the Warrior. Men
have been active in charity work, have helped out people down the
block, and have been involved in church, synagogue, or ashram

committees. Just as women brought casseroles to the neighbors, men would help build or fix whatever was needed. In the American West, community barn raisings were as much a part of frontier life as the quilting bee. One very successful consultant I know confided in me that his success comes from never worrying overly much about money. When he sees something that needs doing, he does it. Sometimes he is paid very well. Other times he contributes his services. The result is that he is not only affluent, but very respected.

Over the final two decades of the twentieth century, women have entered the public world in greater numbers. At the same time, communication skills and interpersonal intelligence have become essential for leadership and teamwork, rather than the top-down authoritarian approach that used to be the norm. Government programs have been instituted to help the needy. And even though President Lyndon Johnson used Warrior language to launch his "war on poverty," the intent came from the Altruist, not the Warrior, spirit in our country. Increasingly, our soldiers are as likely to be delivering food to starving people as they are to be engaged in mortal combat with an enemy.

It may well be that because of the threat of nuclear annihilation, people in ever greater numbers have realized that, in the poet W. H. Auden's words, "We must love each other or die." In the new global economy, and with our increasingly diverse workforce, learning to care for people who seem very different from us—whatever our background might be—is today's challenge. The picture taken from outer space of our beautiful globe—glowing like a jewel in the sky, but with no sign of national boundaries—is a powerful symbol of how interconnected all our journeys are and have been.

Those in whom the Altruist archetype is expressed fully care about others throughout the world, not simply as a virtuous act of charity but because they really believe that we are family. Coming face to face with a person with a different color skin, dressed in unfamiliar clothes, expressing ideas that seem strange or even uncomfortable, the Altruist sees the brother or sister underneath.

For the Altruist, the challenge of our time is to take the love, the care, the sharing, and the cooperative spirit that always have characterized the private sphere (at least within homogeneous groups) and express those traits in our pluralistic public and business life as well. At the same time, today's Altruists recognize that the imbalance between the Warrior and Altruist archetypes has led to a breakdown in the social fabric of our neighborhoods. While more women have joined the workforce (and adopted more Warrior characteristics), we have not seen an equivalent shift in the amount of male energy refocused on care.

In *The Death and Life of Great American Cities*, urbanologist Jane Jacobs explains that neighborhoods were much safer when older women sat on the front stoop or at their windows and kept an eye on things.[7] Yet, even without reverting to earlier sex roles, our neighborhoods can be safe again. We can make them so when our cultural value for care catches up with our respect for competition and achievement—in short, when the values of the traditional female realm are as respected as those of the male world. When this happens, the core of our families and communities will seem as important as the workplace to men as well as women.

In the past, the psychological development required of people was simplified greatly by assigning different groups roles that used only part of their potential ability as human beings. The increased complexity of life today and the breakdown of traditional sex roles force us to become more psychologically complex and balanced.

However, when the sexes are socialized very differently, there is an inherent limit to the intimacy that couples can achieve. Men and women today can reach greater closeness than in prior times precisely because we are learning to share more experiences and perspectives. Men do not have to feel as though women are an alien species and vice versa. Both men and women have access to the Warrior and the Altruist within.

As women and men balance the demands of "proving oneself" with "living generously," our communities, businesses, and societies can function more harmoniously together. The Warrior takes us part of the way to prosperity by teaching us discipline, skill, and a focus on quality of achievement. The Altruist moves us into abundance by encouraging us to share the wealth.

GIVING AND PROSPERITY

The Warrior lives in a context of scarcity. The Altruist archetype helps us make the transition into abundance. When we learn to give and receive appropriately and skillfully, the result is truly miraculous. A few years ago, I had the opportunity to participate in a giveaway ceremony patterned on those practiced by several Native American peoples. It showed me how letting go of what you no longer need and giving to others what they need can come together magically and painlessly. We had been told beforehand to bring something that was very valuable to us (though not necessarily of monetary value), something that we also were ready psychologically to give up and move beyond. We placed this item on an altar. Then we all walked by and took whatever item beckoned to us. The miracle, we discovered as we discussed it later, was that everyone received just the right gift. What I learned from this experience was that miracles of synchronicity (meaningful coincidences) do occur—regularly!

We all can have enough if we do not hoard. Our job is to appreciate thoroughly and treasure whatever we truly want that we already have and at the same time give up anything we no longer need. *Our capacity to give away speaks to the universe of our willingness to receive.* We do not have to hold on to things, protecting ourselves against a rainy day. If we freely give away, we also will receive freely *just what we need.*

In the 1970s, the United States experienced a series of energy "crises." We believed that gasoline was scarce, even though we still had an adequate supply. People stocked up out of fear. Ironically, this fear that we would not have enough became a self-fulfilling prophecy. When people believe they have enough and share freely, there *is* enough. What Franklin Roosevelt said in 1933 remains true: "The only thing we have to fear is fear itself."

When we get frightened, we hoard. One dollar, kept locked up, is worth only one dollar—for however long we have it. If that dollar is spent, invested, or given away, it might change hands ten times that day and hence be worth ten dollars. Over the course of the year, even if some days were less active, that dollar might be used for more than three thousand dollars' worth of transactions. Very literally, wealth happens when we keep money circulating. The same is true with goods. If all of us hoard goods we have no need for in our attics and basements, many people go without. If we all pass on what we no longer need, there is more for everyone to share. In addition, we have reached such a state of international interdependence that a financial collapse anywhere in the world has an impact on us. We all benefit if every society is doing at least minimally well. The more affluent the people of all nations are, the more they have to lose by going to war. Good trading partners are less likely to become enemies.

Many churches teach people to tithe, telling them that tithing will bring them prosperity. For this truth to kick in, we need not necessarily tithe to churches. The same principle can work equally well if we give money to philanthropic or political causes. Over the years, two people have sent me money with a card explaining that they tithed each week to someone who had nurtured them spiritually. Tithing works because it triggers the sense of prosperity. If I have enough to give away a percentage of my income, I feel psychologically abundant and hence become open to receiving the abundance of the universe.

We all are expected to tithe to the government—in fact, for most of us the tax bill comes to significantly more than ten percent. When the Wanderer archetype is active in our lives, this tends to seem like a great imposition. The Warrior supports taxes for the military and other government functions that help the country maintain a competitive advantage. The Altruist, however, is perfectly willing to pay a reasonable amount in taxes, believing that we have as much collective responsibility as we do personal rights. The Altruist knows that societies do not work unless affluence is shared. If the strong keep winning and the weak keep losing, the eventual result is a world full of crime, poverty, disease, environmental disaster, and the continual threat of rebellion caused by increased political repression. Rather than complain about taxes, the Altruist simply wants them used for the collective benefit, to provide roads, schools, and help for those who cannot help themselves.

When all have what they need to develop their full potential, the combined resources of the society are astoundingly high. When money is available for investment, innovation increases and productivity soars. Making certain that everyone has an opportunity to make a real contribution to the world pays off in universal prosperity.

Although people complain about the commercialism of the Christmas season, it is still a time to give and share. We watch movies like *It's a Wonderful Life* or read Charles Dickens's *A Christmas Carol* and the message is clear: when we hold on to wealth tightly, our lives dry up. When we spend our lives giving to others, we will be surrounded by loving community. All this focus on love and care, it is true, causes people to buy gifts for their loved ones. The truth is, all this spending does boost the economy. However much some might wish for a more authentic spiritual observance of the season, it does teach us about the relationship between caring and prosperity.

While Warriors think of money as a way to keep score in a competitive game with winners and losers, the Altruist sees money as a thank-you note from a person or from society for a job well done. This money then can be spent or contributed to thank others for what they are giving to the world or what they mean to us personally. The money paid is completing the cycle of giving and receiving that helps our self-esteem and our relationships grow. Thus, in the Altruist's worldview, we do not need the threat of poverty to keep people productive. Have you ever had the experience of believing that your contribution to an enterprise mattered greatly? If so, you know how motivated and how productive you can be. The more freely and fearlessly we give, the less it feels like sacrifice and the more it seems like a way to generate incredible abundance for us all.

GETTING ACQUAINTED WITH
THE ALTRUIST ARCHETYPE

To familiarize yourself with the Altruist archetype, make a collage out of Altruist-like pictures from magazines; make lists of songs, movies, and books that express the Altruist; collect pictures of yourself, relatives, colleagues, and friends in an Altruist mode. Practice noticing when you are thinking or acting like an Altruist.

Altruist Exercises

Step One: Look for opportunities to be kind and caring to others. Every day, try to help someone. Make it a point continually to open your heart to give not only to those you love, but also to strangers. In every situation, think what the most loving thing you can do in this encounter is. Be particularly attuned to people who depend on you: a spouse or partner, parents, children, friends, and employees. Be attentive to what they need from you.

Step Two: Pay attention to all the people, activities, and places you love. Notice especially when love simply lights you up or gives you energy. Take time to be grateful for these experiences. Notice how just paying attention increases the satisfaction you receive from them (as you stop simply taking them for granted). Begin increasing the time you choose to spend doing things and being with people you value.

Step Three: Think of yourself as a philanthropist. Pay attention to how you can contribute your time, money, and expertise to benefit the larger society. Pay attention to what issues, causes, and organizations tug at your heartstrings. Decide what percentage of your time and money you are ready to give away. Consider how your own talents and abilities can be used to benefit society. Act on this to the best of your ability.

Step Four: Remember with all these efforts to begin by loving and nurturing yourself. Notice how giving to others, in a way that comes from your genuine altruism, enhances your self-esteem and quality of life. Discontinue any ways that currently are giving you no satisfaction. Replace them with more authentic modes of giving.

CHAPTER 6

Achieving Happiness: The Innocent's Return

> She was the single artificer of the world
> In which she sang. And when she sang, the sea,
> Whatever self it had, became the self
> That was her song, for she was the maker. Then we,
> As we beheld her striding there alone,
> Knew that there never was a world for her
> Except the one she sang and, singing, made.
>
> —Wallace Stevens, *The Idea of Order at Key West*

The hero finds the treasure.

Are you ever filled with yearning for a better life? Do you believe life does not have to be hard? If these feelings are strong in you, or if you have many moments of true peace and contentment, you are ready for the return to innocence. This means that you can have the happiness you always wanted—that is, if you are willing to allow yourself to be transformed in the process.

Before the journey, the Innocent lives in an unfallen world, a green Eden where life is sweet and all one's needs are met in an atmosphere of care and love. The closest ordinary equivalents to this experience occur in early childhood—for people with happy childhoods—or later, in the first stages of romance or in mystic experiences. Even when people have had no such idyllic experiences, they may be propelled forward by the hope of attaining a peaceful, happy, secure life.

Stories that teach us that we can be cared for can be very comforting. In Shel Silverstein's award-winning children's story *The Giving Tree*, a young boy plays in a tree's branches and eats her apples. When he grows up, she gives him her branches to build a house. Many years later, when he yearns to sail the seven seas, she gives him her trunk to make a boat. Finally, when he returns to her in old age, she is sad because she has nothing left to give, but he explains that he only needs a place to sit down. So he sits upon her stump and, like every other time she has given to him, "He's happy and she's happy."

If only life were that easy! The skeptical among us might question whether anyone is cared for this well or whether the tree is really that happy. Does she in fact want to sacrifice herself to the boy? From this vantage point, we also might wonder about the boy's narcissism. Has he no awareness of the cost of his behavior to the tree?

INNOCENCE AND DEPENDENCE

Before the journey, innocence is experienced in a childlike way, which means that it involves a good bit of unconscious or even conscious dependence. It is appropriate for infants and children simply to assume that others will take care of them. Even as an adult, the Innocent who has not experienced the Fall takes the earth and its resources for granted and imagines God as an all-powerful Father (or Mother) whose purpose is to keep one safe—that is, if one is good.

Such innocence is a natural state for infants and small children, and throughout life a part of the self needs to hold on to the experience of being totally safe, totally cared for, and totally loved. Many people believe they can retain this kind of innocence by following all the rules set by parents, religious authorities, teachers, and bosses about what they should be. Ironically, the very attempt to hold on to innocence ultimately subverts it. Some people become bitter when they try so hard and then others who break all the rules get the girls (or boys), make more money, or receive more attention. Even worse, they may find that all this focus on being perfect calcifies their lives.

If we do take our journeys, however, there will be times when we return to Eden: in those precious moments when we are infatuated with a new friend or new love, when life glitters with possibilities, or when we are filled with awe at the beauty of a pristine lake, a towering mountain, or a lovely rose. We also may reexperience what it is like for a small child to feel safe and cared for—with a friend or loved one, in a therapeutic or workshop environment, or in those spiritual moments when it seems as though we are being held in the hands of a benevolent God or Goddess.

In the main, however, growing up—for much of the journey—requires us to know life in a more fallen world, where many others do not care about our welfare, where even our friends and lovers can betray us or let us down, where predatory people attempt to take advantage of us, where we can be seriously hurt and damaged, and where God sometimes feels very far away or nonexistent. Yet, despite all this, something in each of us rejects the persistent message that it is a tough world. Part of us, at least, continues to search for more utopian possibilities.

The promise of a return to the mythic Edenic state is one of the most powerful forces in human life. Much that is harmful in what we do—and what we fail to do—is defined by it. We objectify the earth and each other in a frantic attempt to get what we think we need to be happy. The irony is that *we can and do return to safety, love, and abundance, but only as a result of taking our journeys.* Understandably, most people seem to want to skip theirs and go straight to the reward!

The child in us imagines paradise as the place where all our narcissistic whims are satisfied. Growing up requires us to let go of this fantasy so that we can do the hard work of gaining competence in both the inner and outer worlds. The reward at journey's end is the experience of entering the promised land. However, this does not mean that we get all the toys we ever wanted. Rather, it is a state of consciousness that requires a deep acknowledgment of, and reverence for, ourselves and others.

This return heals the wounded inner child and frees us from a victim mentality. No program seeking to cure dysfunction or empower students, workers, or citizens will be successful unless this return is accomplished. Moreover, it cannot be accomplished when spirit is denied. Only when we begin to see ourselves as spiritual beings can we trust in the universe enough to take responsibility for healing ourselves and the planet.

THE GIFT OF SPIRIT

Virtually every religion in the world has a way of describing a state of oneness with the divine, the achievement of which inspires this kind of trust. Buddhists call this enlightenment; Christians call it conversion. Most religions prescribe practices designed to help us achieve this state. Jewish Kabbalistic writings, for example, teach meditative practices that lead to union with the divine. Moreover, many people experience it spontaneously. You may have had such an awakening in one of the following ways:

- a religious conversion
- a mystical experience
- a sense of "Aha!" in which the meaning of the universe or your own life is revealed
- a sudden welling up of joy or peace
- a feeling that the divine is within you or another person

- a sense of awe at the wonder of nature, the universe, or life itself
- a feeling of being absolutely where you ought to be

These are examples of the treasure the hero seeks. In the Camelot stories, the knights and ladies do not search for the Holy Grail because of its material value. Rather, they undertake the quest because an encounter with the grail entails a visionary moment that radically changes the lives of those who experience it. Lancelot is so overcome at finding it that he goes into a coma for twenty-four hours.

In the Fisher King myths, which are closely related to the Camelot stories, the object the hero finds is a sacred fish. The identification of the fish as the treasure sheds new light on the use by early Christians of the fish as a kind of secret sign. (They would, for example, draw a fish on the ground to identify themselves to one another.) Just as fish come from beneath the sea, the visionary moment comes out of the depths of the unconscious to transform our conscious lives. If we think of this from a religious perspective, such moments connect us with the divine (in a Christian context, with Christ).

In many fairy tales and legends, the hero finds a buried treasure. After a long quest, Santiago, the hero of Paulo Coelho's *The Alchemist: A Fable About Following Your Dream*, discovers a treasure chest of Spanish gold coins hidden in the roots of a sycamore tree. The tree is growing out of the sacristy of the ruined church where his own journey had begun. Santiago wonders, like many heroes before and since who find their treasure in their own backyard, why the journey was necessary. Then he realizes that his pilgrimage, which took him to the pyramids, itself was the treasure. While the coins make him wealthy, it is not the money that makes him happy. The journey had filled his life with joy. In fact, he finds the money only after he has attained happiness.[1]

Stories of spiritual heroes help us find that pristine place from which all invention and creativity and life come. In this stillness, we can experience the god within ourselves. This time, however, we encounter the sacred not as children, looking up to a parental figure, but as adults, realizing that we are, indeed, part of the divine.

When we grow up, we begin to see ourselves as partners in the ongoing creation of our world. We no longer act like childlike dependents. In fact, we take responsibility for caring for others and the planet. This return requires a recognition of interdependence, which necessitates not only the claiming of personal responsibility for maintenance of our earthly paradise but also knowledge that some pain and suffering are rightly a part even of Edenic life.

TRYING TO LOOK GOOD

The return can be derailed if the Innocent tries to be good by conventional standards. Our culture is full of messages that if only we are virtuous or accomplished enough, we will be spared the trials and pains other people are forced to endure.

As Innocents learn that more is required of life than waiting passively for rescue, they tend to seek some program that promises them success or happiness—either in this life or, failing that, in the next. Accordingly, Innocents work very hard to please God, their employers, their mates. What they want is the reward of love and esteem. If life does not work out this way, they can feel entitled to do anything they need to do to get the outcome they believe they deserve.

The film *Amadeus* illustrates this tendency in pathological extreme. Salieri, the protagonist of the movie, bargains with God while a boy, saying he will give his industry, obedience, and chastity if God will make him a great composer. In short, he will be virtuous so that he can be great. He becomes a fine composer and is very pleased with himself and with God—until he meets

Mozart. Mozart is disobedient, disrespectful, undisciplined, and certainly not chaste, yet when he composes, he doesn't even have to make corrections. Salieri, who sees himself as an ideal man, concludes that God has made the infamous Mozart, instead of the virtuous Salieri, into a divine instrument. The injustice is too much for Salieri to bear, so he declares war on Mozart and on God and steals Mozart's requiem from him on his deathbed.

The truth, however, is that while Mozart may not seem good to Salieri, he is genuinely an Innocent—that is, he simply trusts the inspiration he receives. For all his apparent immorality, he truly does live for a mission greater than himself. He cannot stop composing, even on his deathbed. In his case, this is not workaholism, but the compulsion of the creative genius to express the art for which he lives.

Virtue often is used to camouflage cowardice. Much of the appeal of dogma in religion is that it gives its followers rules to follow that rescue them from having to find out who they are and what they really think. Organizational development approaches that offer an easy right answer attract a ready following, as do books that promise instant success or enlightenment. Similarly, many people are attached to traditional sex and work roles because they provide a surrogate identity that makes the uncertainty of the journey appear unnecessary.

If a woman is having trouble in her career—if she fears failure, for instance, has trouble with the Warrior culture she finds in the male work world, or is exhausted because she is doing all the housework in addition to her job—she has the option of a seemingly virtuous escape. She can always decide to quit and stay home for the good of her children, because the traditional role still is identified with virtue in our culture. While in some cases it certainly is appropriate to decide to stay home with a child or to care for elderly or infirm relatives, it is dishonest to use them as excuses for the fear of failure, for not asserting one's own needs and values in the workplace, or for not insisting that one's partner or family share responsibility for domestic tasks.

In Washington, D.C., these days, virtually every man who resigns from high office announces piously that he wants to go back to private life to spend more time with his family. Occasionally this may be true. It also is a fact that this "mom and apple pie" statement frees him from having to declare the real reasons he is leaving, whether they be disagreements with the White House, disgust with politics, inability to rise to the occasion and do the job adequately, or failure to assert that men in government also have the right to balanced lives.

If we try and try to be good based on other people's notions of virtue, we also can end up losing our chance at reentering paradise. Gertie, the protagonist of Harriette Arnow's novel *The Dollmaker*, is a six-foot-tall hillbilly who is extremely wise but habitually discounts her wisdom. Her idea of paradise is buying the Tipton Place, a family farm, and working it with her family as she also pursues her talent as a sculptor. Although she had saved enough money for the purchase, she allows others to tell her what she should do. As a result, she slowly loses almost everything she loves.

First, Gertie listens to her mother, who says a woman's duty is to be with her husband. Gertie's husband had moved to Detroit to find work, and when she joins him, she misses her chance to buy the Tipton Place. Then she loses her favorite daughter because she believes a neighbor who tells her she must not let Cassie play with the doll that is her imaginary friend. So Cassie sneaks off to play with the doll and is run over by a train.

Gertie is a talented sculptor, but she doesn't take her vocation seriously, calling it "whittlin' foolishness." As a poor Appalachian woman, she receives no encouragement to see her own inner calling as mattering. Her vision is to sculpt a "laughing Christ" that communicates her own life-enhancing view of Jesus, in contrast to the suffering crucifixes that represent to her the deathly Puritan legacy of her mother. Gertie's ultimate act of self-disrespect is chopping up a block of fine cherry wood to make cheap figurines and crucifixes—because they will sell. This act is equivalent to killing or maiming herself.

The "laughing Christ" is an image of the divinity within Gertie and us all. Earlier in the book, Cassie enjoins her mother to finish the statue and "let *her* out." "Her," of course, is Gertie. The moment in which she chops up the cherry block is genuinely tragic, because in doing so she has denied herself and her own vision. Yet even then she is not without hope. We all have moments of cowardice when we deny our wisdom, integrity, and divinity. Although the novel ends here, the last line lets us know that Gertie's self-destructive act has forced her into a new level of understanding. Her excuse for chopping up the cherry block when her family needed money was that she could not find the right face for Christ. At the novel's close, she achieves the vision of the returned Innocent as she exclaims, "They's millions an millions a faces plenty fine enough . . . some a my neighbors down there in th' alley—they would ha done."

Gertie always works very hard to do right. This is part of the irony of her story. The harder she works at it, the worse her life becomes. The point is not for her to prove her heroism by fighting against her nature, but to claim her nobility by trusting what she really loves. Gertie comes to understand at the end that had she simply allowed herself to be herself and to go for what she honestly wanted, her dreams could have come true. Most likely, she would have been the owner of the Tipton Place, surrounded by her family, completing her sculpture. She realizes in retrospect that she had plenty of support for staying on that farm, but in her self-distrust she listened to those voices that undercut her. Even her husband explains that he would have supported her had she only trusted him enough to tell him what she was doing. So, too, with all of us. A happy ending may well await us if we just have the courage to trust our own journeys.[2]

It would be easy to dismiss this story as simply an expression of antiquated notions that the female role requires sacrifice and the poor have no talent worth nurturing. However, which one of us does not have some of Gertie inside? Generally, we are not defeated in some dramatic and noticeable way. Rather, we are defeated by any number of small acts of self-betrayal masquerading as virtue that add up, over time, to an inauthentic life.

Gertie's dilemma is one virtually all of us can experience, even in the most advantaged circumstances. A man at one of my seminars complained that he had been too busy making yet another million dollars to find his own bliss. He had sacrificed his soul to become the ideal of the successful man, just as certainly as Gertie did to fulfill people's ideal of the self-sacrificing woman. Moreover, as Gertie's life illustrates, often it is the people who love us most—parents, lovers, spouses, children—who most discourage the authentic life. This happens because we so want to please the people we love and because we tend to look to them as mirrors to help us know who we are and what we are here to do. We must remember that no one else ever can tell us what our life is about. Only we can know. Often, our heroic calling will make others around us uncomfortable.

While it is important not to confuse self-indulgence or narcissism with an authentic call, it is equally important not to give our power away to others who are only too happy to tell us what we "ought" to be doing. Returning to paradise, therefore, requires us to take back responsibility for being the authors of our own lives.

CREATIVITY AND NAMING

Every culture has a story about the creation of the world: a goddess lays the cosmic egg or a god speaks the magic words, creating light. God the Creator speaking into the void to create life is a profoundly active image of creation. God says, "Let there be light," and there is light. God names reality, and then it exists. If we think of ourselves as co-creators of our lives, we can interpret this story as a reminder of the need we all have to find our true voices. When we have a vision of what we want and verbalize that vision, we begin the process of manifesting a life just perfect for us.

The goddess giving birth provides a complementary feminine symbol for what creativity is like for many people. When the goddess gives birth to something out of nothing, her creation comes out of her body, not her mind. Similarly, we may labor long to give birth to something, not being quite sure what we are birthing. Our lives may seem to us not so much something we chose as something that has chosen us, and we may fear that the process will miscarry. Few things are certain, and once the process is under way, it takes on a life of its own.

Anyone who writes, paints, or composes knows about receiving help from the muse. The feeling is not so much that you are creating art, but that art is being created through you. If you have no creative art form, think of your dreams. Some part of your psyche creates wonderful stories and images to edify and enlighten you. Some people do not remember their dreams, but we all have them, every night. The fact that we dream means that every one of us has the imaginative potential to spin wonderful stories without any conscious effort at all. We also all know moments when we experience what it means to go with the flow: the ideas we need come to us just in time; we "accidentally" meet the right people; doors open, seemingly by magic. When this happens, we return to the Innocent at a deeper and more sophisticated level. Now when things go wrong, we trust some learning can be gained from the experience.

When we are Orphans, we do not identify with creators. We may see God as a creator, but way above us and distant. We may imagine especially talented people as creative, but we do not regard ourselves as participants in the creative process. Indeed, we may see ourselves as being at the mercy of fate or of people with power. As Wanderers, we flee to save ourselves from those who would define our fate, and as Warriors we fight to protect our boundaries against them. As Altruists, we participate in the cosmic process of destruction and creation by allowing ourselves to be sacrificed, if necessary, to ensure rebirth. Only when we have gone through all of these stages can the Innocent reemerge with the assurance that we are co-creators of our lives. When this happens, we are ready for the return from the journey.

THE RETURN TO PARADISE

Every year, Jews throughout the world celebrate the Passover seder. During the service, they retell how the Hebrew people escaped from slavery in Egypt to find the promised land. At the end, they affirm "Next year in Jerusalem," expressing solidarity with all people, everywhere, who yearn to be free. Fundamentalist Christians pray for the second coming of Christ to establish heaven on earth. People in the New Age movement predict a transformation of consciousness. The legendary Grail knight transforms the wasteland kingdom so that it blooms again. Dorothy hopes the great wizard of Oz can help her find her way home and eventually discovers the secret in her ruby slippers. She clicks them together and immediately is transported back to Kansas.

Most of us long to find a place where we will feel, finally, at home. We seek and seek and seek, until one day we realize that the secret is within us. On the journey, we learn that we have choices about what worlds we wish to inhabit. When we take our journeys we begin to know who we are, what we value, and how we feel. Then, as we express our truth in the world, we attract to us others, like ourselves, who want to live in the same kind of happier way. Together, we form mini-kingdoms, communities of like-minded people who experiment with new ways of living. This process seems miraculous—like the transformed kingdom at the end of the hero's journey.

Even though the information always has been available to us, often we do not register the existence of all these simpatico people, groups, or books—until we are psychologically ready to experience them. Think what happens when you learn a new word. You never were conscious of it before, but after you learn it, you hear it all the time. It always was there, of course, but not for you. You did not notice it because it did not exist in your world. Similarly, early in our quest we feel lonely and alienated, assuming that to fit in, we have to conform to what we believe to be "reality." As we change, however, reality changes, too. The reward for taking the journey is finding communities that do not require us to lop off parts of ourselves to belong.

You may remember examples of the classic plot in which the hero is an orphan or is oppressed and unappreciated in the family and searches for his or her true home. As we become more and more who we are, and hence link up with others with whom we feel a deep connection, we have more, and more satisfying, relationships. The reward for the hero's inevitably solitary journey, then, is community—community with the self, with other people, and with nature and spirit. At the end of the journey, the hero feels and *is* at home.

This does not bring an end to problems. Taking our journeys does not exempt us from life; illness, mortality, disappointments, betrayals, even failures are part of the human condition. But if we have faith in ourselves and in the universe, they are much easier to bear. Further, because heroes confront their terrors, they are not limited so much by their fears. We can act without the continual tape in our heads questioning whether we are doing the right thing, whether someone else will disapprove, or whether someone else is out to get us. If we imagine God as distant and judgmental, we also may worry that God will abandon us. As Gerald Jampolsky explains in *Love Is Letting Go of Fear*, all these layers of fear keep us from experiencing the love underneath. The more we are able to let go of our fears, the more we can tap into the life-force energy that keeps us healthy and vital and alive. This also allows us to experience joy.[3]

A very spiritual and creative woman confided in me that she had no religious training as a child. She asked a neighbor about God and was told only one thing: "God is love." This was all the theology she needed. She grounded her life and her actions in being loving and, as she did so, found God within herself. As a result, she felt at home in the world. In a similar vein, Ntozake Shange's play *for colored girls who have considered suicide when the rainbow is enuf* ends a heart-rending soliloquy with the line "I found God in myself, and loved her fiercely."[4]

In a slightly different version of the heroic myth, the hero becomes the king or queen. Updated to contemporary terms, it means that the hero often gravitates to leadership roles. The journey increases our ability level, making it more likely that we will rise to positions of power and authority and be successful in our endeavors. As we take our journeys, it becomes natural to assume more responsibility—not only for our inner reality, but for the way our outer worlds mirror that reality.

Typically, we have the confidence and ability, at this point in our lives, to provide leadership in the world. This empowered attitude means, too, that we understand the cyclical nature of the journey. Thus, whenever our kingdom feels like a wasteland, we recognize that we may have become too comfortable and stopped growing. Then we know it is time to hit the road and continue our quest.

THE INNOCENT AS NAMER

I always have found it interesting that God charged Adam and Eve with the task of naming all the creatures of the earth—including plants, animals, and their own progeny. The Fall occurred when they ate of the apple of the Tree of the Knowledge of Good and Evil. Humankind fell from grace the minute we began to name some of our experiences as evil. We return to paradise when we regain the ability to name (without denial) all of our experiences as good.

The wise Innocent knows that our lives are defined not by what happens to us, but by how we think about what happens to us. Paulo Coelho's *The Alchemist*, mentioned earlier in this chapter, offers a wonderful parable illustrating this truth. Santiago's parents want him to become a priest, but he prefers to travel, so he becomes a shepherd. This life suits him for several years, until he has a recurring dream of going to the pyramids and finding a treasure. Trusting the truth of his dream, he sells his sheep and takes a boat to Tangiers, where someone steals all his money. He falls asleep in despair and awakens in an empty marketplace, completely penniless. He feels the way anyone would—angry, hopeless, victimized.

Reflecting upon his situation, he realizes he must "choose between thinking of himself as the poor victim of a thief and as an adventurer in quest of his treasure. . . . 'I'm an adventurer, looking for treasure,'" he says to himself. [5]

Wise Innocents understand that many realities exist simultaneously. We cannot always control the events that happen to us. However, we choose the world we will live in by our interpretation of these events. Santiago utilizes spiritual principles when he affirms his real nature and his destiny to find a treasure. We can do the same by creating and repeating positive sayings like: "I am filled with joy and light," "Perfect health and abundant energy are flowing through me," or "I have the perfect work for me right now."

Santiago also uses the spiritual principle of denial. Spiritual denial should not be confused with psychological denial—that is, pretending that things are different than they are. Santiago does not pretend that the thief did not steal his money. Rather he asserts appropriately that the thief's action has no power to determine who he is. Santiago may be set back temporarily by his loss, but he refuses to think of himself as poor. Indeed, he affirms that he is in the process of finding a treasure.

When we are working to create the perfect life for ourselves and those we love, we can use these two techniques daily. We can affirm the life we want to have and declare that the demands on us that are inconsistent with our journeys have no power over us. Our lives also will lighten the minute we think, as Santiago does, of our experiences in terms of *adventures* rather than obligations and as *a source of potential learning* rather than frustrating distractions from the life we believe we deserve.

On his journey across the desert toward Egypt, Santiago travels for a time with an alchemist who teaches him that the proper purpose of alchemy is not creating gold but understanding the soul of the world and, through that study, finding the sacred. Santiago worries that he does not have access to the great alchemical texts. His companion assures him that every one of us always has access to the truths we need on our journeys:

> Perhaps, if you were in a laboratory of alchemy, this would be the right time to study the best way to understand the Emerald Tablet. But you are in the desert. So immerse yourself in it. The desert will give you an understanding of the world; in fact, anything on the face of the earth will do that. You don't even have to understand the desert; all you have to do is contemplate a simple grain of sand and you will see in it all the marvels of creation.[6]

The alchemist concludes by reminding Santiago to listen to his heart. Because his heart is part of the soul of the world, it too knows all things. Thus, when we follow our hearts and commit to the road that truly beckons us, we will learn everything we need to know to be wise.

In *Knowing Woman*, Claremont de Castillejo explains that when a village in India experiences a drought, they send for the rainmaker. Rainmakers do not do anything to make the rain happen; they just go to the village and stay there—and the rain comes. They do not make the rain come, they allow it, or, more exactly, their inner atmosphere of allowing and affirming what *is* creates a climate in which what *needs to be* happens.[7] Perhaps you have known people like that. It is not that they make the sun shine, the rain fall, or people in their office work harder, but when they are there, things work right—and, apparently, effortlessly.

SUFFERING, EROS, AND CREATIVITY

At the basis of life is Eros—passion, life-force energy. This energy is present when we allow the natural process of spontaneous creation to occur. To do that, we need to be courageously open. Sometimes, though, we get hit with genuine tragedies. To continue the metaphor of birth, the events that change us most can feel more like rape than love. While the pain and suffering involved is not invited or deserved—it simply may be the price we all pay for living in a world still at a very primitive stage of development—catastrophes can be used by the psyche for growth and eventually to bring us treasures, if we permit that growth to take place.

The major temptation of the Innocent is to ignore pain and suffering. Joanna, the title character of May Sarton's novel *Joanna and Ulysses*, learns to reframe suffering without pretending it isn't real. She chooses to celebrate her thirtieth birthday by going off by herself for the first time in her life. Although she always has wanted to be an artist, she is a clerk, and she travels from Athens to the island of Santorini in the hope that there she will be able to paint. Her goal is to really *see* objects as they are, so that she can paint them. To her surprise, she finds that in doing so, she breaks through her denial systems and sees more than she is conscious of wanting to see.

On Santorini, Joanna befriends a small boy, who asks her why she never married. In answering, she tells a story she never has told anyone. Her mother had been a resistance fighter. Captured by the Fascists, she was forced to watch while guards stuck cigarettes into her son's ears until he was made deaf. All the time, the son shouted, "Mother, don't talk." Then they tortured her until she died, but she never talked. The son was released and told the family the story. Joanna put off her hopes of becoming an artist to take care of them all. While her father sat alone much of the time in a darkened room, she took a dull job. The whole family went through life numbed by the tragedy, putting one foot forward at a time.

At thirty, arriving on Santorini, the first thing Joanna sees is a donkey covered with sores and piled high with baggage, being beaten. This scene is the last straw for her. She cannot stand any more inhumanity and runs up screaming for the donkey's owners to stop. They explain that they are poor people and do not have the luxury of coddling animals. They just want the donkey to get to the top of the hill before he dies. Finally, in exasperation, she buys the animal at a ridiculously inflated price. This is how she begins her vacation—leading a dying donkey, which she christens Ulysses.

To Joanna, Ulysses represents the part of herself that is an artist, the part that has been starved, neglected, and mistreated. She chooses the name because she recognizes her own potential for heroism, but she also chuckles at the appropriateness of her repressed self being symbolized for her by such an ignoble beast, especially since she regards her aspirations as so ridiculous that she is afraid to speak of them.

She begins to paint and nurses Ulysses back to health. When she tells the young boy her tragic history, she expects him to be shocked or aggrieved, but instead he reacts with exultation, saying, "I am so proud of your mother. I am so proud of your brother." His response jolts her into seeing things differently, into remembering how passionate her mother was, how she loved flowers, and how she loved freedom enough to die for it. Actually telling the story and hearing the boy's liberating response makes her feel as if "she were being brought out at last from a dank, dark cell where all she could think of was suffering, the endless chain of suffering."

When she returns to Athens, Joanna brings Ulysses with her and hides him in the basement, but he chews through his rope and surprises her and her father upstairs. She and her father speak honestly for the first time since her mother's death, and she shows him her paintings. They talk about her mother, and she exclaims: "If you shut out pain, you shut out everything, Papa! . . . Don't you see, how everything stopped—my painting became trivial, my life too. I could not remember Mother as she was. We shut her out like shutting out life itself!" To deny the pain was to hold on to it. Only by going through it, allowing it, feeling it, speaking aloud about it, could Joanna learn from it and go on to feel joy and power in a new way.

Equally important to Joanna's honoring and affirming both the pain and the joy is her commitment to her art and what that art means to her. To be a great artist, she must be able to see the whole expanse of what is real. But repression takes away our lives and traps us into our illusions. Joanna shares the gift of the artist both when she shows her father her paintings and when she explains to him what she has learned. By expressing her truth, she changes not only her own reality, but his as well.[8]

Joanna's creativity is released by the power of "naming"—first by the spontaneous innocence of the boy, who immediately sees what is glorious in a tragic situation, and then by her own more mature innocence as she consciously transforms her life by changing the way she views it.

ASK AND YE SHALL RECEIVE

In *Collections 1978*, psychotherapist Shirley Luthman argues that we choose our lives. To illustrate the psychological consequences of this idea, she shares reflections about how she would react if she discovered she had a brain tumor. She would be quite shaken up, obviously. Nonetheless, while allowing those feelings, she maintains that she would not do anything until she could focus inward and get clear enough to understand what was going on. Had her being decided that it was time to die? Or, if not, what was the tumor trying to tell her? Only when she was clear about where she was going would she determine what to do. That might mean deciding it was time to die. It might mean finding some alternative treatment.[9]

Fundamental to Luthman's approach is a strong belief that at the deepest soul level of our beings (which is not always accessible to our conscious minds), we choose what happens to us—including choosing our illnesses and our deaths. We make these choices, she says, not out of masochism, but because they will teach us what we need to learn. Therefore, it is important to respect everything that happens to us as a way of honoring our choices as the teachers of needed lessons.

Now, the Orphan will not agree with this Innocent archetype perspective because for her, choice means blame: if I choose to be a battered woman, that means I am to blame for my own suffering. But to the Innocent, blame is irrelevant, and the search for a culprit is a useless diversion. "Who is to blame?" is not a useful question. Better ones are "What can I learn from this experience?" and "Given the wisdom I have gained from it, what do I want to choose now?"

From the vantage point of the Innocent, a woman may make meaning of the horrible experience of being abused by thinking that she had long had a batterer in her own head, telling her she was too fat, too selfish, too pushy. By getting into a situation in which she is physically or emotionally battered by someone else, she finally comes to the point where she says, "Enough. I may be bad, but I am not bad enough to deserve this kind of treatment." So she finds help, gets out of the relationship, and works on her self-esteem to the point where she does not spend so much of her time at the mercy of her internal batterer. Although the external situation is painful, it produces a crisis that forces on her the opportunity to opt for growth, change, and eventually less pain in her life. Thus, attracting a battering relationship in the long run can be seen as bringing her health. In such ways, wise Innocents regard even their most difficult experiences as examples of Eden unfolding.

In "My Own Journey—New Life," an autobiographical chapter in *Energy and Personal Power* (a sequel to *Collections 1978*), Luthman tells about the pain she endured when she lost her husband. They had had a deep and fulfilling relationship, and when he died, she was grief-stricken. She still believed that we choose our own lives, but she felt like a victim anyway. Later, she confronts the idea that "on a deep level of my consciousness I may have known I was marrying a man who was going to die and leave me, even though I had no cognitive awareness of such a possibility." Asking herself why she would do such a thing, she concludes: "My ability to be alive, intense, and to relate deeply is connected to me and not dependent on a particular person or place, on anything external to me."[10]

When the Innocent is activated, some people believe, as Luthman does, that at a deep soul level we choose our lives. Others believe that such losses as she describes happen for reasons that have nothing to do with our choices, but nevertheless can be used to stimulate growth. Still others resist the idea of choice, but see a pattern of meaningful coincidence in the universe.

Synchronicity is a term coined by C. G. Jung to describe such causal connections. While the Warrior learns the lessons of causality, the Innocent trusts synchronicity. You know those times when you go to a bookstore and just the book you needed (but had never heard of) practically falls into your hand? Or when you run into just the person you need, seemingly by accident? Those are examples of synchronicity."[11]

Mirroring—when the world outside mirrors our world inside—is another aspect of the same phenomenon. Partly, as illustrated by the battered woman, the external world tends to dramatize what is going on internally so that we notice it. Mirroring also works another way. That is, often when we change our inner world, the outer one changes as well. For example, I know men and women who despair about ever finding true love. But once they take their own journey and develop their own capacity for love, they frequently are astounded by how many fascinating and thoroughly admirable people suddenly show an interest in them.

When we are in the Wanderer stage, the world is full of suffering. When we move into the Warrior stage, then the world miraculously changes with us and confronts us not so much with catastrophes as with challenges. In the Altruist stage, we find ourselves surrounded by people needing love and care at every turn. As we enter the Magician stage, we encounter situations and people needing to be transformed. The Innocent will see this as mirroring. Other archetypes might explain it differently—for example, that we notice the parts of our environments that fit our programming.

When, as an Innocent, we do not like what is happening to us, the first thing we will do is go inward to see what inner change might produce an outer change; our assumption is that paradise is possible and is close at hand. We can always do something to improve our situation. We change the world by changing ourselves.

If this idea is not balanced by the perspectives of other archetypes, it can be taken too far or even used in a controlling way. For example, if you work with a person who mistreats you, going home and doing affirmations may not help, unless the affirmations are designed to strengthen your self-esteem so that you will act on your own behalf. However, noticing a prior pattern in your life of abusive relationships can help you see that this relationship may be your chance to free yourself. The issue initially may be that you need to call up your Wanderer to leave or your Warrior to stand up for yourself. Simultaneously, you can affirm your readiness for a healthy work relationship. The Innocent archetype can help you recognize this pattern and trust the process you are in. It may not be able to help you change the individual person who is mistreating you. That person has his or her own journey, with its own timing. However, your Innocent can trust that you have the power to leave this situation and find a better one.

As Orphans learn to allow pain, Wanderers loneliness, and Warriors fear, Innocents learn to allow faith, love, and joy. And the more they let in, the more they attract to themselves. In *Whee!, We, Wee All the Way Home* (a title that suggests its Innocent perspective), theologian Matthew Fox argues that the ultimate prayer is to receive life fully:

> A friend who gives me a record is pleased when he learns of my delight at playing the record. After all, my delight was the very goal he intended in giving me the gift. The Creator can be no different. Our thank-you for creation, our fundamental prayer, therefore, is our enjoyment and delight in it. This delight is called ecstasy when it reaches a certain height, and it is also prayer. Like all prayer, it touches the Creator and we are touched by the Creator in that act of ecstasy and thank-you.[12]

This attitude is important not only for us to receive the delights of the world, but also to realize our potential for our own inner riches.

The Innocent's process is not simply passive receiving, however. It is a matter of asking, with the expectation that we will have what we need. The Christian scripture that most resonates for the Innocent's consciousness is Matthew 7:7–8:

> Ask, and you will receive; seek, and you will find; knock, and the door will be opened. For everyone who asks receives, he who seeks finds, and to him who knocks, the door will be opened.

It is equally important to be grateful for what we receive. A particularly touching part of the Passover seder is the recitation of a long list of things God did for the Hebrew people during the Exodus (for example, bringing them out of Egypt, providing manna in the desert, etc.). As each instance of divine help is recalled, the participants exclaim "*Dayenu!*"—literally, "It would have been sufficient." It would have been sufficient even if God had not performed the next miracle. Yet, God performed them all. Collectively, this catalogue of interventions inspires awe.

A novel that illustrates the process of the return is Margaret Drabble's *The Realms of Gold*. Its central character, Frances Wingate, thinks back over her life with a humble sense of wonder at all she has received. Frances has a rather unusual capacity to trust herself and her vision, the result being that she habitually has asked for what she wanted—and gotten it. She is aware that she never has made things happen; they just have. She is an archaeologist who became quite famous when she discovered the ruins of an ancient city in a desert. Actually, one day in an airport she realized that she simply knew where it was. Of course, this knowledge was grounded in all her study of the ancient culture of the

Phoenicians, but it was the intuitive flash that made the difference. Furthermore, she unquestioningly followed her hunch and then found and excavated the site. She wonders:

> If I hadn't imagined it, it wouldn't have existed. All her life, things had been like that. She had imagined herself doing well at school, and had done well. Marrying, and had married. Bearing children, and had borne them. Being rich, and had become rich. Being free, and was free. Finding true love, and had found it. Losing it, and had lost it. What next should she imagine?

The enormity of this power frightens her. She worries that she might imagine something frightful, and that would happen too. Accordingly, she comes face to face with her sense of responsibility for her own life and her contributions to the world. It also is true that Frances is looking back over her life with the Innocent's consciousness as she ponders. Events may not feel so fortuitous and easy when they are happening. Yet had she not learned the lessons of the Warrior, she could not have followed up on her hunch so confidently, organized an expedition, and proceeded to dig. Similarly, she would not have had the independence of mind and courage to take her career seriously at a time when women were not expected to be able to combine a career with a husband and family.

Her life is an interesting example of the consciousness of the return, and a very human one. She is not "perfect." In fact, she drinks too much and in other ways is prone to self-indulgence. But that is part of the point: she is *not* better than other people, and she *does* know how to create paradise in her life. She visualizes what she wants and takes action to get it with a simple, relaxed confidence that it will happen, without falling into denial or escapism. For example, she sends a postcard to a lover from whom she had parted saying she wants him back. The card is delayed in reaching him, and her response when she does not hear from him is puzzlement. After all, he always said he would come back if she asked him to, and she believed him. Finally, he receives the card and returns to her side, and she has her wish—a truly satisfying, intimate relationship.[13]

Perfectionism can hold up our journeys. For many people today, life is one self-improvement project after another. We believe we cannot win the treasure until we have it all together. That is not the point at all. The return asks us to recognize the good that has always been in our lives. In *The Wizard of Oz*, Dorothy sees Kansas very differently at the end of the story than at its beginning, when she felt victimized and alienated. Her side-kicks symbolically represent the potential inside her that is realized through her journey: the cowardly Lion, who wished for courage, saves the day; the Scarecrow, who wanted a brain, makes all the plans; and the Tin Man, who wanted a heart, cries so much, is moved so easily to sympathy, that he rusts his armor. Dorothy herself wants to go home and discovers that she could have done so anytime she wanted to—at least anytime after she killed the wicked witch and gained her ruby slippers. As she clicks her heels together, she affirms, "There's no place like home," and finds herself back with her Auntie Em.

When Dorothy had left Kansas, it seemed like a wasteland to her, simply because she was unhappy there. When she returns, Kansas has been transformed into the promised land—not because Kansas really has changed, but because *she* has. Experience has helped her appreciate what she formerly took for granted. She wakes up, of course, surrounded by people who love her—as they always did.

The Innocent archetype helps us change the filter through which we see our lives. Most of us take all the good in our lives as our due, focusing therefore on things that frustrate, annoy, or disappoint us. If we make the choice to appreciate what we have and resonate with positive events and circumstances, we suddenly become much happier.

Such wisdom is influencing management theory and practice today. Consultant David L. Cooperrider helps organizations put aside their problems long enough to find out their strengths and their values. He calls this approach "appreciative inquiry," noting that organizational systems have their own logic, just as do individual souls. He explains that "any system or society flourishes only so long as it has a positive image of itself—its past, present, and future." Cooperrider's approach helps us find the soul of the organization, its deepest values and commitments. Any desire to change an organization that does not honor its core truth and that does not trust in its own worth and that of the people in it eventually will do more harm than good.[14]

The wise Innocent understands and appreciates organizational, family, and social systems on their own terms. Rather than trying to make change occur, we can promote positive outcomes by encouraging, through our attention and support, the positive forces that can be found in any and all situations.

In our personal lives, the Innocent archetype can help us achieve happiness even when we do not yet have what we want. It provides us with the faith that we always will have what we *need* to grow. We pick up from the culture a constant pressure to live up to certain standards of normalcy and success. We can relax into our lives only if we are able to trust that each life has its own logic and each gift has its own time.

The Innocent tells us that we can reenter paradise whenever we are ready to do so. We do it not by controlling what happens to us, but by learning to recognize possibilities we have not previously seen. The Warrior believes we have to force people to move into the new world; the Altruist believes that social change requires sacrifice; the Magician explores the limits of our abilities to redeem the world. The Innocent, however, knows that we need only to be presented with an option. People are attracted to increased life. Left to themselves, they will gravitate to it.

Mary Staton's science-fiction classic *From the Legend of Biel* describes a civilization that slowly grows to encompass most of the universe, yet never fights a battle. The civilization is peaceful, egalitarian, and complex. Other groups join it not because they are forced to, but because their curiosity always eventually leads them to it. When they get there, they find themselves in the Hall of a Thousand Chambers, where they experience many adventures. In the process, they evolve and discover who they are on a deeper level, moving from dualistic, hierarchical, patriarchal consciousness to a more complex, multidimensional, and egalitarian perspective. Once they have advanced to that level, they cannot imagine going back to their former ways of doing things. That would be like crawling after they had learned to walk—or fly.[15]

Innocents do not try to force social change on others, because they recognize that people need to take their journeys to be able to live in a humane and peaceful world. On the other hand, they also recognize that many things in the culture artificially retard people and keep them stuck unnecessarily. Innocents act as magnets who attract and galvanize positive energy for change. They do this by identifying the places where growth can occur for individuals, institutions, or social groups, and then by fostering it. Although they may or may not be the leaders in a particular political, religious, or intellectual movement, they act as rainmakers. When they are there, growth occurs.

Because so much of what we believe about the world really is projection, wise Innocents are able to inspire hope in others because they *know* it is possible to have a peaceful, humane, just, and caring world. After all, they have learned to be peaceful, caring, and respectful of others and themselves! Further, they attract what they are, so they also have many areas in their lives in which they experience such a world as their reality.

Wise Innocents trust that when we open our hearts, we always have enough love; when we stop hoarding—talents, ideas, material goods—we always are prosperous. They know that we create scarcity through our fears. But when we relax into our lives, we experience the fullness of our true nature—which always is good. The result is happiness.

GETTING ACQUAINTED WITH THE INNOCENT ARCHETYPE

To familiarize yourself with the Innocent archetype, make a collage out of Innocent-like pictures from magazines; make lists of songs, movies, and books that express the Innocent; collect pictures of yourself, relatives, colleagues, and friends in an Innocent mode. Practice noticing when you are thinking or acting like an Innocent.

Innocent Exercises

Step One: Every day, spend as much time as you can appreciating what you have. Thank people who are helpful to you.

Step Two: When you have a problem, affirm the outcome you want as if it were present in your life already. Hold the vision of your ideal outcome. Write a sentence that describes what you want, but phrase it in the *present tense.* When thoughts of fear or luck begin to make you anxious, deny their power over you and return your focus to more hopeful words or images.

Step Three: Trust your inner guidance. Practice prayer and/or meditation to listen for guidance. Remain open to hear this inner voice as you go through your day.

Step Four: Keep a record of your dreams, treating them as letters sent from your unconscious mind to make you aware of what your conscious mind may be missing.

CHAPTER 7

Transforming Your Life: The Magician

... Out beyond the shadows of our old thinking, a wholly different world appears. A world that delights in our explorations, our desires, our need to join with others. A world that welcomes and supports our endeavors. The world knows how to grow and change. It has been doing so for billions of years. Life knows how to create systems. Life knows how to create greater capacity. Life knows how to discover meaning. The motions that we sought to wrestle from life's control are available to us to support our desires if we can stop being so afraid.

—Margaret J. Wheatley and Myron Kellner-Rogers, *A Simpler Way*

The hero returns to a transformed kingdom.

Does your life seem out of control? Are you having difficulty keeping up with the demands of work, your responsibilities to family and friends, and your own needs for physical exercise as well as spiritual/psychological development? Do you feel as though you are being run by your life? Are you surrounded by people and situations that need transformation? Even though you may be very sophisticated and successful, does it sometimes feel as though you need a miracle?

Modern life is fast-paced and complex. People everywhere are having a difficult time simply keeping up with its demands. Moreover, you cannot do so if you overwhelm yourself trying to please your boss or teacher totally, prepare adequately for your next career move or school assignment, satisfy your parents, be a perfect parent/friend/partner, and attain the ideal of physical and spiritual beauty, while also trying to find yourself.

The Magician archetype is associated with the human will, the capacity for free choice, and the decision to take control of one's life. It is only human to make excuses, blame others, or complain about the times when we are scrambling to catch up with our lives, but the Magician in all of us knows that any lack of balance in our external world reflects imbalance inside. To do magic we must focus our energies so that they are not dissipated.

When our lives feel unmanageable, one or more archetypes is dominating the others. For example, we are out of balance in:

- the Innocent, if we try to be perfect and please everyone;
- the Orphan, if we are distracted from the tasks at hand by our fears and anxieties (so that we worry rather than make progress);
- the Wanderer, if we spend endless hours on self-improvement projects in the hope of someday being "good enough" to get everything done;
- the Warrior, if we are driven to achieve, and just cannot stop striving to be the best;
- the Altruist, if we spend time doing for others what they could and ought to do for themselves;
- the Magician, if we are so inflated that we think we can do anything and everything.

Most of us do not even realize that we *can* make choices to have the kinds of lives we want. We do not have to take the advice of (or please or impress) the experts, relatives, and friends, however well-meaning they might be. Many people today are like a motorist who sits in the passenger seat of his car because a whole group of people are hogging the driver's seat, fighting for control of the wheel. The car, of course, careens all over the highway with so many people steering. The motorist complains from time to time that he is getting farther and farther from his destination, but no one in the driver's seat seems to notice.

Perhaps he eventually kicks them all out and manages to get into the driver's seat. He steps on the accelerator, but nothing happens—the car is still in neutral. Only when he shifts into first gear and, at the same time, steers the car does it begin to move toward his desired destination.

Similarly, when the Magician archetype is activated, you feel confident that you know what ought to be done to transform your life or your world. You stop letting others make your decisions, and you develop a vision for where you want to go. You also are willing to risk action—to get behind the wheel of your life. You activate the gear shift of magic when you begin to act in keeping with your values and your life purpose. It is as if you place yourself in just that magical position that allows the gears of the universe to align with you and support your efforts. When you do so, you find that fortuitous coincidences begin to occur that open a path for you.

Modern chaos theory in the social and natural sciences asserts that everything in the universe is interconnected and hence profoundly interdependent. For example, to dramatize the radical complexity of weather prediction, chaoticists say that the fluttering of a butterfly's wing in Tokyo affects the weather in New York. Many of us like to think that some equivalent of a great wizard is pulling the strings of the world, but the reality is that each of us runs our own command central. The universe is not a static thing. It is in the process of being created all the time—by all of us.

We experience social interdependence in its negative form all the time. For instance, if we work so hard that we neglect our children, chances are that other people are having the same problem. If this pattern continues unchecked, the entire society will face the challenge of dealing with a whole generation of troubled young people. If your company is so obsessed with making a profit that it does so at the cost of environmental damage, the resulting ecological imbalance can affect the whole community. Yet it is easy enough for most of us to remain oblivious to the ways we are helping to create social problems.

The Magician archetype helps us take responsibility for existential choice. You might think of yourself as like a shaman stepping to the center of a medicine wheel, or magic circle, to do magic. Virtually all magical traditions teach that each individual is a microcosm of the universe. If we want to change the world, we must start with ourselves. Scientists tell us we live in a relativistic universe where no person, planet, or star is any more central or intrinsically important than any other. None is higher or lower either. We step into the point of power inside our own magic circles when we act on the knowledge that we have as much right as does anyone else to determine the world's future. There are many possible outcomes for humankind. Nothing is locked in. We cast our vote for the world we prefer for ourselves and our children with every choice we make every day.

The best of contemporary career counseling encourages people to trust that their lives—no matter how difficult they have been—have prepared them to do something only they can do. When you find work that uses all your prior experience, it feels incredibly magical, like you are a puzzle piece dropping into place. As more and more parts find their right spaces, a structure emerges that others can use to orient themselves, just as the emerging pattern makes a puzzle progressively easier to complete. Moreover, as you do the work that you most love, you undoubtedly will do it very well. As you become more successful, you increase your contribution to a flourishing economy.

The quest for an authentic sense of purpose often brings people to their knees—or their meditation cushions—seeking to connect with some higher or deeper wisdom. Some talk about seeking the will of God, others about finding the truth within them, still others about being in tune with "the force" or the processes of the universe.

The Magician archetype exists within every major religion that has stories of holy figures who do miraculous things. In indigenous traditions, prescience and healing abilities demonstrate a call to shamanism. The dominant religious figures of the world were all miracle workers; Jesus, for example, healed the sick, fed the multitudes, and raised the dead. The Red Sea parted for Moses, and manna came to him from heaven. Krishna, the Buddha, the Goddess Tara—all are credited with miracles. Moreover, in virtually every spiritual tradition, people with special healing or psychic powers are seen as particularly close to the divine.

Most ordinary people are able to find balance and meaning in their lives precisely because they have faith that they are receiving supernatural help. When we have faith, it is not so important that we drive an expensive car, impress the neighbors, or win a Nobel Prize. It is okay just to be who we are. Living in harmony with God and our own natures allows us to simplify our lives.

In our culture, we tend to seek "magic" answers and expect them to be easy. Thus, the Orphan sees the Magician as someone who makes difficulty go away—as in "Poof!" and it disappears. However, in most spiritual traditions, magical abilities are a result of disciplined study and practices designed to help individuals align their wills with the divine. In the alchemical tradition, the ideal of changing lead to gold (by a kind of telekinesis, or mind over matter) was not so much about chemistry as it was a sign that the consciousness of the alchemist had become golden as a result of long and disciplined practice.

From this perspective we can think of our difficult experiences as providing cauldrons that help refine our consciousness. Several people I have worked with have complained initially about the fast pace of their highly successful lives. One woman said she did not have time to write speeches in advance or prepare for meetings. She simply had to be ready to be "on" at any time. In part, she could do this because her prior experience had prepared her so well for her high-powered job. However, she also realized that this lifestyle meant she had to let go of control. In fact, she now prayed for divine assistance before each major event—and help always seemed to be there. She just knew what to do.

The Magician shares a basic worldview with the Innocent, but claims a greater amount of power. Innocents go with the flow and trust God, the universe, and/or the process of history. Magicians take responsibility in a more active and immediate way for the state of their lives or of the planet. This means that they often add a revolutionary consciousness to the hero's journey. They say: "When things are not all right, I will stand and be counted."

SETTING THE WORLD RIGHT

When the Magician archetype is active in your life, you may sense an inner call to make a difference in the world—in ways that might seem risky. You might even feel inadequate to the task. Martin Luther King Jr. is an example of a modern-day Magician whom everyone knows. Thinking about his story can help to activate your own magical potential. Nurtured by a strong faith in God and in the process of history, yet faced with the reality of racism in America, King said "No!" Segregation was not acceptable. It simply had to end. Your own "no" might be about something much different. If you are feeling angry about a family, school, organizational, or societal problem of any kind—especially if you feel passionate about that particular issue—this is *your* call to action. Remember, Magicians change history when they refuse to let their own lives and the lives of others be determined by social inertia. Rather, they demand that change take place—now!

Magicians are able to effect seemingly magical change precisely because they do not give away their power. Most of us imagine that other people are driving the car of history. Certainly, Martin Luther King Jr. had every reason to think of himself as in the back seat, if not completely outside. When he wrote his famous "Letter from Birmingham City Jail," people tried to discredit him as an outside agitator, since Birmingham was not his hometown.

As an African American in a time of segregation, it would have been easy for him to identify himself as "other," as the outsider and hence someone unable to make a difference. But King identified himself as central everywhere he was. He was central as an African American, as an American patriot, and as a Christian minister. Therefore, he could speak for, and lead, the black community. He could call on all Americans to fulfill the promise of democracy and on all Christians to act on the trust that all of us are God's children and therefore one family. Equally important, he did not make anyone else the enemy (as a Warrior might have). Instead, he called on people of all backgrounds to be true to the values they already espoused. Magic happens when we stand up not only for ourselves and our own group, but also for the promise that exists in every one of us.

In challenging the American people to put an end to segregation, King did not just enjoin others to change their behavior, he took the wheel and began to drive, setting in motion a process that changed the nation and the world. The civil rights movement not only ended segregation but sparked, by its example, the women's movement, the antiwar movement, the men's movement, and the gay rights movement. Its impact spread beyond our borders, leading eventually to the end of apartheid in South Africa. Of course, this ripple effect had started much earlier. Martin Luther King Jr. was influenced by Gandhi, who was influenced by the American transcendentalist Henry David Thoreau. King also could not have had the impact he did without the prior work of any number of other civil rights activists who helped to create his moment. The point is that anyone who takes a stand for justice anywhere, on behalf of anyone, contributes to our liberation from the insidious idea that some people are intrinsically better than others.

The Magician archetype demands that we move out of alienation and take the wheel of our own destinies. This, in turn, requires us to think of ourselves as being at the center of life, determining the future. Therefore, to be a Magician, it is essential to know what you stand for. You can begin with what bothers you about the world. Listen to what you complain about and you will know what you are called upon to use your magic to rectify.

It is the Magician's task to make it right when we err and, in doing so, to restore the balance of our lives and in our worlds. In *The Tempest*, his final dramatic statement, Shakespeare provided us with a case study for setting the world right when things have gone awry. As the play opens, we find Prospero, the former duke of Milan, in exile with his lovely daughter, Miranda. Prospero lost his crown when he was deposed by his brother, Antonio, who, with the support of the king of Naples, banished him to a far-off island. Prospero could have spent his life crying in his beer, as he certainly had the right to feel very aggrieved. However, he takes responsibility for his own part in this seemingly unfair fate. In retrospect, he sees that he neglected his duties as duke to pursue his study of the magical arts, leaving Antonio in charge. In his preoccupation, he created a vacuum that Antonio filled.

Prospero's situation illustrates two principles. First, we violate the order of the universe when we fail to be true to our purpose for being here. Second, we create disorder when we allow others to harm us. Prospero takes responsibility for committing both errors and thus is able to forgive Antonio. Then he cleverly sets in motion a series of events that restore the proper roles in the external world.

Once Prospero's internal consciousness has changed, circumstances that occur seemingly accidentally provide the opportunity for him to set external events on course. Fate brings a boat carrying Alonzo, the king of Naples; his son, Ferdinand; Antonio; and others near Prospero's island home. Enlisting the aid of the sprite Ariel, Prospero uses his magical powers to create a storm that leaves them marooned. In ways too complicated to detail here, Prospero makes Alonzo and Antonio believe that Ferdinand is dead, and plants the notion that this may be their punishment for wronging Prospero. The two conspirators then repent of their wrongdoing and speak of their desire to set things right. By the close of the play, Alonzo and Prospero are reunited, and Miranda and Ferdinand are betrothed. The conflict between the brothers and the exile are ended, and they prepare to sail back to Milan together. [1]

While most of us do not have the powers ascribed to Prospero, we can restore the appropriate order to our lives by doing what we can to make things right when we err. Most religions provide some ritual to help with this task. In Judaism, the ten-day period between Rosh Hashanah and Yom Kippur is set aside for people to atone for anything they did wrong and make it right. In Catholicism, the function of regular confession to a priest is to enable people to return to alignment with their spiritual nature. In Protestant religions, confession is made in prayer directly to God. In many Eastern religions, meditation as a regular practice keeps people connected to their own inner knowing, so that they will act mindfully, in ways that set things right. In feminist Goddess circles, women are taught never to do anything that harms another, for what we do comes back to us magnified threefold. The only way to protect oneself from unwanted consequences of negative behaviors is to make things right as quickly as possible.

The Reverend Eric Butterworth, author of *Discover the Power Within You*, likens the return to spirit to turning on a light switch.

"Sin" simply means being "off the mark." When we stray, Butterworth says, it is not required that we beg God's forgiveness. Spirit, he notes, is like electricity. We routinely will get off the mark when we forget to turn on the switch. We do not have to beg the light to come back on, we just have to notice it is off and turn it on again. Reconnecting with spirit is like this. As we align once again with our spiritual nature, we will know intuitively what to do, and the mischief we have caused by our lack of consciousness generally is righted, at least over time.[2]

The Chinese *I Ching* was designed as an aid to leaders. It did not so much tell people what to do as it helped them stay in alignment with the Tao. Then as now, reading the *I Ching* enables people to make choices consistent with the spiritual order of the universe at a particular moment.

Using more psychological terms, many people today right their consciousness by centering. When we lose touch with our centers, we feel unbalanced—because we are. We may even be careening off course at breakneck speed, pulled in every direction by the magnetism of other people's demands and the attraction of the newest gadget, toy, or experience.

It is important to recognize, as does Prospero, that we disturb the order of the universe not only when we harm someone else, but also if we allow anyone to take advantage of us. I frequently see managers who are willing to overlook nonproductive and noncollegial behavior in employees—especially if these supervisors are afraid of being charged with racism, sexism, or general unfairness, or if they fear challenging someone with connections to powerful people. These ineffective employees, then, never learn how to be productive and successful in the workplace. We also know how easy it is to enable other people's addictions, with the result that they do not face the logical consequences of their behavior—consequences that motivate people to seek recovery. This is why twelve-step programs have participants regularly conduct a moral inventory and make amends to anyone they have harmed. If doing this can help keep alcoholics and drug addicts sober, imagine what it can do for people who are not, or not yet, addicted to anything. The point is, people are designed to be moral. If we do not do what's right by our own lights, we not only mess up our own lives, we mess up the world. Certainly, we are more likely to abuse drugs or alcohol—not to mention falling prey to workaholism or codependence—if we have reason to want to be distracted from facing the truth about ourselves.

There is a magic in making things right that tends to put our lives in order. Most employers highly value employees who simply show a willingness to take responsibility for their mistakes and learn from them. Indeed, successful people are not necessarily any more able than others; they just are more willing to see their mistakes as opportunities to grow. Magical people do not simply sit around blaming others. They recognize their own part in any difficult situation and change what they are capable of changing—themselves.

INTEGRATING THE SHADOW

When the Magician archetype emerges, the shadow aspect is never far away. This can be a dangerous time, because we can be possessed by its negativity and live it out. The shadow-possessed Magician can be truly evil, using the power of charisma to seduce, manipulate, and destroy, rather than to elevate. Intent makes a great difference. If your intent is to use your power for greed or ambition, the emergence of the Magician archetype tips the balance and throws you over into doing evil. However, if your intent is positive and you have committed your life to good, you can face and integrate the shadow side.

This transformative journey begins when problems occur that help us see qualities in ourselves and others we might rather not. The movement from Warrior to Magician archetype hinges on the ability to stop regarding the enemy out there as "not me" and to begin seeing the shadow in oneself. In the great *Star Wars* trilogy, when Luke Skywalker finally gets the chance to kill his nemesis, Darth Vader, he discovers that the enemy is his own father (a relative, someone like him, whom he cannot easily kill or punish). More typically, on the journey, we have to face the fact that we have evil within ourselves. Something happens that discloses our culpability, and we are forced to acknowledge our own faults. Often this occurs when a spouse or lover walks out, our child gets in trouble, we fail in business or lose a job, or we fall prey to any kind of addictive, compulsive, or self-destructive behavior.

This is a dangerous moment. In *People of the Lie*, M. Scott Peck shows that the more unwilling individuals are to look at the harm they have done, the more evil they tend to become. As they become defensive, covering their tracks, they sink in deeper and deeper. Therefore, it is absolutely essential that we neither make excuses for ourselves nor give up believing in our ultimate good intent.[3]

Whenever individuals or groups identify with any kind of worthwhile purpose, their first challenge is to recognize and integrate the shadow. Something inevitably will go wrong. I recently was with a group of wonderful people committed to an equally wonderful cause. Within months of founding a utopian organization, they were at each other's throats. Moreover, individuals were reacting to others who simply had a different point of view as if they were dangerously naive, verbally abusive, or politically oppressive. In short, they were acting out old battles on one another. In similar situations, many such groups either disband or exile scapegoats who get blamed for all the problems (which then continue to plague the organization until they are dealt with). Individuals often blame others and go to war, or they blame themselves and lose confidence in their ability to keep faith with their vision.

The truth is, any time we take a risk to act, we will be challenged to integrate some shadow element of ourselves. This is an ongoing process. What differentiates magical people from others is their capacity for honest self-reflection. They neither shrink from seeing negative truths about themselves or their group nor banish aspects of themselves that seem troubling. Rather, they seek to find the gold in the shadow.

Achieving balance is not simply about finding a way to get to work, picking up the cleaning and the kids afterward, and getting home in time for dinner. Much more profoundly, it is about recognizing and finding a place for the whole of who we are. Several years ago, a man came up after I had given a speech and told me that he had been in recovery for twenty years and spent much of his time helping other alcoholics into recovery. He was particularly effective, he said, because he did not judge them at all. There was nothing anyone could say to shock him because there was nothing so depraved or bad that he had not done himself. The interesting thing is that as long as he was drinking, he was not clear enough to face the enormity of how terrible his life had become. When he sobered up and faced the full horror of his life, he discovered that he had an equally immense capacity for goodness, love, and care.

These undeveloped shadow qualities possess us in monstrous form until or unless they begin to be admitted into consciousness. Of course, under ideal circumstances this man would have been able to avoid the depth of suffering he experienced through his addiction. Many addicts tend to be perfectionists. Paradoxically, the harder they are on themselves, the more likely they are to become addicted. The alcoholic I just discussed became one because initially he was unable to integrate his pain or his vices into his self-concept. It took a twelve-step program, many years later, to help him learn how. When we can accept our sadness, our loneliness, our anger, our self-destructiveness, and our childlike wish to be cared for, we do not have to anesthetize ourselves. Moreover, we can open up to respect our childlike vulnerability, our independence, our appropriate moral outrage, our willingness to give, and our faith—that is, the positive poles of the negative traits just listed. This is why taking the Orphan's, Warrior's, Wanderer's, Altruist's, and Innocent's journeys prevents addiction.

We also can create a shadow identity by repressing desire. For instance, our culture is just moving out of Puritanism to deal with the shadow of sexuality, which often manifests itself in perverse yet extremely powerful forms. Sex is used in advertising to sell everything from cars to power tools, either by subliminal means or by having scantily clad women (or men) standing by the object being sold. Such juxtaposition makes no logical sense unless we understand that we quite simply are possessed by our repressed sexuality. In contemporary movies and in contemporary life, sexuality often is accompanied by violence. Rape, violent seduction, child molestation, pornography, and sadomasochism all speak to the reality of our culture's shadow possession, as do the more subtle but even more pervasive sexual relationships in which one or both of the parties is objectified. Integrating the shadow, in this case, can lead to ecstatic experiences of healthy and spiritual eroticism.

The Innocent teaches us to love the world just the way it is. If our Magician is balanced by a strong Innocent, we can take steps to make our dreams come true without feeling overly attached to doing so. However, if we become compulsive about getting our way, we subtly undermine any magic in our lives. Instead of linking easily and effortlessly with those who genuinely share our goals, we run the risk of getting bogged down in Pygmalion projects, trying desperately to change others (or the world) so that we can have what we desire. When we become hooked on manipulation, magic turns sour and controlling. The wonderful visions that could empower our lives are transformed into obsessions that run them. At this point, the Magician can become an evil sorcerer.

People with a Warrior mind-set assume that the appropriate response when we see the shadow within or without is to slay the dragon—to get rid of the sexuality or the obsessiveness. What happens then, however, is more repression, and the dragon gets bigger, and the possession gets more pronounced. When the Warrior/Altruist resolution is achieved, we learn to face the dragon and to recognize that it is dangerous—to ourselves and to others—but then to transform the monster by affirming it and acknowledging it as our own.

Violence is caused in large part by the repression of assertiveness. We learn to be nice, to give in, that we do not have the right to ask for what we want. Many of us are not taught skills for recognizing and asserting our needs. Consequently, emotions build up like an internal time bomb. The result is an explosion—anger, perhaps emotional or even physical violence inflicted on ourselves or another person. Paradoxically, the antidote to violence is not just self-control (which by itself can lead to repression), but self-knowledge and the skills of self-expression and assertion.

Magicians understand the courage and audacity involved in asserting themselves and their will on the universe when they themselves are not yet whole. To do so means letting loose their demons upon the world. Actually, because we all are co-creators whether we want to be or not, we always run this risk anyway. However, Magicians take responsibility for this process and basically trust it. If dragons are but their shadows, their unnamed, unloved parts, then the only way to transform them is to act, and by acting bring them into the light of day.

Yet, some discretion is required in the scope of their action to avoid calling forth demons too great for them to handle. In Ursula Le Guin's science fiction novel *A Wizard of Earthsea*, the main character, Sparrowhawk, believes, in his youthful arrogance, that he is powerful enough to call forth the dead. He succeeds, but in doing so lets loose a monster from the underworld that threatens to destroy the world. Young and inexperienced though he is, Sparrowhawk understands that it is his responsibility to find this demon and to confront and disarm it. He spends years on this lonely journey. When he finally tracks the monster down and confronts him, he realizes that the way to gain power over him is to speak the demon's real name. Facing him, he calls him Ged (Sparrowhawk's real name), and in acknowledging his shadow as a shadow, the two parts of himself are unified and the threat is no more.

Le Guin writes, "Ged had neither lost nor won but, naming the shadow of his death with his own name, had made himself whole: a man who, knowing his whole true self, cannot be used or possessed by any power other than himself, and whose life therefore is lived for life's sake and never in the service of ruin, or pain, or hatred, or the dark." After this triumph, Sparrowhawk sings a sacred song that celebrates paradox: "Only in silence the word, only in dark the light, only in dying life: bright the hawk's flight as an empty sky."[4]

The Magician comes to understand the precious balance in the universe and how individuals help to either foster that balance or disturb it by the choices they make about their lives. In *The Farthest Shore*, the third in Le Guin's *Earthsea Trilogy*, Sparrowhawk rights the balance again. Cob, a great mage gone evil, has decided to use his power to conquer death and to give people immortality. The result, of course, is that they have become possessed by death's shadow. Everywhere Sparrowhawk finds the walking dead: alienated, listless, many addicted to drugs, no one taking pride in work or loving one another.

He explains that what has caused the problem is that people desire "power over life," which he calls "greed." The only power worth having, he notes, is not "power over," but "power to" accept life, to allow it in. The desire to control life and death in order to attain immortality creates a void within and throws the cosmos out of balance. Sparrowhawk explains to Cob that "Not all the songs of earth, not all the stars of heaven could fill your emptiness," for Cob, in going for "power over," has lost himself and his true name.[5] Magicians, then, give up the illusion of control to allow life in themselves and in others. When they do so, they right the balance of the universe.

In contemporary times, the Shadow is visible for all the world to see. People bare their souls on talk shows. We know about the violence, incest, and despair in the family that before was hush-hush. Our politicians' vices are displayed before the world. Sex and violence are portrayed regularly on television and in the movies. It is a very difficult time in which to keep children innocent or hold on to adult ideals. Living near Washington, D.C., as I do, on some days it is difficult for my own cynicism to keep up with the news in *The Washington Post* that I read over my orange juice in the morning.

The shadow is visible, in part, because the Magician archetype is emerging into our collective consciousness. Our task is to integrate the shadow by finding the positive energy behind the negative behavior. For example, it is negative to beat someone up, but the desire to do so comes from an impulse to destroy something. What needs to be destroyed are many of our old habits of mind.

MAGICAL NAMING

The Magician uses the power to name differently than the Innocent. The Innocent names the world as good. The Magician often begins by identifying problems and then moves to exploring new avenues of perception. Many people today are afraid to call a spade a spade. For the Warrior, calling a dragon a villain is a prelude to attack. To be honest is to make oneself vulnerable in the pecking order. Honesty is very threatening, especially because people usually are trying to seem more than they are in order to rise in the hierarchy. It means having one's failings exposed. The Magician's way of talking about problems is tempered by love, supported by the belief that none of us is intrinsically bad or wrong. We all have a positive reason for being.

In Philip Ressner's wonderful children's book *Jerome the Frog*, a playful witch tells Jerome she has turned him into a prince. He still looks like a frog, but the townspeople begin sending him on quests just in case he really is a prince. He has several successes, so finally they send him to slay the dragon, who is always breathing fire and destroying villages. Jerome finds the dragon and draws his sword, but the dragon asks why. It is, after all, his nature to breathe fire and burn villages. Jerome ponders this and they discuss things a while and finally come up with a solution agreeable to all. The dragon will burn the town garbage every Tuesday and Thursday and lounge around and tell lies the rest of the week. Jerome does not try to convert the dragon or convince him to be "good," but instead helps him to be more fruitfully who he is, since dragons not only love to breathe fire and burn things up but also like to be admired and appreciated.[6]

Jerome's kind of victimless, villainless problem solving is predicated on the assumption that none of us is wrong or bad. We may, however, be repressing who we are and acting out of our shadow, or we simply may lack skills to express ourselves in a socially responsible manner. When either of these is true, we may cause difficulty for ourselves and others. Nothing is inherently wrong with dragons when their true natures are discovered, developed, and usefully channeled!

It is not just honesty, then, that is important, but the energy that surrounds it. If honesty comes out of a desire to cut someone down, it can be very destructive. However, enveloped in the faith that everyone has the potential for good, it has quite a different effect. The Magician's goal is not to slay but to *name* the dragon—to reinstate community through communication.

Madeleine L'Engle's novel for adolescents, *A Wind in the Door*, illustrates the power of positive naming, even when dealing with evil—if that naming is honest and not enabling of self-destructive attitudes or behaviors. The hero of the story is Meg, the adolescent daughter of parents who both are prizewinning physicists. The problem is that her beloved younger brother, Charles Wallace, is dying. Her mother has discovered that something has gone wrong with Charles's farandolae. Inside every human cell are organelles with their own RNA and DNA called mitochondria, without which we could not process oxygen. Inside the mitochondria, Meg's mother posits, are farandolae that have the same relationship to the mitochondria as the mitochondria have to the cell.

This vision of the interdependence of all life runs throughout the novel. Meg is visited by people from outer space and by a cherub, who explains that size makes no difference. Everything in the universe is just as critical as everything else, and everything is interconnected. They also explain that she can save Charles Wallace, because she is a Namer. A Namer, it turns out, is someone who helps things and people know who they are. For example, Meg's friend Calvin is a Namer to her because she feels more like herself when she is with him than at any other time.

The source of the problem is the Echthroi, the "Unnamers," who are responsible for things like black holes, alienation, despair, and crime, because they try to keep people, stars, trees, etc., from claiming their real identities and, therefore, from making their contribution to the universe. After practicing naming on a few people, Meg goes down into the mitochondria and talks with the farandolae. It turns out that the Echthroi have been there and convinced the farandolae that they need not take their journeys, that they are the greatest thing that exists. When the farandolae take their journeys, they sing with the stars. If they do not, the whole organism they are a part of dies.

Meg succeeds in naming the farandolae, but then realizes she must face the Echthroi themselves to free herself and her friends.

When she does so, she does not try to kill them as a Warrior might. Instead, she begins a litany of naming, ending with "Echthroi. You are named! My arms surround you. You are no longer nothing. You are. You are filled. You are me. You are Meg."[7]

Meg implicitly understands the principle of the microcosm and the macrocosm that is basic to magic. If she is a microcosm of the universe, then anything "out there" is also "in here." We all have some part of oursleves that we might call our "self-hater" that seeks either to tempt us with visions of grandeur or undercut our belief that what we do matters. Thus, we all have an Echthroi part seeking to divert us from our life purpose. As we learn to love the enemy without, we also learn to love (and in this way domesticate) the enemy within. The fearsome dragon we most fear, outside ourselves, holds the key to the shadow within.

Facing the shadow expands our capacity for love, so that eventually we can love everything inside and outside of us. However, doing so does not require us to enable bad behavior in ourselves or others. In the familiar story "The Frog Prince," a young princess drops her golden ball into the pond and is inconsolable. A frog appears and says he will get it for her if she promises to let him eat from her bowl and sleep on her pillow. She agrees, and he fetches the ball. Then, to her horror, her father insists that she keep her word. In the version I heard as a child, the frog turns into a prince when the princess kisses him. Lots of jokes have made the rounds about how many frogs women kiss, hoping one will be transformed into a prince, but little attention has been paid to the princess's suppression of disgust. The princess is repulsed by the frog, and implicit in the story is a message that the proper young princess should repress those feelings.

A contrast with a similar fable is helpful here. "Beauty and the Beast" is a prototypical Magician story. In this tale, too, the Beast

is transformed into a prince by the princess's kiss, yet the circumstances are quite different. The Beast acts quite princely toward
Beauty: he is always kind and generous to her. True, he asks her to
marry him every night, but she stays with her feelings and always
says no. He respects her right to do so even though he knows it
means he may stay a beast always, because only love will undo the
spell and make him human. Finally, when Beauty agrees to marry
him, she *does* mean it. She sees his inner nobility and comes to love
him. Then, and only then, is he transformed.

"Beauty and the Beast" suggests that we can transform not only
ourselves but others by loving them just as they are—"naming"
them as lovable, even with all their imperfections. "The Frog
Prince," though is a different story. The frog takes advantage of
the princess; she is emotionally younger and not so wise as Beauty,
not so able to love the frog as a frog. However, Madonna
Kolbenschlag, in *Kiss Sleeping Beauty Goodbye*, explains that in the
original version of the Frog Prince story, the frog was transformed not by a kiss but only when the princess acknowledged
her disgust, picked him up, and threw him in the fire.[8] (I like to
think she shouted "Yuck!" as she did so.)

In our culture, love often means indulging people, allowing
them to mistreat you. Such passivity involves a subtle kind of
despair. Magicians challenge people precisely because they trust
that there is more to them than their current self-indulgent or
self-destructive behavior. I have seen more men changed, I think,
when their wives stopped putting up with their chauvinism than
when they just accepted it. I have seen women change when their
husbands stopped sacrificing their own journeys to make enough
money to support them in the style to which they had become
accustomed. I also have seen children change when their parents
have stopped spoiling them and have set appropriate limits on
their behavior and spending. Wise love sometimes demands a
transformative toss into the fire, rather than the reinforcement of

the beastliness or froggishness in people. The toss into the fire also was a statement of self-respect for the princess. She had enough respect for herself not to force herself to kiss a frog—no matter *what* her father said! No matter what she had promised!

The Beast is transformed through the love of Beauty, and the frog is transformed only when the princess vehemently rejects him. Both women are Magicians when they fully trust and assert their own integrity. Now, this is not the Warrior's view of integrity—which requires keeping one's word, whatever the cost—but integrity that means living fully in keeping with one's deepest self. (Although keeping one's word is important to Magicians, too. They cannot trust their capacity to name and to create their world through naming it if they speak carelessly.) The young woman princess in "Beauty and the Beast" turns the Beast down night after night as long as it does not truly fit for her to be his bride. She does not force herself to do some goody-goody rescue number. What saves him is the genuineness of her love, just as the frog is so much better off after knowing the princess's honest disgust.

BEING REAL, BEING VULNERABLE

Being ladylike or gentlemanly and denying one's anger simply results in the unconscious sabotage of relationships. Expressing one's anger is transformative because it allows for a true and open, honest relationship. It makes way, therefore, for love. Margaret Atwood writes in *Lady Oracle* about a protagonist who lives several lives, all versions of the roles she has been taught to play. It is only the explosion of her anger at the end of the novel that makes any real relationship possible. Mistaking a reporter for her husband, she hits him over the head with a wine bottle. She visits him in the hospital and notes that they have become great friends. He is, after all, the only person who knows anything about her.[9]

The Magician is not sentimental or romantic. The goal of the

Magician is to recognize what is true about oneself and others. While at root we are all one in love, many layers exist above that reality—layers it may be inappropriate to overlook. It takes so much courage and discipline to live with true integrity moment to moment that we cannot do it without having gone through the stage of being a Warrior. To be honest and open in the moment is to be profoundly vulnerable. It does not allow for manipulation and control, but it does allow for intimacy, for love, and, occasionally, for magic moments.

Bonanza Jellybean, a character in Tom Robbins's novel *Even Cowgirls Get the Blues*, reassures us that we can move from hell to heaven simply by changing our attitudes. People have different ideas about the afterlife; however, most of us know that life right here on earth can feel like "heaven" or "hell." "Hell," Jellybean argues, "is living your fears. . . . Heaven is living your dreams."[10]

Shug in Alice Walker's *The Color Purple* is a powerful example of a Magician who transforms hell into heaven for a whole community. Shug lives with almost total fidelity to who she is—even though she breaks many of the social and gender rules of her time. She is a rather small-time blues singer with no great power in the world. Nevertheless, she transforms a patriarchal, oppressive environment in which little or no love or happiness can be found into a true community. She does not set out to change things. They change because she is who she is—which includes qualities of independence, assertiveness, gentleness, and care.

Celie, the main character in the story, begins as a molested and battered child who is married off to Albert, a man who does not love her but just wants someone to care for his children. He beats her because of his rage that she is not Shug, for he loved Shug although he did not have the courage to defy his father's wishes and marry her. Celie knows all about Shug, knows how free and honest she is, and instead of being threatened by her, gets courage just from seeing Shug's picture.

Celie already had gained some self-esteem from a choice she made to be an Altruist when, as a teenager, she dressed up to attract her father so he would not also molest her little sister. She chose to sacrifice her own body for her beloved sister. Later, from Shug, she learns to stand up for herself. Shug at first is hostile to Celie because she is married to Albert, but after Celie nurses Shug through an illness, Shug comes to love her. In this beauty-and-the-beast situation, Celie comes to value herself because Shug cares about her, and eventually they become lovers. Shug helps Celie learn to love and value her own femaleness and to find her own gifts: she makes wonderful, custom-made, comfortable pants. Finally, Celie learns to love without dependence when she discovers that she can survive and be content even when Shug leaves her.

Albert's fate is more like the frog's. First Shug confronts and rejects him when she learns he has beaten Celie, and then Celie confronts and leaves him, cursing him all the while, saying that everything he ever has done to her will rebound karmically on him. He is healed in part by having to face the damage he has done and in part by the love and care of his son, who does not give up on him, even after all the harm he has caused.

By the end of the story, all three—Celie, Shug, and Albert—care about one another. Albert has given up his pretensions to being the patriarch and Shug has returned to Celie. Ultimately, Shug, as Magician, redefines not only individual relationships but also the social paradigm for her community.

The most effective leaders I encounter in my executive coaching practice have an unself-conscious trust in their own instincts. Like Shug, they expect things to work out and do not agonize about their responses. Even so, I have observed patterns in what they do. They believe in people, notice them as individuals, and show that they care. They also have no difficulty setting boundaries when someone is not performing. People know they will have all the support they need if they are doing their best. However, if employees are not performing competently in their current jobs, the manager talks to them about whether this job is right for them. If so, training options are considered to help them become more successful. If not, they might be moved to another position or let go (with active encouragement to find fulfillment elsewhere). But most of all, such managers save a lot of time that others spend worrying, because they expect to succeed—and typically do.

Beyond that, when problems occur they do not respond by saying, "Someone should do something." Rather, they step up to the plate themselves and get started doing what they can to hit a home run. Warriors also act immediately when change is needed. The difference is that Warriors strategize to make change happen, while Magicians envision the desired outcome and get moving, trusting synchronicity to help them work out the details. When things go wrong, Warriors struggle to exert more force or control. Magicians pull back to be certain that their goals are congruent with the true needs of the time. When things become difficult, the Magician may accept that magic currently is not working in the outside world. Often what is happening instead is that the magic is working inside. We are being initiated to a higher level of consciousness by the difficulties we are experiencing. As our consciousness is transformed, the outer world changes accordingly, though sometimes this process takes time and ingenuity.

If what you want (and what fits with your journey) does not exist yet or is in very short supply, you may need to invent it or just wait. Magicians know that timing is critical. Sometimes the partner you want is there, but not yet at the right place in his or her journey to meet you. Perhaps the culture you live in does not have a standard form of employment to match your vocation. For example, one woman I know felt very aimless and went to a psychic, who told her that her problem was being by nature a temple-keeper in a world with no temples. There are no ads in the paper for temple-keepers. She became a massage therapist and healer practicing out of her home, which she redesigned to be a sanctuary in the midst of a chaotic, high-pressure city. This is where it is helpful to remember synchronicity. Rarely are persons so far ahead of their culture that they are not, at least in some ways, a microcosm of it. Temple-keepers may not find literal temples, but they can maintain figurative ones when they find out what they revere as sacred; then they can keep those things safe.

Recognizing our interdependence may feel limiting because we can go only so far into a new world by ourselves. However, first it is important to understand how profoundly our lives can be changed even in our present society. I have noticed people in the same country who seem to be living in different realities. There are those whose lives are defined by scarcity, loneliness, fear, poverty (of goods or of spirit, which makes even the wealthy feel poor), and ugliness; and there are those who are surrounded by love, beauty, and abundance and who feel befriended, prosperous, and happy. Similarly, some people are living mentally and emotionally in the nineteenth century, while others are living in the twenty-first. In many ways, we truly inhabit different worlds.

When the Magician is active in our lives, we choose the world we live in. In the developed world this is easy to see. We resonate to different possibilities, and we have options. We affiliate with those parts of society that correspond to our own consciousness. We know that many people in the world have fewer or perhaps even no options. However, if we remember that the tradition of shamanism thrives in what we regard as underdeveloped cultures and countries, we can see a form of the Magician that prevails even in situations that appear to be enormously limiting, at least in a material sense.

In virtually every indigenous tradition, the shaman travels between the worlds. Healing occurs because the shaman goes into a trance and enters another reality, another world, independent of our everyday social roles. In this reality, he or she removes the cause of the illness on the mental, emotional, or spiritual level. Entering this other dimension also allows for the development of psychic ability, for the shaman "sees" events and forces that are invisible to the eye. Such shamans understand that we live in only one dimension of many. There are many ways to inhabit other worlds, only one of which is in the physical body. Every one of us has the capacity to journey in our imagination and, in doing so, to change our consciousness.

Moreover, we can see the Magician archetype in transformative world leaders, even those whose commitment to societal change has led to exile or imprisonment, such as Nelson Mandela. His twenty-five years in prison not only did not break his spirit, they created the opportunity for an incredible expansion of consciousness that prepared him for eventual leadership in post-apartheid South Africa. The legacy of the Magician is that if we are willing to experience whatever initiation it takes to become magical ourselves, there are no odds too great to stop us.

CREATING CAMELOT

Creating our own utopian worlds is an ongoing, daily process. We can activate our inner Magician by thinking of legends and stories of great wizards. One example virtually everyone knows is Merlin, who provided the vision for the creation of Camelot.

The great Camelot legends, which emerged in oral tradition in a way that charted a path for hope during the Dark Ages, provide metaphorically rich teachings about how to use magic to transform our lives. The story begins when society is crumbling. The old king has died and, in the feudal system, rival lords begin fighting to succeed him. The war creates so much social disruption and bloodshed that many are disheartened completely about the future of Britain. (You might see that as analogous to the state of many of our organizations, families, and communities today.)

Merlin has retreated to a cave in the forest, where he is fighting off serious depression. His attention is captured for a moment by the glitter from a crystal in the wall of the cave. Suddenly, he has a vision of the just and humane society that ought to exist instead of the petty infighting he sees all around him every day. What happens to Merlin here exemplifies the shaman's practice of leaving the everyday world to move into the imaginal realm. All of us can do this when we shift from focusing on problems to imagining the world we would like to inhabit.

Often, we dismiss our moments of vision simply as escapist daydreams. Merlin, however, takes his seriously, calling the vision Camelot. For the rest of his life, he holds up all choices against this vision, deciding to act consistently in ways that lead to its realization. You and I can do this by taking visioning seriously in our work and our private lives, living every day as if we were bringing into being our own personal Camelot.

After a time, Merlin leaves the cave and begins to "sell" his vision to others. Of course, he has no idea how the society will move from anarchy to Camelot, but he trusts it will. He begins to identify the key players, most importantly King Arthur and Queen Guenevere. Together Merlin, Arthur, and Guenevere assemble the lords and ladies of Camelot, identifying those who share their goals and ideals. While Merlin articulates the vision in ways that engender commitment, Arthur matches talent to task, helping people to know what they can do to make this dream a reality. Guenevere focuses on forming a genuine sense of community among those assembled so that they care about one another and are loyal to their communal cause.

The lesson for us today is that no one creates paradise alone. It is essential to link up with others who have similar dreams and values and to organize both a collective effort (with an emphasis on accomplishing goals) and a genuine, caring community (with a primary focus on the nurturance and development of individuals).

The key players of Camelot also find or create sacred objects that facilitate the work: Arthur's magic sword, which comes from the Lady of the Lake, a Celtic goddess of great power; the Round Table, which is part of Guenevere's dowry when she is betrothed to Arthur; and the castle of Camelot, which Arthur and Merlin design and have built. Similarly, each of us needs to find or produce the forms that perfectly match their function. In the modern world, this might include the right office or home environment, the appropriate technological support, and any and all physical structures that grease the wheels of success.

For visions to succeed in the long run, they must give expression to our higher values. The Camelot legend tells us that Guenevere develops the code of chivalry, providing the values statement that inspires the imagination of the knights and ladies of the court. They promise to serve God, to be kind to those in need, and to create the most just society that ever existed. They are loyal to the vision of Camelot because it gives them a way to act in keeping with their own vision. Eventually, of course, the knights go in search of the Holy Grail, which provides each with a knowledge of the meaning of his life. This teaches us that no matter how powerful our collective visions may be, they hold our allegiance only to the extent that they coincide with our sense of individual purpose.

If you are in the process of creating your own personal Camelot and things do not go smoothly, you can do a rough check to see what might be out of balance. Have you committed to a clear vision? Do the other stakeholders share that vision with you? Have you matched talents to task to get things done? Do all of you share a genuine sense of community? Are the physical structures and technology appropriate to realizing your vision? Is that vision congruent with the values of all concerned?[11]

The most central quality of the Magician is the willingness to undertake honest self-examination. Recently, I facilitated a truly magical team-building retreat in an organizational setting. The participants came in angry because some of their co-workers had split off to form a competing enterprise and did so at a critical time for their organization. They knew they had every right to sit and complain about what had happened to them. Instead, however, they looked inward at what they could change about how they did business and then outward to emerging market needs. As a result, rather than falling into cynicism and blaming, they came up with a new vision that held the promise of getting them ahead of the curve, thus ensuring the market share they needed to succeed. In the process, they also managed to increase camaraderie and commitment among their team members. During the debriefing session, several of them mentioned that the difference between those who succeed today and those who don't is their willingness to learn from whatever happens and change the only thing they can: themselves.

In the madcap contemporary world, we can apply these same principles to balancing our professional and personal obligations. First, visualize what it would be like to have a life that is in balance. Second, make a clear decision to commit to balance "no matter what." Third, share your positive intent with those around you, asking for their input and support to manifest this sane and enjoyable life. Fourth, take action to reflect this commitment in the actual structures of your life. (For example, you might negotiate to work part-time, stop rescuing others when they fail to meet their obligations, or hire or collaborate with others to pick up some of what you have been doing.) Fifth, tune in to your deeper values, allowing back into your life those activities that reflect them. (For instance, you might want to spend more time with your children or friends, take walks in nature, meditate, or express your creativity through music or art.)

And finally, if you seem to subvert your own efforts in some way, take responsibility for the shadow-you that is creating that difficulty. Since the shadow never goes away, pay attention to what it wants from you. (For example, if you decide to cut back how much time you work, you may find that a part of you is more committed to achievement than you had realized. Or you might identify some part of you that is afraid of empty time. In the first case, you might want to rethink your ideal of a balanced life to include more focus on achievement. In the second, you might work on learning to deal with the pent-up feelings—or the sense of disorientation—that emerges when you have unscheduled time.)

THE TRANSFORMATION OF SOCIETY

Political leaders today speak frequently about the cultural and economic transformation afoot in the world. In recent decades, the rationalist paradigm has had such a strong hold that it was seen as unsophisticated to believe in energy, healing, spirit, souls, or even God. Today, things are different. Books about soul are on the best-seller list. People talk about spirit in the workplace. Scientists now recognize that matter essentially is an illusion. Everything actually is made up of mind stuff, information. Every particle that ever interacted with another particle still spins in relationship. Moreover, the results of scientific experiments seem related to the expectations of the researcher—which means that even at the level of physics, our minds influence the world (or, at least, our expectations predetermine, to some degree, the results of our laboratory experiments).[12]

In the first edition of *The Hero Within*, published in 1986, I noted that we were in the midst of a transformation from a Warrior to a Magician culture. In such an environment, people who have little or no access to the Magician archetype have difficulty keeping up with the demands of the time. In the current milieu, we regard it as axiomatic that systems are changing and that individuals must reinvent themselves to keep pace. It is not so much that our environments determine consciousness or consciousness determines events. Rather, individuals, organizations, and society as a whole are in dynamic interaction as the pace of change speeds up.

Part of the issue we all face is how to maintain our equilibrium when everything around us and in us is changing. Only those who are willing to let go of their attachment to the illusion of permanence and stability have a chance to succeed. By temperament, however, Magicians like to make change happen. The secret is to withdraw your resistance to being transformed. Shevek, the central character in Ursula Le Guin's novel *The Dispossessed*, sums up the Magician's wisdom when he says, "You cannot make the Revolution. You can only be the Revolution."[13] When you do so, your world changes—as if by magic.

GETTING ACQUAINTED WITH THE MAGICIAN ARCHETYPE

To familiarize yourself with the Magician archetype, make a collage out of Magician-like pictures from magazines; make lists of songs, movies, and books that express the Magician; collect pictures of yourself, relatives, colleagues, and friends in a Magician mode. Practice noticing when you are thinking or acting like a Magician.

Magician Exercises

Step One: Describe what it would be like to have an ideal balance in your own life; then live in a way that is congruent with your vision.

Step Two: Visualize the world as you want it to be; then cast your vote for this outcome by how you live your life every day.

Step Three: Identify people and groups that you judge negatively or dislike, as a way to identify your own shadow. Explore how you might see the shadow in yourself—either in your own behavior or what you feel but fear to express. Think of responsible ways to affirm the more positive aspects of this shadow and integrate them into your life.

Step Four: Practice standing up for your principles without making anyone else wrong or bad. Make clear to others what you believe in and where your commitments are, but act lovingly as you do so.

Step Five: Be honest with yourself about your own failings and atone for any misdeeds. Notice what part of you is responsible for the negative outcome. Then pay attention to the positive desire beneath the negative behavior and act to fill this underlying need.

Step Six: Practice seeing the positive potential in people and situations, "naming" that potential in nonshaming, nonblaming ways (while also holding boundaries to be certain that you and others are not harmed by current negative behaviors).

PART 2

Personal Mastery: The Guidebook

Introduction

Personal Mastery:
Inner Resource Development

> Problems cannot be solved by the same consciousness
> that created them.
>
> —Albert Einstein

Part One of this book provides a map to the hero's journey and the archetypal guides that help us on our way. Part Two explores the practice of personal mastery. It contains crucial information about strategies to increase self-awareness and, in so doing, to become more capable of living a successful and happy life.

Some people tell me they do not believe in archetypes. Unfortunately, what you do not see or think is real can still trip you up. Such people often are controlled by the archetypes within them: they cannot stop trying to achieve every minute (Warrior), they obsessively take care of others (Altruist), they always seem to be victimized (Orphan), and so on. Failure to understand the dynamics of the inner life can retard our progress just as much as if we did not believe in learning to read or do math.

You can utilize information in Part One simply to understand what archetypes have been expressed in your life thus far and to appreciate people who are different from you. If this is all you do, it still is valuable. Understanding what motivates you and appreciating the perspectives of others are important ingredients of career and life success.

Part Two, however, invites you to go deeper with this material. If you do, you can gain the personal mastery necessary to take charge of your life at a more profound level. In classical Jungian analysis, you find meaning in life by attending carefully to your dreams and the archetypes that populate them. This practice is an important aspect of inner resource development and is highly recommended to readers of this book.[1] The goal is individuation, which means simply that you find out who you are at a very fundamental level.

As we become aware of archetypes—in Jungian analysis or by applying the concepts in this book to our lives—our relationship to them shifts. Eventually, it is possible not only to honor their presence, but also to cooperate with them consciously. At this point, we are partnering, or even dancing, with our inner guides. In the process, we reach a new level of freedom and power. The more familiar with our inner terrain we become, the more conscious and liberated we can be.

There are many more archetypes than the ones described in this book. These six, however, provide an inner structure that allows us to develop ego strength, which in turn makes it possible for us to work safely with other archetypal energies. Many people today do not go further than this in their development, in part because they do not believe in anything beyond material reality. As the returned Innocent and Magician are awakened in us, we move into a deeper, more spiritual and soulful level of being.

In the final chapter of Part One, we learned about the Magician's role in achieving balance. Personal mastery means that we are capable of becoming conscious of any discrepancies between our outer role commitments and our emerging inner archetypal realities. We stop trying to be all things to all people and focus instead on expressing our own inner truth and meeting the challenges that are meaningful to us.

In today's world, it also is helpful to have each of these six archetypes available to us. When this occurs, life begins to have greater ease. Although there is no prescribed order that must be followed for the journey, personal ease and mastery are fostered when the archetypes are in relative equilibrium.

Wholeness in the psyche traditionally is symbolized by a sacred circle that is inherently harmonious because it is a microcosm of the universe. Jung described how patients approaching wholeness spontaneously drew mandalas—that is, circular figures with four outer parts arranged around a center. In virtually every indigenous shamanic tradition, the medicine men or women create a magic circle (or medicine wheel) of some kind, with the four directions and the center, to invoke balance between the human, spiritual, and natural worlds. In *Projection and Re-Collection in Jungian Psychology*, Marie-Louise von Franz writes:

> One primordial image in particular has survived in scientific tradition for a greater length of time than most, one that has appeared as a visual image of God, of existence, of the cosmos, of space-time, and of the particle: the image of a circle or of the "sphere whose center is everywhere and whose circumference is nowhere." Over the centuries this image has undergone many transformations, until finally it was understood more and more as the image of the endopsychic reality in the human being.[2]

The circular diagram on p. 221 is a visual summary of Part One of this book. Before the journey, our consciousness is defined by the society around us. The Orphan emerges when we fall from innocence, when something happens that undermines our faith—in our parents, authority figures, God, even life itself. As we face our disappointment at living in a fallen world, the Wanderer escapes from captivity and prompts us to head out on our own to discover what is possible. However, we soon learn that we cannot always leave when things do not go right. At this point, the Warrior helps us learn to stay and assert ourselves. But in the normal progression of life, if we are always battling, we find ourselves isolated and alone. When the Altruist emerges, we discover the joys of giving to and caring for others. By this time, we no longer feel so vulnerable. The return to innocence heals the wounded inner child and allows us to trust life. Then the Magician appears, and we gain personal mastery and the ability to make life-affirming choices.

This process creates an inner "family" that can compensate for any deficits in our family of origin. That is, when you gain a family within, your life no longer is limited by what you had or did not have as a child. You carry a healthy family with you always.

THE INNER FAMILY

The Orphan archetype teaches the inner child to survive difficulty. The Wanderer differentiates the adolescent from parents and others and promotes the sense of adventure we need to face the unknown. The Warrior activates the inner father so he can protect and provide for us. The Altruist supports the inner mother so she can nurture and comfort us. (Here, of course, I am using the traditional attributes of mother and father. They may or may not correspond to qualities of your actual parents. It is not important which parent carries which qualities as long as a child is safe, loved, and challenged.)

As we build an inner family, the inner child does not feel so lost, alone, and dependent. Thus, we no longer have to be so reactive to what our families of origin, and particularly our parents, did or did not do. Though most of us project issues with our parents onto other authority figures as well as onto organizations, we can learn to defuse this process by building an inner archetypal magic circle that allows us to withdraw these projections.

It is important to remember that these inner figures are archetypes—and archetypes are both within us and around us. When we return to innocence, the universe itself begins to feel

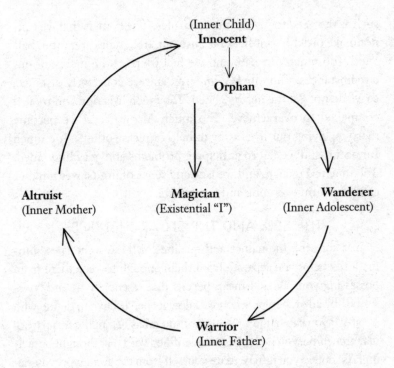

like a more friendly place. Having found out who we are, it is not such a stretch to imagine that everyone is precious, because others, like us, have something unique to give. Having developed boundaries, it does not seem so frightening to open our hearts to receive. We know that if anything hurtful comes our way, we can defend ourselves. Having opened our hearts to care for others, it seems logical that others will love and care for us as well.

When this circle is complete and the inner child is healed, the Magician steps to the center to hold the other archetypes in balance. It also supports choice and the inner mastery that allows us to create the lives we truly want to live. Most of us think that our lives are spinning out of control because of external pressures, such as the need to juggle multiple roles. The truth is that we cannot make order in our lives because our archetypes are not in balance. Too much Orphan, and we feel we're at the mercy of our circumstances. Too much Wanderer, and we constantly distance, so we do not get the help we need. Too much Warrior, and we feel compelled to overachieve. Too much Altruist, and we become martyrs, giving our lives away to help or please others. Too much Innocent, and we fail to anticipate problems and get blind-sided. Too much Magician, and we lack any sense of limits: we think we can transform everyone and everything.

THE SELF AND THE SIX ARCHETYPES

Just knowing the names and qualities of these archetypes automatically helps you separate from them enough to keep them from possessing you. What I mean here is that essentially we are "possessed" by an archetype when we allow its perspective to define who we are. If you can name a feeling or thought as belonging to a particular archetype, you no longer are identified with that thought or feeling. As soon as you differentiate yourself from the archetype, you can influence the degree and quality of its expression in your life.

Not too long ago, I was leaving work after a particularly rugged day. I thought to myself, "I'm depressed." I realized that I easily could talk myself into getting more and more down if I kept up this thinking pattern. Using *The Hero Within* model, I remembered to ask myself, "What part of me is depressed?" I then realized that my Orphan was unhappy because I had been mistreated by some colleagues. The unfairness of what had happened stung me so badly that it immediately threw me psychologically out of balance, and I began identifying with just one archetype.

As I thought about it, I realized that the rest of me was fine. Differentiating the self from the Orphan brought immediate relief from identifying who I was with this negative feeling. I could call on my inner Altruist, who recommended a good chat with a friend, followed by a bubble bath. Then my inner Warrior gave advice on how to defend myself from the nefarious political maneuvers going on in my workplace. Finally, I could call on my Innocent to remind me to choose inner peace and trust the process of the interaction.

When we recognize the archetypal basis of all thoughts, we develop the capacity to identify the structures beneath them. No longer trapped in one point of view, we can switch mental models to solve problems when one of our habitual approaches is not working. This is why the capacity for inner resource development is essential for anyone in a leadership position today. The great problems of our time cannot be solved by people in the grip of any one archetype's way of seeing the world.

LIFE STAGES AND ARCHETYPAL STRENGTHS

Archetypes also tend to emerge at predictable life stages, unless they are repressed by our conditioning or current environmental pressures. Although archetypes can be present at any time, we need certain ones to help us face key developmental challenges. Therefore, we are not out of balance if, at particular times, these archetypes take a more active role in our lives than others. For example:

- The Innocent and Orphan archetypes always are present in childhood. They give rise to continuing inner-child issues until both are integrated into the psyche.
- The Wanderer tends to be activated in adolescence and the mid-life transition. If its lessons are not learned during these key passages, we can be left with an unnerving lack of direction and self-knowledge.
- The Warrior and the Altruist dominate in early life, as we learn to take on family and career responsibilities. If they are not expressed at this time, we are likely to be plagued by feelings of powerlessness until both are activated.

- The Innocent reemerges and the Magician appears in mid-life and later, if not before. Without these archetypes, we cannot resolve issues of spirit and soul and are left with a sense of meaninglessness.

It also is true that we always have access to every archetypal mode. What "stage" we are in has to do with where we "hang out" the most, where we spend the greatest percentage of our time. The most oppressed victim will have moments of transcendence. And none of us gets so advanced that we stop feeling, every once in a while, like a motherless child. In fact, each stage has a gift for us, something critical to teach us about being human. Most of us have a favorite archetype throughout life, but we need access to all the others to traverse predictable life passages successfully. If we continue to grow in this way, we will gain wisdom as we age.

The fact that people address certain developmental tasks in a predictable order *does not mean that we leave one archetype behind in a linear fashion and go on to another.* We attain deeper levels of understanding and higher levels of performance associated with any one of the archetypes only by intensifying our investment in the others. We continually sharpen and refine skills in each category, for the journey truly is a process of high-level skill development. Ultimately, we gain a repertoire of possible responses to life, giving us incrementally more choices about how we can react in any given situation. Accordingly, over time, we tend to achieve greater archetypal balance, simply because the pressures of maturation expand our range of options.

You can use the archetypal wheel to analyze the overall balance in your life. Leading a full and complex life requires the following:

- The ability to anticipate problems so that you can avoid over-load (Orphan);
- Some form of authentic self-expression (Wanderer);

- Clear goals and the will to achieve them (Warrior);
- Generosity toward family, friends, and colleagues and concern for the good of the whole society (Altruist);
- A sense of faith and trust in a God, Goddess, Higher Power, or simply life itself (Innocent); and
- That you take responsibility for existential choice and creating or restoring the balance that is right for you at any given time (Magician).*

INNER ENERGY AND OUTER ROLES

When the outer roles we are living conflict with our inner energy dynamic, we can feel stale, burned out, as though the meaning has gone out of our lives. This can happen because, while those roles once fit us, we have changed inside or because we are making choices based on what others want for us, what seems expedient, or what might work in the short run, rather than what we genuinely desire. Our lives seem manageable to the degree that we are able to express our inner realities in the outer roles we play. If the energy within us is moving naturally toward outer activities that we are repressing, we will have no energy for what we in fact *are* doing. As a result, we feel either exhausted or hyper all the time. When the energy of our inner archetypal potential matches our outer activities, our work proceeds with ease and we experience life as pleasant. Sometimes we can alter our outer roles to fit our inner lives, and sometimes our challenge is to awaken an archetype within that is needed to fulfill our external commitments.

Part Two is a guidebook for developing personal mastery. Chapter 8, "Honoring Your Life," offers an opportunity for you to use the hero's journey map as a way to celebrate the route you have

---

* See Appendix C for information about how to use the archetypal wheel to create environments that promote heroism—in families, schools, workplaces, psychotherapy, recovery, and politics.

taken—one that is uniquely your own. In the process, you can explore the archetypal influences upon you of your gender, your family of origin, and your current workplace. Chapter 9, "Troubleshooting When You Get Lost or Stuck," provides a compass to help you find your way when you are lost or to find the way out when you feel stuck. Finally, Chapter 10, "The Ethics of the Journey," explores the heroic code, since nothing throws us off balance as quickly as violating our principles and values. As a whole, Part Two is designed to give you the tools necessary to work with your own heroic journey and in this way to take greater control of your life.

Exercise A: If you have not taken the Heroic Myth Self-Test in Appendix A already, now is the time to do so. To explore the balance in your life right now, look at your results on Part One. Compare the archetypes within you to the roles you actually play at this time. For example, if you score high on the Altruist and are engaged in parenting or otherwise helping or developing others, you would have archetype/role congruence on this measure. However, if you scored low on Altruist and your major role is a caregiving one, you may experience stress. Then you might look at your current activities more generally to see how your inner archetypes are, or could be, expressed in your outer life. If some of your archetypes are evidenced primarily in their negative forms, you also might explore ways they could be expressed more positively. The chart on the following page provides examples that might stimulate your thinking. It is not meant to be exhaustive.

Exercise B: Part Two of the Heroic Myth Self-Test tells you what archetypal behavior others see in you. Look back at your results on Part One and compare them with those on Part Two. First, notice whether you see yourself more or less positively than others do. Second, pay attention to whether others are seeing an archetypal expression in you that you are missing. Third, if some archetype you know to be active within you is not apparent to others, analyze why this might be. Perhaps you are not acting in external ways that show this inner strength. Perhaps others are not open to noticing this archetype. Perhaps they see you through their own archetypal lens. If others see you very differently than you see yourself, however, you may want to work on aligning your everyday personality and behavior with your inner truth.

Internal Archetype	Possible Outer Expression
Orphan	Participation in therapy or a recovery program, reaching out to others in need, work that provides job security, involvement in liberation movements, learning about ways to live more effectively
Wanderer	Solitary endeavors, travel, exploration of new ideas or experiences, following your own interests, differentiating yourself from others, starting a new endeavor
Warrior	Competitive endeavors, persevering in difficult circumstances, setting and achieving goals, asserting your needs and keeping strong boundaries, building physical strength
Altruist	Taking care of children, the elderly, or the ailing, volunteer and community services, philanthropic efforts, nurturing yourself or others
Innocent	Prayer and meditation, creative/artistic pursuits, learning from others, celebrating, having fun
Magician	Being a catalyst for change, exerting influence or leadership, making big decisions, helping others work well together, creating new models, practices, or approaches

CHAPTER 8

Honoring Your Life: The Route

Trust your process.

—Anne Wilson Schaef

The map of the hero's journey connects you with all the heroes of all times and places. The map, then, is the same, but only you can choose the route you want to take through this varied terrain. This chapter is designed to help you appreciate the life you have lived thus far and what gifts you have received from it. When we measure our lives against an ideal, we almost always come up lacking. Then we feel bad about ourselves. However, if we receive our journey as a sacred experience, we can marvel in its mystery without judging overly much. My hope is that this chapter can help you honor yourself and the life you have lived while also providing a baseline to help you make life-enhancing choices for your future.

The hero's journey is developmental, but not linear. No rule says that we all have to travel through it, lockstep, the same way others do. The trick is to understand the unique form and logic of your particular journey. The circular diagram of the sacred wheel described in the introduction to this part is a two-dimensional model for a three-dimensional process. Actually, it would be more correct to envision it as a cone or spiral, in which it is possible to move forward while frequently circling back. Each stage has its own lesson to teach us, and we reencounter situations that throw us back into prior stages so that we may learn and relearn the lessons at new levels of intellectual and emotional complexity and subtlety.

It is not so much that we go anywhere, but that we fill out. You know how some people feel shallow to us, as if there is not much there? Their souls seem thin, anorexic. The journey fills people out and gives them substance. Those who have taken their journeys feel bigger—even if their bodies are slender or they are small of stature. We feel the size of their souls.

As we move through the spiral, the "stages" of our journey become flowing points on a dynamic, spiraling wheel of interaction with the world. Every time we experience something that makes us feel disillusioned and/or powerless, we put to use the lessons we learned as Orphans—we mourn our loss and, recognizing that we do not have the skill or knowledge to deal with a situation entirely on our own, we seek help. When we feel alienated, we focus inward and ask ourselves, "Who am I this time?" We must take the time we need to keep up with our changing identities.

When we feel threatened and angry, we know that we are not living exactly the way we wish to or believe in. Then we assert ourselves and our values, taking the risk of stepping off the edge of conventionality to live the life of our choosing—and to accept the consequences of that choice. When we feel maimed by giving too much or inappropriately or feel put upon by other people's demands, it is time to explore what gifts are truly ours to give. We must ask, "What do I really need to give to this life, and what is just placating others?"

The first swings through the spiral take some time and energy. They are experienced as hard work. It is a bit like riding a bicycle, however; once you get the hang of it, it comes quite naturally. As we learn the lessons that are the gifts of each archetype, they become a natural part of who we are. It's not so much that we leave the hero's journey, but that it becomes so much a part of us that we no longer are conscious of it.

Moreover, our individual journeys recapitulate aspects of the evolution of archetypes (to the degree that they remain relevant to our time and place). In our first tries at warrioring, for example, we may come on like Attila the Hun, but later we may learn to assert our own wishes so appropriately and gently that we can negotiate for what we want without any noticeable conflict. We then have the Warrior to protect our boundaries as we focus our energy on accomplishment.

Each archetype gives us gifts that have resonance with aspects of the other archetypes. For example, the Altruist helps us learn to sacrifice for others out of love for them. Orphans sacrifice, in part, to propitiate the gods or some authority figure, so they will be safe. Wanderers sacrifice community to find themselves. Warriors risk their very lives (or their jobs) to prevail. Magicians, believing that nothing essential ever is lost, may welcome the organic and gentle letting go of the old to make way for new growth, new life.

FINDING WHOLENESS

Most of us are used to thinking that higher is better, so we want to move out of the "lower" archetypes to develop the "higher" ones. But the spiral pattern is not so much about advancing as it is about expanding. It might be helpful to think of the spiral growing wider and wider as we become capable of a larger range of responses to life and thus are able to have more of it. We take in more and have more choices. The circular diagram reminds us that we do not have to choose the "best" archetype. Rather, we can seek to balance our expression of all of them. While this schematic is helpful conceptually, human development rarely is that neat and tidy. The point, however, is that the archetypes are interrelated, and often we cannot resolve the psychological or cognitive dilemma embedded in one without working through another. For example, if you are focused on achievement but are not willing to help others, you are likely to be distrusted by others and hence be less successful than you could be. Conversely, if you give to others but have no boundaries, you may be run over by others' demands. The Warrior and Altruist are two complementary ways of making a difference in the world. When they are in balance, life is more satisfying and fulfilling—not only for individuals but for groups. (Similarly, the Innocent and the Orphan seem like polar opposites, but both share a desire to find a way to be safe in the world. Together, they help us discern tempters from guides, so we develop street smarts.)

We go to school with each archetype many times in our lives. Further, events influence the order and intensity of our learning. Any massive change, commitment, or crisis requires a reconsideration of identity issues. Each time we encounter the same archetype, we have the opportunity to do so at a deeper level of understanding.

The virtues that the hero learns in each guise never are lost or outgrown. They just become more subtle. As Innocents, heroes demonstrate the simple faith it takes to begin a journey. When troubles inevitably come, heroes lose their innocence, at least temporarily. As Orphans, they learn to be careful and to sympathize with one another. As Wanderers, they find and name their own truths. As Warriors, they learn to prove themselves in the world through making a positive contribution. As Altruists, they learn to love, to commit, to give, and to let go. Returning as Innocents, they appreciate the beauty and wonder of the world and trust in divine help. As Magicians, they change the world by first changing themselves.

When a new stage is appropriate, any archetype can renew us. But when those who are at an earlier stage of development jump prematurely into a role that requires an archetype or archetypal level that is beyond them, their growth can be stultified. For example, parents who are Altruists may teach their children the virtues of giving unselfishly to others without realizing that children and adolescents also must develop some assertiveness, spunk, and competence; otherwise their overly stimulated Altruist can cause them to be used by others, to martyr themselves, and to give their lives away.

ARCHETYPES AND POLITICS

The point of archetypal awareness is to be more complete, to be more whole, to have a wider repertoire of choices—not to be higher up on a developmental ladder. We do not outgrow any lessons. A good example of this can be found in politics. Each archetype has its own contribution to make. Innocents tend to want to have great excitement about candidates. At worst, they imagine their candidate will rescue them, but at best they simply work hard for the best person to win. Once the candidate is elected, Orphans will be quick to spot his or her Achilles' heel. At worst, they will sit around whining about the state of the world. At best, they will help others balance their enthusiasm with a proper awareness of the official's weaknesses and vulnerabilities. At their worst, Warriors jump on the bandwagon to launch an attack designed to bring the flawed leader down. At their best, they see to the nuts and bolts of managing campaigns, lobbying for change, and crusading for justice. At worst, Altruists get burned out struggling to work hard enough to make up for the flaws of the system (or the leader). At best, they give a reasonable amount of their time and money to foster the common good.

At worst, Wanderers abdicate responsibility for the political process; but at best they serve as pioneers, seeking out new political experiments. In times of major cultural transformation such as now, Wanderers also may remove themselves from direct political action, yet address identity and value concerns to help make new politics possible. (When I wrote the first version of this book, I fit into the latter category; seeing the need for a change in consciousness that would help make a renewal of the political process possible, I took a break from political engagement to focus on fostering the inner life.)

Magicians are more likely to emphasize the creation of new or alternative communities, institutions, and ways of relating to one another, or to work at the local or organizational level until grassroots efforts make major change at the national and international levels more likely. At worst, such changes are quirky, naive, or cultlike. At best, they provide the seeds that sprout into the creation of a new world.

None of these responses by itself is adequate; yet all are useful—at least in their positive guises. There are times for recognizing when others know more or are better leaders, and you should follow them. There are times when it is best to remove yourself from the action to be sure of your values. There are times for political engagement. There are times to focus on what you can create right where you are. And there are times to call attention to every positive sign on the horizon.

ALL THE ARCHETYPES ARE VALUABLE

However, we do not always feel so tolerant and appreciative. Sometimes, when we move into the first stage of an archetype, we are a bit dogmatic about it and see it as the only way to be. When we leave that position, we usually flip-flop and reject where we have been. For people just moving out of the martyr stage of the Altruist mode, any positive statement about the value of sacrifice is likely to seem masochistic, sick, or codependent. Of course, such sentiments generally are right, at least for the person expressing them. If we are just moving from Altruists into being Wanderers, the temptation to stop the journey and give to others is an ever present and real threat.

Leaving an identification with an inner ally's perspective is like leaving a love affair or marriage. Few of us can just say to a partner or lover that we are ready to move on and leave with a simple thank-you for what has been. Instead, we spend a great deal of time chronicling the faults of our former lover and how bad the relationship was. Often, we create high drama to divert ourselves from our fear of the unknown or because we do not believe we have a right to leave anything unless it is absolutely awful.

We also may reject stages we are not ready to move into yet—the ones we have had little or no experience with. Instead, we may redefine them in terms we know and thus completely misunderstand the point. That is all right, too, because at that point the truth we do not understand is not yet relevant to us developmentally. For instance, to a person first confronting the fall from Eden, the returned Innocent's trust in the universe may seem to be dangerously deluded.

As I have shared these ideas over the past several years, people always seem to want to advance immediately to what they consider to be the higher or better archetypal positions. Not only that, they want others to skip the unpleasant stuff, too. I once was working with a management team that identified one of their units as strong on the Orphan archetype. The president looked at me in frustration, asking, "Can't we just kick them out of Orphan?" I do not believe that can be done—or if it can be done, it cannot be sustained over time. We do have to pay our dues by spending some time in each stage. What I hope, in such cases, is that knowing where we likely are going will free us up somewhat from the fear that often paralyzes us as we confront our dragons.

A paradigm shift occurs when people move through these stages. Eventually, their perception of reality actually changes. Most important, they come to understand the difference between objective reality and the perception of reality. Often, they realize (sometimes in one great "Aha!") that seeing the world as a place full of danger, pain, and isolation is not realistic but only their perception of it during the formative parts of their journey. This new knowledge can be very freeing, as it allows us to understand the power we have by simply disciplining our own thinking. Every thought essentially is a vote for the life we want to experience, because we strengthen what we focus on in both our inner and outer worlds.

Exercise A: To recognize the route you have been traveling, draw or write the story of your life up to this point. To the degree you can, identify when and where each of these archetypes has been active in your life. (You can find the archetypes that are active right now by looking back at your results on Parts One and Two of the Heroic Myth Self-Test in Appendix A.) Then imagine that your life had to be exactly as it has been to create you as you are now. After that, summarize the wisdom you have gained on your path as well as what you know about your gifts and abilities.

Some of you might be able to do this in one sitting. Others will find it better to work on it every day for a while, examining different chronological periods and/or different aspects of your life—love, work, friendship, learning, spirituality, recreation, etc.

The remainder of this chapter focuses on the collective nature of the journey: how we are socialized by gender expectations, family and ethnic group identification, and workplace experiences.

HOW GENDER AFFECTS YOUR JOURNEY

Archetypal expression is influenced by socialization patterns—for example, in our development of gender identity. The Warrior archetype is aligned closely with masculinity and the Altruist with femininity, so little boys tend to get reinforcement for Warrior behavior and little girls for Altruist behavior. This results in an asymmetry in gender development. Whatever else men do, they often feel they need to act tough, or they will not seem like men. Whatever else women do, most conclude that they need to act caring, or they will not seem like women. Women, therefore, tend to linger in the stages that emphasize affiliation (Altruist and Orphan) and men in those that emphasize separateness and opposition (Wanderer and Warrior). As Carol Gilligan shows in her classic study of moral development, *In a Different Voice*, women are more likely to see the world in terms of nets or webs of connectedness, men in terms of ladders and hierarchies where people compete for power.[1]

When we look at where most women and men are without seeing the overall developmental context, it may appear as if there are distinct and different male and female paths. But the patterns are incredibly variable. Many men and women do not follow the predicted path at all, yet they still live happy and productive lives. Therefore, what I am describing is a tendency, not some absolute rule.

Alternately, if one looks only at the archetypes being expressed and not at the different order and the intensity of commitment to each, it appears that men and women are developmentally the same. Yet men and women have both a different biology and different cultural experiences, which influence the order and style of their journeys.

The Wanderer and the Warrior experience themselves as separate from the world, and thus, to them, too much closeness can be seen as a threat. These archetypes, then, hold the "masculine" quality of separateness. The Altruist and the Innocent experience themselves most often in bonded community (and the Orphan also wants that sense of connection and interdependence with others). Therefore, isolation is perceived as a danger. Thus, these archetypes hold the "feminine" quality of affiliation. The Magician, occupying the position at the center, is androgynous. (The alchemical symbol for the attainment of higher consciousness was the picture of the androgynous monarch that appeared on the cover of prior editions of this book.)

Until we integrate the perspective of the other sex, women and men tend to suffer in different ways. Too much separation (without room for real relationships) and life can become unbearably lonely. Too much closeness (without room for individual expression) and life can be intolerably stifling. Neither the masculine nor the feminine principles by themselves can fulfill us as human beings. When the masculine energies (Wanderer and Warrior) are balanced with the feminine ones (Altruist, Innocent, and Orphan), human wholeness becomes possible. Although wholeness eventually requires androgyny, the styles of men and women tend to reflect cultural assumptions about how the sexes should behave. That is, men who act in ways that the culture sees as gender appropriate display the more masculine archetypes, while women often exhibit the more feminine archetypes. However, in a mature and solid human being, all the archetypes in this book are integrated into the individual's conscious life in some way.

These indicators of gender difference and sameness are shared, of course, in the context of a pluralistic society. Each individual and social unit inevitably is changing at its own rate and expressing archetypes at its own unique level. The result is that every imaginable stage on the human journey (including archetypal stages) is being expressed somewhere by someone. Because technology rapidly informs us of the bewildering array of human possibilities, we also know that we do not have to remain where we are, doing what we have been doing. This gives us options to break the old molds that tell us how we have to be.

However different men and women look on the surface, we are similar under the skin. Both sexes have equal access within themselves to all the archetypes, even if some environments discourage their outer expression. This means that men and women can understand one another, because we are not as different as we sometimes appear to be. For example, knowing this, we can understand a popular book like John Gray's *Men Are from Mars,*

Women Are from Venus within its archetypal context, noting that the Warrior (Mars) and the Altruist (Venus) are archetypes available to both sexes.

Exercise B: Examine your Heroic Myth Self-Test results (especially Parts One and Two) and your autobiography through the lens of gender. How has gender influenced your development? Does your life illustrate the predictable gender pattern, or has your route been more individualistic? To what degree are you pleased or displeased with your gender identity? Are you relatively androgynous at this time in your life? What is the ideal gender balance you would like to express in your outlook and behavior?

THE INFLUENCE OF FAMILY BACKGROUND

Our journeys are affected by our family background as well as by gender. Part of this background includes our ethnic heritage. For example, I grew up in a Swedish-American family. Like most European cultures, Scandinavian culture has much in common with the dominant culture in the United States. When my ancestors moved to the Midwest, they must have felt right at home. However, they also brought with them cultural values that were somewhat different—at least, different from contemporary American ones. American culture generally emphasizes both independence and achievement. However, if you are Scandinavian, you are taught never to stand out. In fact, in our family we heard of relatives who discouraged their children from continuing to play musical instruments if they began to get too good! The fear was that people who excel might make others feel bad, so it was part of good manners not to be conspicuous.

On the face of this, I could say that my cultural heritage discouraged the Warrior and the Wanderer in favor of the Altruist. Yet I can fine-tune this generalization a bit by looking at my own family. All four of my grandparents emigrated from Sweden to the Midwest. My parents moved from Chicago to Houston. In fact, my personal heritage had plenty of Wanderer, so I have little difficulty being independent. The Altruist comes naturally to me because it was encouraged by my cultural roots and my family. I had to make a conscious effort to awaken the Warrior because that archetype was not valued in my culture or family—especially for women. (Men could be Warriors, but only when they actually were soldiers.)

Think of archetypes as seeds planted in the ground of your psyche. Your culture will water those archetypes it values and, likely, try to weed out those it disdains. As each of us learns to appreciate the value of cultures different from our own, it also is easier for us to express archetypes that are not encouraged by our own subgroup.

Your particular family refines the cultural pattern, making it specific to a smaller group of people. What is strong in and what is missing from your family of origin leave imprints on your life. People generally take for granted the archetypal strengths of their family, even though they tend simply to soak them up. Generally, the archetypes that are strong and healthy in your family are allies for your journey. Those that are missing or that are expressed in their negative forms motivate you to embark on a path of healing and development.

We contribute to the evolution of our families when we are able to express the positive aspects of the absent or wounded archetypes. Healing our families as well as ourselves is a powerful, if largely unconscious, motivation for most of us. The following chart can be used to identify your family's archetypal balance. You might check or circle all that apply.[2]

Family Archetype	Family Values	Strengths Fostered	Weaknesses Fostered
Orphan	Survival, loyalty, adaptability	Resilience, realism, empathy	Low expectations, victim mentality
Wanderer	Independence, self-reliance	Adventurousness, individual expression	Inattentiveness to children (loneliness)
Warrior	Achievement, competition, justice	Achievement, discipline, assertion	Workaholism, stoicism, perfectionism
Altruist	Caring, giving, philanthropy	Unselfishness, generosity	Weak boundaries, martyring self
Innocent	Stability, faith, optimism	Spirituality, creativity	Denial, naïveté, superficiality
Magician	Transformation, consciously creating your life	Vision, innovation, charisma	Weird, esoteric approaches, lack of common sense

Exercise C: Think about your family of origin and the archetypes active in it (with reference to your results on Part Three of the Heroic Myth Self-Test). Referring to the chart above to stimulate your thinking, identify the values of your family of origin, remembering to note major differences in your father's, mother's, siblings', or other family members' values. Then, thinking about yourself and your family members, reflect on the strengths and weaknesses that were fostered by your family of origin. Now, consider your current family, referring to your results on Part Four. (Feel free to define "family" loosely—as the group that provides your primary support and to which you are close.) Pay attention to its values and the strengths and weaknesses it perpetuates. How is your current family similar to and different from your family of origin? To what degree do you carry on the positive legacies of your family of origin? To what degree have you moved beyond its deficiencies?

THE CRUCIBLE OF WORK

Most of us are aware of the importance of socialization in childhood. Many of us forget, however, that we always are being socialized, at every stage of life. Every time you take a new job, adopt a new friendship network, engage in any kind of organized activity, or move to a different place, you are affected by your environment. Very typically, you will show the world archetypal characteristics that are valued by those around you—particularly those in power. (Of course, if you are oppositional, you will do exactly the opposite of what is wanted just to "show them.") The archetypes we allow to be expressed in our lives tend to evolve more than those we repress, hide, or deemphasize. Thus, every time we make a choice to place ourselves in a new environment, we affect our archetypal development. With this in mind, it is important when making life choices to recognize their implications for who we want to become.

In a quickly changing workplace (and also in school), your archetypal development is tested continually. Your success and failure result not only from your technical competence, but also from deeper archetypal qualities. For example, when we do not succeed, one or more archetypes often is missing:

- Without the Orphan, we are unlikely to anticipate problems.
- Without the Wanderer, we are too likely to go along with others, even when we know they are wrong.
- Without the Warrior, we may let people walk all over us.
- Without the Altruist, we cannot work well with others.

- Without the Innocent, we fail to persevere because we lack faith.
- Without the Magician, we allow ourselves to be swept along by circumstances without stopping to make conscious decisions.

Analyzing where your performance fails can help you know which archetype might help you become more successful.

Most schools and workplaces have an archetypal bias. If you cannot express the archetype that is displayed most clearly in an organization, you are unlikely to succeed there (even if you have the archetypes that the organization needs most). You can see the archetypal elements in the values and taboos that characterize each organization's culture. With reference to the chart below, consider the archetypes that have been most active in the schools and workplaces in which you have studied or worked for significant periods in your life.[3]

Organizational Archetype	Values	Taboos
Orphan	Realism, carefulness	Naïveté
Wanderer	Self-reliance, autonomy	Dependence
Warrior	Competition, toughness	Out-of-control feelings
Altruist	Unselfishness, caring	Personal ambition
Innocence	Faith, optimism	Negativity
Magician	Transformation	Being dull, ordinary

Exercise D: Exploring your school/workplace history and your results on Part Five of the Heroic Myth Self-Test, notice the archetypes that have been dominant and taboo in this environment. Those that have been active around you tend to this encourage their development in you. Being in environments in which an archetype is taboo retards your development of that archetype (unless you express it in some other area of your life). How do you think these environments have affected you? If any school or workplace environment currently is problematic for you, remember that each archetype has its own plot. Moving into such an environment is like stepping onto a movie set—you simply have to relate to the plot being enacted there or you are irrelevant and in the way. Of course, you can try to change the plot being acted out, but doing so takes time and skill. Experiment by writing the story of your time on that set in a way that produces a happy ending.

THE CARAVAN: GROWING AND DEVELOPING WITH OTHERS

Using these theories requires an awareness that we are multi-dimensional creatures. Most people work with different arche-types in different arenas of their life. For example, some are highly influenced by the Magician's consciousness when they think about spiritual issues, but not when they think about their health. Exploring possibilities inherent in each archetype in different parts of your life may be a way of broadening your skills, or it may be stultifying. You may find that you are stuck in roles that are defined by the context, and your responses do not, or no longer, reflect your true feelings.

You may fear that people will be thrown off if, say, you experiment with some of your assertive skills at home or your nurturance skills at work. Or you might fear a loss of power, as you put aside highly developed skills to try out what you may be awkward at and unsure about at first. Yet you might find it interesting, challenging, and even fun to vary your repertoire and experiment with new approaches to old situations. Being assertive in your private life, for instance, is different in style and in substance than assertiveness in public life. You learn new aspects of each archetype based on the context you are in.

Also note that people find the more primitive versions of any of the stages jarring simply because they are blunt, not yet refined.

Remember that in their more developed and subtle forms, none of the approaches is difficult for most others to deal with. If people do have difficulty, it may be that they just are disoriented by change of any kind. Or, as you change and grow, a few acquaintances may drift away, but your compensation is that gradually you will attract to you people who appreciate what you are or are becoming.

The fact that we are not alone also means that our journeys are affected profoundly by those around us. There is a limit to how far any of us can develop without taking others with us—and sometimes, if we grow very quickly, we may choose to wait around for others who trail behind. In fact, sometimes we have to wait for environmental factors to catch up if we hope to have an impact. Each of us has the responsibility to recognize that every context we enter has its own archetypal character. No matter how old we get, we still are being socialized by our environments—and we also are influencing those environments, either for good or for ill.

In the Exodus story, the Hebrews leave a condition of slavery in Egypt and wander in the wilderness for forty years; metaphorically there are two important lessons here. First, the Hebrews remain in exile until the last of the those who were slaves die off. So, too, during our own journeys, slavish and childish attitudes in us must die before we can enter the promised land. Even Moses sees the promised land from a distance, but does not enter it. Second, those who are able to reach this goal have gone through experiences in the desert that have changed them all in similar ways. As individuals, we can have brief experiences of the consciousness of the promised land, but it is difficult to sustain it alone. For many, those moments of illumination feel like just a peek at what is ahead. To sustain the experience over time, we need the support of others who see and know this place too. The journey is not just about me and mine. It is about *us*. Thus, it is not necessarily a violation of your journey to wait around for people you care about, or who are dependent upon you, to catch up, instead of moving on without them. If you were climbing in the Himalayas, for instance, all the members of your party would help each other make it. We can take the same attitude on our developmental journeys, giving each other a leg up when we need it.

Exercise E: Make a list of the people close to you—your family, friends, co-workers, etc. How does each of them affect your journey? Who among them is important enough to make you either hold back or pick up your pace to stay together? Are there institutions that you also care that much about—a workplace, a school, a church or synagogue, a political party, a movement? If so, what captures your allegiance in that way?

CONCLUSION

Most of the time, we simply can trust the process of our journeys without thinking much about them. Sometimes, however, things suddenly do not work. We feel lost, empty, or stuck. At these times, it is critical to take a self-reflective stance. If you have completed the exercises in this chapter carefully, you have a baseline of knowledge about your life that prepares you to act freely in most situations. The chapter that follows provides a compass to regain your direction if and when you ever feel that you have lost your way.

CHAPTER 9

Troubleshooting When You
Get Lost or Stuck: The Compass

> Life presents us with repeated opportunities to face what we fear,
> what we need to become conscious of, or what we need to master.
> Each time we cycle around the spiral path to the place that gives us
> difficulty, hopefully, we gain more consciousness and can respond
> more wisely the next time; until we can finally pass through that
> nemesis place at peace and in harmony with our deepest values, and
> not be negatively affected at all.
>
> —Jean Shinoda Bolen, *Goddesses in Everywoman*

Recognizing the archetypal dimension of life can provide a compass to help you navigate through it. At times we may feel lost and not know what to do. Generally, this happens when we are continuing to act as we always have, but suddenly our old approaches do not work. Some people describe this less as being lost than as being stuck. Usually, you are faced with some new challenge; though you try and try, you make no progress. What you are doing is not working, but it is not clear what else might work.

A woman once shared with me that before she read the earlier edition of this book she knew intuitively that she had the capacity to transform her life, but she did not know how to start. The book in general, and the Magician chapter in particular, she said, provided a toehold that allowed her to get her footing. Another reader described the book as a kind of compass that allowed him to orient himself by figuring out where he was on the map. He later compared it with one of those directories in shopping malls with the arrow that says, "You are here."

Generally, when we feel lost or stuck, our natural archetypal development has been interrupted in some way. Such blocks occur for two major reasons:

- we have become overidentified with one archetype to the detriment of others, or
- we have repressed an archetype, so that it is not available when we find ourselves in a new situation, or we become possessed by its shadow form.

As you increase your ability to call up previously blocked archetypal energies, you enhance your power to respond appropriately in changing situations and to have the life that is most authentic for you. Since your journey is both like that of all heroes everywhere and unique to you, the map of the heroic terrain needs to be complemented by your own personal map—which can help you understand how you came to be the person you are.

This chapter, therefore, will identify:

- why you might have overidentified with an archetypal position;
- family and workplace forces that may have caused you to develop an archetypal imbalance;
- cultural influences that might result in your repressing an archetype;
- ways to recognize and integrate the shadow; and
- strategies for awakening an archetype.

WHY YOU MIGHT HAVE OVERIDENTIFIED WITH AN ARCHETYPAL POSITION

It is common to become so identified with one archetype that we block out other archetypal perspectives. For example, Jack not only was the quintessential Warrior, he was extreme even to other Warriors. He slept on the floor because beds were for sissies. He did not bother to cook his eggs in the morning because it took extra time. After he had a heart attack, he put himself on a regimen that included red meat for breakfast, more jogging than his doctor thought wise, and an annual skiing trip (which he took armed with emergency oxygen supplies). He saw illness as an enemy that you simply could not give in to or it would get you. As with many people, going with his dominant archetypal approach worked well for him in some ways. He did, live another twenty years after his first in a series of heart attacks and kept quite active until shortly before his death. However, his identification with the Warrior hurt him in his personal relationships and, as he became older and more infirm, he needed closeness with others. Fortunately, he recognized this and began, consciously, to let people in, becoming more loving with his wife, daughter, and friends. The late opening into new archetypal possibilities required him to move outside his comfort zone, but it also averted a potentially lonely old age.

The felt experience of knowing what it is like to be under the influence of an archetype actually can help you read others. As a result, you will be blind-sided less frequently. For example, when people pronounce that everyone is out to get them, watch your pockets when you are with them! We tend to see the world in our own image. We can call to ourselves anything we focus on. Some people always talk about how hard life is, and sure enough, they endure one catastrophe after another. You might be equally watchful of people who are too positive to be believed. They may attract what they are denying. Someone walking around wearing rose-colored glasses can be a magnet for problems until they grow in awareness.

Moreover, people view the world from the vantage point of their dominant archetype. Those in the Warrior phase may believe that life is a battle or contest. They regard any other way of seeing the world as escapist or naive. If you tell them about abundance, sharing, and love, they will think you are deluded. Do not even try to provide Orphans with empowerment options until you have met them where they are and empathized with their pain. Otherwise they might write you off as not understanding what they have been through.

People might confuse an archetypal position with who they are for a variety of reasons. When they do so, their lives become one-sided and unbalanced and they lose touch with the more complex reality around them.

First, if you are socialized strongly to be one way, you may have a lot riding on thinking you are that way. The high-achieving male may get so much reinforcement for acting like the stoic tough guy that he fears deviating from this masculine ideal. A woman who nurtures and serves others may be praised as "good," unlike other "bad" or "angry" women. The fear of seeming unfeminine or selfish can keep her in a box.

Second, you may overly identify with an archetype because it is dominant in the world around you. The major reason people today experience such difficulty maintaining balance in their lives is that the competitive values of the work world have taken over our culture: we are what we do and we are measured by how successfully we do it. As a result, we tend to be addicted to success—whether mildly or severely—and to identify with the Warrior archetype and its need to be victorious.

The only way to achieve balance in our outer lives is to attain greater archetypal balance in our inner worlds. If the Warrior archetype has crowded out every other, you will be happiest when you are producing and achieving. Therefore, you will not really want to leave the office—and when you do, you likely will use the cell phone, fax machine, and e-mail to be certain that you do not lose the competitive edge during your supposed "downtime." Stress management experts can preach to you all day about taking real vacations and having quality time with your family or friends, but you will be unable to do so unless and until other archetypes have equal room in your psyche.

Our archetypal natures are affected strongly by every social system we spend our time in. If, for example, you take a job in an environment in which the Warrior predominates, you will need to have a strong Warrior to survive. The more reinforcement you get from those around you for acting one way, the easier it is to start thinking that that part of you is all there is to you.

Similarly, if you are surrounded by friends or co-workers who think of themselves as either sick or oppressed, you are likely to overidentify with the Orphan archetype. I remember a woman who introduced herself at one of my workshops as an adult child from an abusive home. She explained that she had been told (and clearly believed) that it would take many years before she could get a handle on this problem and that, during this time, she would not be able to focus on much else. Certainly she would not be able to undertake a demanding job or enter into an adult love relationship. Her entire social network included only other adult survivors of dysfunctional families, and their conversation revolved around their most recently recovered traumatic memories and how they were doing and feeling in response to them.

I want to be clear here that many people exhibit extraordinary courage in dealing with childhood traumas—some of which are almost unbearably horrific. I do not in any way intend to demean the importance of this work or the courage it takes to do it. Nevertheless, my own experience is that people recover much more quickly if other archetypes are active for them in addition to the Orphan.

The psyche is incredibly wise. The reason some people "forget" or repress difficult childhood memories is that they are not yet strong enough to deal with them. Those who have activated their Warrior and Wanderer, for example, before they confront their childhood traumas have an easier time recovering than others for whom only the Innocent and Orphan archetypes are functioning. Moreover, they are more likely to be able to continue to have fulfilling lives at the same time as they recover from the abuse. However, in an Orphan culture, bonding occurs around wounding. When we share our suffering, we feel close to one another. Anyone who brings in a great success story, however, may find him- or herself subtly undercut by friends. To stay close, then, we unconsciously may repress other potential parts of ourselves. This is a major reason why recovery often takes longer than it needs to for many people.

All the archetypes have gifts. When we tap into their energies, they help us. As a result, we can fixate on the one that helped us in some dramatic way. Then we become true believers, and movements that once were liberating become cults.

Third, you can get stuck in an archetype because an authority figure told you that is who you are. Take the case of a young woman in therapy who was very fearful and avoided leaving the house. She wanted to have a job, but was too frightened. Her therapist noted to herself that abuse may have been responsible for the woman's current timidity, but focused with the client on her assets. It turned out that the client had a well-developed Altruist. She cared for herself and her children quite effectively. Together, she and her therapist realized that she needed to awaken her Warrior to be able to set boundaries. Before she could be ready for the work world, the woman had to become tougher. But she did feel as though she could sign up for a women's martial arts class. After focusing on developing her Warrior in such ways, the client eventually got a job.

Later she pieced together the reason she was so timid. Her mother had been terrified that something would happen to her and got anxious every time the daughter went anywhere alone. Because her mother died when she was only twelve, the woman had not linked her fear with her mother's implicit message that she was fragile. She naturally romanticized her mother, and never had criticized her in any way. Of course, once the woman put the pieces together, she realized that her mother never intended to limit her potential. She then conducted a ritual honoring her mother and declaring her intention to become the brave woman her mother undoubtedly would have wanted her to be.

You might be fixated on an archetype because your parents thought of you as the loving one (Altruist), because a teacher saw you as standoffish and independent (Wanderer), because your classmates thought you were a tough guy (Warrior), or because your boss relied on you to be the miracle worker (Magician). If so, you can begin to notice other archetypal qualities in yourself and find ways to show them to the world.

Fourth, you can overidentify with an archetype because you did not have the support you needed, growing up, to find your own identity. This can be true for those of us who came from dysfunctional homes, who grew up in a context that was turbulent and chaotic (such as a family with many losses or a community torn apart by crime or war), and/or who lived in times and places that did not value individual gifts and perspectives. Actually, people from stereotypically "good" families are about as likely to have stultified journeys as people from unhealthy families, simply because they experience such pressure to measure up to standards of "goodness" (defined variably in terms of morality, achievement, propriety, or responsibility).

It is human nature to be imperfect. It is equally human to hide one's imperfections when we know we will be judged harshly for them. Cathy came from a religious family that tried very hard to provide a safe and loving environment for her. However, their idea of good parenting was to try to make her completely good, like Christ. In the process, they discouraged her from following her bliss because they feared that her desires would lead her into temptation. From her church, she picked up the impression that the only way she could be good enough was to be martyred like Christ or many of the great saints. She concluded that any concern for her own desires was selfish. Indeed, nothing she did ever was quite enough, because she was not perfect and no amount of ordinary altruism adds up to being crucified for others. Not only was she unhappy, she also felt guilty about feeling miserable.

This deeply religious woman eventually gravitated to a church that was archetypally more balanced. Here she was taught that the divine could be found within as well as beyond. The minister also emphasized many aspects of Christ's life other than his death. Stories of Christ tossing the money changers out of the temple gave Cathy permission to awaken her Warrior. Stories about Christ going alone to the desert helped her know it was all right to embark on her own Wanderer journey, which she did by going off to read books that expanded her horizons. Stories about Christ feeding the multitudes and healing the sick inspired her to awaken her Magician. With more than one archetype active in her life, she achieved much greater fulfillment. In doing so, she increasingly was able to differentiate between each archetypal position and her own budding individuality.

Her wise minister helped this process by encouraging her to check what really fit for her in different areas of her life. As a result, she became a more authentically giving person. As long as she struggled against her own nature to care for others, she could not succeed. It was only when she learned to trust her own process that she could love others and give to them with sincere joy.

Charles came from a very different background, but had a similar problem. A survivor of a dysfunctional family from a poor, crime-ridden neighborhood, he identified with the Outlaw (which is the shadow side of the Warrior). He prided himself on being tough and doing whatever he needed to make his way in the world. As a child, he stole hubcaps and other items for small change. As a teenager, he sold drugs and was a leader in a local gang.

On the outside, Charles looked like he might be headed for a life of crime. However, a judge saw potential in him beyond his current behavior. She referred him to a court-mandated drug rehabilitation program. At first, Charles was not consciously aware of any discrepancy between his tough-guy Outlaw image and his real self. Fortunately, he had been sent to a very good program. In group therapy and one-on-one counseling, he began to recognize his vulnerabilities (Orphan). Then he recalled that he once had aspired to play in a jazz band, a life very different from the one he currently was living (Wanderer). As part of this program, he worked to help younger boys. He discovered that the more he did for them, the better he felt about himself (Altruist).

At a major turning point, Charles had a dream that he and all his immediate friends died, some from AIDS, some from drug overdoses, and some from gang warfare. About the same time, he attended two funerals in the same week for friends no older than himself. The shock of the dream coupled with the deaths in real life helped him decide to reinvent himself. He recognized that his enemies had little to do with anything real about himself and everything to do with the social conditions around him. As part of this metamorphosis, he determined to hang around with kids who were committed to doing something with their lives. As he changed, he noticed a ripple effect as his life influenced some younger boys to stay out of the gangs and remain in school (Magician).

Cathy and Charles illustrate extreme but still common situations. All of us have been hampered by circumstances that discouraged our journeys in subtle if not overt ways. Every time we make a choice to continue in an environment or to seek a new one, we choose how we will be socialized in our immediate future.

Exercise A: Notice if you are overly identified with one archetype. If so, which archetype? Why do you think you developed this attachment?

CULTURAL INFLUENCES ON DEVELOPING AN ARCHETYPAL IMBALANCE

As discussed in the previous chapter, every family has archetypal strengths and archetypal weaknesses. What worked in our family provides us with the sword and shield that accompany us on the journey. Our family's weaknesses cause the wounds that motivate us to set out and seek our fortunes. On the journey, we also may face challenges that help us access archetypes that were missing in our families.

Suzanne came from a very dysfunctional family. Her mother was an untreated schizophrenic, given to bizarre behavior. Because the family was wealthy and powerful, no one did anything to rescue the children. Suzanne was conscious of the wounds she carried, but took for granted her more positive inheritance. Her father was a very influential lawyer who fought for justice in the town. Suzanne ended up being a crusader, carrying the positive Warrior potential in her family. She was motivated on her journey by the damage done to her Orphan self. Beyond that, she felt herself drawn to shamanistic practices. Working on these issues, Suzanne realized that mental illness can be a shadow side of the Magician. Her interest in medicine men and women reflected a need to find the healthy aspect of this archetype. Through this process, she healed herself.

Doing so enabled her to pass on the positive potential in both the Warrior and the Magician to her own children.

Wherever a vacuum exists in a family—when some important archetype is missing or virtually absent—one of the children almost inevitably will be drawn to that archetype. In the case of Suzanne, she was surprised to discover a powerful pull to the Innocent archetype. In exploring this attraction, she realized that what her family lacked completely was faith.

Awareness of your early family imprint can help you anticipate ways you may be unbalanced. It also can help you identify which archetypes you simply can count on, which ones were expressed in their negative poles and need developing, and which ones you might want to awaken for the first time.

Similarly, anytime you enter a social system, your own archetypal balance is affected by its invisible archetypal structure. For example, whenever you take a new job you are in dynamic interaction with the organization's archetypal structure. The unwritten rules of organizations all have archetypal roots. Some archetypal qualities are valued and others are taboo. For instance, if the organization comes from an Altruist stance, you will be valued if you seem to be motivated primarily by the desire to help other people. If you seem to be doing the job just for the money, you will get little respect.

Deborah took a job in a sales operation with Warrior values, even though she was totally noncompetitive and unassertive. She hated the people she worked with and they treated her as marginal to the team. She was extremely unhappy in her job until she realized that she was there to develop her Warrior. When she started to show more toughness, she began to be treated more collegially by her co-workers.

Organizations with archetypal structures opposite to your own can feel very uncomfortable, but they do help you balance out your archetypal wheel. Organizations that are an exact fit—archetypally unbalanced in the same way you are—will feel very comfortable to you, but will tend to retard your development. The ideal situation is the environment that is like you in enough ways to make you feel at home, but different enough to cause you to stretch.

Jim went to a public high school that was academically very competitive. He was a kind young man whose greatest wish was to help others. It would have been easier for him had his teachers thought to motivate him by asking him to tutor less gifted students or work collaboratively with his peers. However, Jim's mother understood archetypes. She explained to him that although they could not afford to put him in private school, much as she would like to find a place that fit him better, his current school provided an excellent opportunity for him to develop his Warrior archetype, which would help him navigate his way through life. Jim then took the reigns to motivate himself; he volunteered to tutor students after school and he opened himself to learning about the potential exhilaration of competition in his classroom setting. Although the Warrior never was primary for him, he gained enough access to the archetype to develop good boundaries and a faculty for succeeding in competitive situations.

When organizations are significantly out of balance, people who carry the missing archetypes are extremely important to their survival. For example, Burt served on the board of a church that taught positive thinking (Innocent). His own dominant archetype was Orphan, so he always anticipated future threats. While he was not popular, he did provide an important early signal that averted financial difficulties for the board. In the process, he learned from the church how to have more faith in life.

Exercise B: With reference to the charts on pp. 241 and 243 of the previous chapter, identify any ways in which the systems of which you have been a part have thrown off the normal development of your archetypal balance.

SOCIETAL INFLUENCES ON
ARCHETYPAL REPRESSION

Our psyches can be thrown off balance if an archetype that we ideally need for the next stage of the journey is repressed. People tend to repress archetypes that they believe to be either inappropriate for them or actually bad or wrong. Generally, we hold these beliefs because of messages we receive from the culture.

First, archetypes can be valued in others but inappropriate for us. Sex roles are one, but not the only, reason we repress archetypes we regard as inappropriate. The most unconscious kinds of repression begin when we are children, when we are too young to be conscious of what we are choosing not to be. For example, in spite of the considerable influence of the women's and men's movements, almost all men in our culture are essentially shamed if they demonstrate much vulnerability. If it does not happen in the home, it happens on the playground. Boys are told that if they cry, they are sissies, wimps, or worse. When they pick themselves up and go back to playing without a whimper, they are praised. The result is that most men have repressed Orphan archetypes and difficulty expressing their vulnerabilities.

Girls can cry pretty much all they want. But society comes down on them if they demonstrate much anger or desire to win, especially if it means someone else feels threatened or loses. (Girls are supposed to care more about others' feelings than their own.) Therefore, girls repress their Warrior with an attendant suppression of anger and assertiveness. When they defer to others and swallow their anger and ambition, they are praised as examples of true femininity.

The negative qualities associated stereotypically with men and women show what happens when we do not allow the full expression of our femaleness or maleness and become possessed by the shadow side of our sexual identity. We see this equally in Mr.

Macho or Ms. Bimbo. People also can become possessed by the shadow of their countersexual identity. For example, men who have little conscious access to their feminine side often become very moody. Women with little conscious relationship to their masculine side more typically become very opinionated. This explains the man who goes on a tirade about how emotional women are, or the woman who demands that everyone act in a politically correct manner in order to resist patriarchal oppression. Such shadow possession explains how unconscious each inevitably is about evidencing the traits they disdain.

The alchemy of romantic love can help men and women awaken their repressed parts. To be close, people must be willing to show their vulnerabilities; they also must have good boundaries so that they can assert their own needs. This means that neither men nor women can have the love they want without leaving their psychological comfort zone. Typically, men need to develop the courage to risk showing where they are vulnerable, while women need to take the risk of threatening their men by being more outspoken about their wants and needs.

For example, Margaret was getting more and more unhappy with her life, but put up with her inner sadness because her husband seemed to be enjoying their life just the way it was. Then, suddenly, his work situation changed. He got a new supervisor who was unsupportive. Margaret and the children encouraged him to leave and find a position where he would be valued, so he quit. After that, however, one part of her began to feel even more depressed.

Her husband and children had heard her complaining about her job for several years, but no one encouraged her to quit! For a time, she felt sorry for herself, wondering why no one seemed to care whether she was happy or not. Then it hit her. Her husband had higher self-esteem than she had. As a Warrior, he expected to be treated well, and his Wanderer hit the road when he was unhappy. The answer, she realized, was not to judge her husband but to become more like him. Therefore, she began looking around for work that would really excite her even if it did pay somewhat less than what she was making before. When she found it, her husband looked a bit pale. However, she simply told him how much better she felt and how happy she was to have such a supportive spouse!

Same-sex relationships also have their own built-in pressure to balance the psyche. When the "other" sex is not present, the range of human qualities represented by that sex needs to be carried by someone. A lesbian couple, for example, needs to handle all the roles and traits traditionally assigned to men. Gay males have the same challenge with the more traditionally feminine traits and roles. Either one partner carries the countersexual qualities, both develop them equally, or there is some combination thereof. In the same way, single people, whatever their sexual orientation, are pressured by the demands of their lives to develop their androgynous potential.

Exercise C: Notice what qualities attract you in the other sex—or, if you are gay or lesbian, to your same-sex partner. Pay special attention to the qualities that you believe you do not have. Could developing these qualities in yourself enhance your life and/or improve your romantic relationships?

Notice also qualities you judge negatively in the other sex—whether as romantic partners, friends, or in any other area of your life. Often we disdain what we need to develop in ourselves. Can you see any way your life might be better if you became more androgynous?

Second, archetypes can be repressed because the culture does not value them in anyone. For example, in our culture today the Orphan archetype often is viewed negatively. People are expected to be self-reliant and not to need undue help. When any of us, male or female, represses our inner Orphan, we are likely to be insensitive to others. Or it could mean not noticing when we are being mistreated by others, such as allowing a spouse, partner, boss, or colleague to get away with minor put-downs. People who are used to being treated like objects find it natural to treat others the same way. Think, for instance, of the stoic executive declaring "my way or the highway" without any apparent concern for his employees. At the same time, he may be oblivious to the impact on his health of his driven, workaholic, hard-drinking ways.

In extreme form, repression of the Orphan archetype can lead some people to victimize others (and in doing so, to dehumanize themselves). For example, men who sexually abuse their daughters or sons very often are unrepentant because they are cut off completely from the ability to empathize with what those children must be feeling. In treatment, they get in touch with how they have been abused themselves. As they thaw out their frozen feelings, they suddenly can recognize the harm they have done, and to someone they likely actually care about—that is, to the degree they have been capable of care. As they are able finally to empathize with their victims, some feel incredible grief and remorse. In extreme cases, they feel so bad that if they are not stopped, their remorse can lead to suicide.[1]

The Orphan archetype also may be projected onto others. A savior fixation can result when a person is split off from his or her own pain but is aware of pain in others. When this happens, the person may be powerless against the urge to help—even when it is irrational or enabling to do so. Orphan projection can lead to sadistic acts, in which one quiets one's own Orphan, feeling powerful temporarily, by demeaning or brutalizing another who seems in this instance at one's mercy. We see this in extreme cases in political torture and in abusive families. In everyday situations, we witness it when a frustrated mother hits her crying child, a teacher shames a student, or a boss humiliates an employee.

In some families, for religious or political reasons, assertion is seen as wrong (not simply inappropriate for girls), since it can lead to violence. When the Warrior archetype is repressed, anyone, male or female, will be manipulative and/or passive aggressive. A wonderfully sweet young woman subtly criticizes her husband until, over time, he loses confidence and does whatever she wants. Or she becomes increasingly sick and helpless until others take care of her and follow her wishes. At work, while she never would take leadership directly, she may use gossip to elevate or undermine others, subtly taking power behind the scenes. Or she may project the Warrior archetype onto others, attaching herself to protectors who seem strong where she is weak. If we want peace, it is better to develop the Warrior archetype beyond its violent and ruthless potential, so that we can assert our own needs and work through conflict honestly and openly. Ironically, peace comes not through repressing the Warrior but through developing its higher expression.

ASPECTS OF SHADOW FORMATION AND INTEGRATION

First, when repression of an archetype is strong, it can create a personal or collective shadow. When we repress archetypes we believe to be bad, we are likely to project them onto others—seeing the evil in them, not ourselves. For example, Liza could not stand Jenny. Jenny was a classic Valley Girl airhead. In the terms described here, she was an Innocent, caring about superficial matters: nail salons, hair products, activities that were "in," and boys who were "hunks." Liza did not just dislike Jenny casually. She woke up in the middle of the night deriding her. In her mind, Jenny was shallow, vacuous, and vain. Encountering ideas about the shadow such as those in this book, Liza began to think about herself. Yes, she was a good person. She was a serious student and a social activist who would not think of wearing makeup, wasting her time on frivolity, or giving the time of day to a guy who was not politically committed.

Liza knew many people who morally were much worse than Jenny, so she could think of no apparent reason she should be more down on her than on them. Finally, it hit her! Although she did not want to be like Jenny, she could use a dose of her qualities. "Lighten up a bit," she told herself. "I don't always have to date boys who are pale and thin. I could go to a movie that was not serious once in a while. And perhaps it *is* time to get a good hair-cut!"

Exercise D: To identify the archetypal qualities you have repressed, make a list of all the people you judge negatively and determine which archetype they most resemble. Refrain from listing serial killers or people everyone would agree are bad. List only those people you dis-like but others find quite acceptable. If you can imagine how others see them, it may help you to integrate those positive qualities or behaviors into yourself.

Second, repression of archetypes can lead to intolerance between groups. Sometimes we will repress archetypes because they are associated in our minds with people we think of as different than ourselves. We can, therefore, identify what archetypes we are repressing by areas of discomfort—either things other people do that we cannot do comfortably or ways others act that bother us, or that seem exotic or strange.

In an increasingly global economy, most of us interact, at least at work, with people from cultures very unlike our own. Different cultures encourage and discourage different archetypal positions. For example, Japanese and Latinos are more relational and group oriented than Americans of European descent. Therefore, they have greater ease subordinating the individual to group needs (Altruist), but may repress the individuality of the Wanderer. The dominant culture in the United States prizes individual rights over group responsibility (Wanderer) with an attendant potential for repressing the Altruist and Orphan archetypes.[2]

Integrating the Shadow

In an increasingly complex and quickly changing society, we continually encounter new challenges. We can feel the most stuck when we find ourselves in a situation that requires us to activate an archetype we have so repressed that we do not respect its potential usefulness. For example:

- If you hate dependent, whiny people, eventually you may find yourself in a situation where you are being mistreated and there simply is nothing you can do—unless, that is, you are willing to throw yourself on the mercy of a higher authority and complain vehemently about how bad things are. Or you find yourself being victimized time and time again, so you do not know what to do other than just cry.
- If you cannot stand aggressive people, you undoubtedly will find yourself pushed around at some point. In fact, until you learn the lesson of the Warrior archetype, you will be faced with situation after situation that requires you to fight for yourself.
- If you look down on people who martyr themselves for others, sooner or later you will have someone dependent on you get sick or need help, and you will have to drop other activities you really want to do to be there for that person. If you declare that you do not want to give, you soon may find yourself needing the help of others.
- If you think people who are outsiders are irrelevant or self-indulgent, sooner or later you will find yourself on the outside

looking in. Or the more urgently you want to belong to a group, the more likely that the demands on you to conform in ways that do not fit for you will increase exponentially until they begin to feel oppressive.

- If people who seem wide-eyed and innocent or who appear to have an irrational faith in the divine drive you up the wall, gradually you will find yourself in tougher and tougher situations until you call out for divine help.
- If you think ideas about magic are flaky and irrational, you will find yourself desperately in need of a miracle. In fact, the more tightly you hold to a rationalistic view of the world, the more irrational the events of your life will seem.

Such differences can be dealt with in a variety of ways. For example, one culture can scapegoat another by defining that culture's archetypal attributes as "other" or "inferior." Such collective shadow projection can cause otherwise civilized people to act in intolerably brutal ways (as in Nazi Germany, with the persecution of Jews, or in the United States, with its mistreatment and brutalization of African Americans and American Indians). In such cases, the society degrades and even kills people associated with the archetypal qualities they deny in themselves.

Such instances are powerful reminders that we cannot maintain genuinely democratic communities without understanding the dynamics of our inner lives. If we begin to recognize the psychology of projection and scapegoating, we do not have to make people wrong just because they are different than us. While certainly there are limits to tolerance, living as we do in a global society offers us opportunities to awaken in ourselves qualities that have been cherished and developed by cultures other than our own. In this way, we increase our ability to honor different gifts and perspectives.

Ultimately, the challenge is not only to value difference, but also to recognize our projections for what they are. The changing perceptions of American Indians are a good case in point. In the colonial period and through much of United States history, whites regarded the indigenous population as primitive savages and associated them with nature (in opposition to mind and spirit). Given the dominant psychological theories of the time, whites felt free to kill and contain American Indians, just as they attempted to stop or repress their own desires. More recently, American Indians have been romanticized; this revisionist image of the Noble Savage projects onto them the hunger whites feel to live more in harmony with nature and more in keeping with their instinctual, natural behavior.

Neither view has much to do with how American Indians see themselves. Eventually, one can hope that white Americans will withdraw both projections. When they do so, they can grapple with both their ambivalent feelings about nature and their feelings about their own bodies and desires. Only then will it be possible for them to recognize fully the incredibly diverse nations that make up the somewhat artificial category of American Indian.

If we look at the course of human history, we see endless examples of how different peoples have scapegoated and then oppressed other groups. All these situations are characterized by failure on the part of the dominant groups to develop enough self-awareness to withdraw their projections. When we do withdraw projections, not only do we stop oppressing others, we also gain access to the positive pole of the archetypes that we have been repressing.

If we open up to learning from others, multicultural experiences expand all our horizons. Most contemporary societies have a Warrior bent to them. Beyond that, Western cultures have nourished the development of the Wanderer archetype and the gift of individualism. Many indigenous shamanistic cultures throughout the world have much to teach us about the Magician. Eastern cultures, as well as others that give priority to group over individual needs, exemplify the gifts of the Altruist.

Often the people with whom we have the most difficulty trigger our own shadow side. If we cannot abide political "hawks" or Pentagon generals, we may find that the vehemence of our feeling declines as we take a strong stand fighting for a world free of nuclear threat. If our teeth are set on edge by dependent, whiny people, we may find that as we acknowledge our own dependency and sense of powerlessness, we have more empathy with them. As we expand our own repertoire of behaviors and allow ourselves to be more whole, we attract to ourselves more interesting people— or we are able to understand how interesting other people have been all along. For example, many women who have been socialized to be competitive with other women think that other women typically are competitive, backbiting, and untrustworthy. As they begin to find value in their own femaleness, most of the women around them seem suddenly and quite miraculously to have become sisterly and honest. If this does not happen, they might then take responsibility for attracting shadow-possessed women, asking, "What is this mirroring in me?"

Ultimately, all the archetypes bring us treasures if we hang in there and learn from them. We scorn the "gods" (that is, archetypes) at our own risk. When we refuse to honor an archetype, we find ourselves in situation after situation that requires that gift. We can enter its story over and over again— until we get it right.

Exercise E: List the qualities you value in other cultures or groups and identify their archetypal roots. What do you judge negatively in other cultures or groups? Often we see the negative qualities of archetypes in others and their more positive manifestations in ourselves. You might use the following chart to stimulate your thinking about what archetypes may be calling you through your aversion to certain types of people. Generally, when we awaken these archetypes, we suddenly have greater appreciation of the individuals, cultures, and groups we previously disdained.

Disdained Quality	Call to Archetype	Gift
Victim mentality, complaining, sense of entitlement	Orphan	Realism, empathy
Self-involvement, lack of planning, selfishness	Wanderer	Independence, individuality
Ruthlessness, ambition, greed	Warrior	Discipline, excellence
Conformity, laziness	Altruist	Care, intimacy, teamwork
Naïveté, dogmatism	Innocent	Faith, optimism
Weirdness, seemingly "out to lunch"	Magician	Transformation, new perspectives

SEVEN STEPS TO ACTIVATING AN ARCHETYPE

Society used to change rather slowly. Now the pace of change has quickened. The resulting demands on the psyche are great. It used to be that access to just one or two archetypes would suffice. Today we need access to all of them, at least to some degree.

If you find yourself in a situation that calls for an archetype that is not yet active in your life, probably this archetype is blocked. It is doubtful that you can call up an archetype that is not right for you. However, if the archetype would be coming to your aid organically were it not blocked in some fashion, then you can use consciousness to move beyond that obstacle.

The first step is to identify the positive qualities of the archetype. You can do this by paying close attention to people who express it in ways you admire. Read books and watch television shows and movies based on that archetype. Put up photos, paintings, or posters that illustrate that archetype in your environment. Listen to music that evokes the archetype while you do your mundane tasks. After reading the chapter on the relevant archetype, notice people, books, songs, movies, etc. that reflect its plot and virtues. I strongly recommend keeping a journal or making a scrapbook detailing your findings.

The second step is to think consciously like the archetype you need. Begin by substituting the desired archetypal thought patterns for your more habitual ones. For example, perhaps you typically think like an Orphan and you want to awaken your Warrior. Every time you say to yourself, "There is nothing I can do. I just have to live with this," quickly stop yourself and say, "I have the strength and courage to follow through on standing up for myself and getting what I want." Then imagine yourself putting this new attitude into action. If you wish, you even can devise a small ritual to honor the archetype and invite it into your life. For instance, light a candle and invoke sacred space (in whatever way is congruent with your belief system). Then write down on a small piece of paper what you value in the Orphan. Thank the Orphan and burn the paper, saying good-bye for now. Then pick a symbol for the Warrior and put it in an honored place in your home or office and light a candle to it. Express out loud or to yourself the virtues of the Warrior and ask the Warrior to be your ally. Then blow out the candle and consciously move back into ordinary space.

Most importantly, make a habit of imagining yourself succeeding in expressing the archetype in your life.

The third step is to identify the cause of the inner block to expressing this archetype. If you feel blocked, ask yourself, "Who told me that this behavior is not appropriate for me?" Perhaps the first time you stood up to your father, he took out the whip. You may have concluded that Warrior behavior might get you killed. That conclusion might have been reinforced by watching war movies in which soldiers are, indeed, slaughtered. With this understanding, you might talk with the part of yourself that believes that being a Warrior will result in death about how your lack of Warrior energy has kept you from getting what you want. You might talk about how dead you feel and explain that your father never would have killed you and you are not planning to go to war, noting that the worst consequence is that you will lose your job and your spouse. Or if you are planning on signing up for the military or the police force, you might talk to the scared side of yourself about the necessity to face one's fear of death in order to be free to take risks.

You also might dialogue with the archetype in a journal, asking its advice on how to handle the events of your life. Doing so gives permission for that archetypal energy, which already is a part of you, to share its wisdom with the part that has been running your life.

The fourth step is to begin talking the talk. Listen to yourself and consciously talk in ways congruent with the archetype you want to express in your life. For example, perhaps you typically engage in Warrior talk and want to be more of a Wanderer. Instead of telling a friend, "I'm really going to get that guy who's bugging us," say, "Listening to him helps me recognize that I want to do things very differently than he does them." If you are hanging around with a crowd of people who bond around their wounds, practice saying positive, upbeat things instead. Go ahead and be cheerful, even if doing so feels a bit forced at first.

The fifth step is to be around archetypal role models. The best way to start is to associate with people who evidence the archetype's positive traits. For instance, if you are awakening the Warrior archetype, you might sign up for a martial arts or assertiveness class, or take a job, volunteer, or engage in recreation in a Warrior culture environment. Archetypal energies are contagious.

To awaken the Innocent, you might take a class in positive thinking, sign up for A Course in Miracles[3] class, spend time with anyone of deep religious faith, or simply take time to enjoy and appreciate your life.

If you want miracles in your work life, find someone in your field of endeavor who seems magical to you and ask him or her to mentor you. Read books about new paradigm thinking and connect up with people whom you see as doing cutting-edge work. Volunteer or take a job with a work team that is committed to living its vision and values in everything it does.

The sixth step is to begin walking the talk. Start acting like the archetype even if it feels awkward to do so. Think of this as method acting. Mentally reach down into your psyche and find the part of you that knows how to act this way, then express it. You even can consciously call up the archetype to be expressed through you. For example, a high-level career woman I know imagines herself calling on the spirit of the lion or the wolf when she needs to stand up for a compelling vision in a staid bureaucracy. Invariably, she prevails. Another woman working in a hospice program told me that she connects with her own compassion by thinking of Princess Diana and Mother Teresa. Adolescents might think of superheroes like Superman or Zena or (thinking of *Star Wars*) invoke the Force to be with them.

Some people find it helpful to have some object around them that symbolizes the archetype or to dress in a manner that calls up the archetype (in conservative ways if you want to blend in or in more dramatic ways if you want to call attention to your metamorphosis). Others consciously call on an archetypal energy.

Of course, the most important way to walk your talk is actually to begin doing what the archetype does. If, for example, you want more Warrior energy, stop letting small slights pass. Stand up for yourself or for others. If you want more Magician energy, seek win/win solutions.

The seventh and final step is to fine-tune your skills. When we are new to the Warrior stance, we may fight every battle that comes along. Veteran Warriors, however, choose their battles carefully, being willing to accept a short-term loss to gain long-term strategic advantage. The ability to name the archetypal energy within you provides a small distance between you and the archetype. This distance helps you remember that the archetype is not you. If you can become the scientific observer of archetypal successes and failures, you can influence the level of expression of an archetype in your life. This provides reasonable protection against archetypal possession and helps the archetype be your inner ally.

The more buried the archetype, the slower the process should be for awakening it. For example, in awakening the Warrior, you do not want to pick fights with everyone in sight. If you have some time to integrate the archetype into your life, it is good to express it first in an art form of some kind—a poem, song, painting, etc. The artistic process helps refine and integrate the archetype so that it does not emerge in your actions in an inappropriately primal way. However, if an archetype is dormant, but not really repressed, no intermediate step is necessary, for it has some connection to your conscious mind.

Exercise F: Choose an archetype and go through the steps above to awaken it. Generally, it is wisest to do this only with those archetypes that would be expressed in your life had they not been repressed in some way. Otherwise you might be forcing a process that is not right for you.

Often archetypes are awakened as a natural part of ongoing inner work. You may not even notice that you are engaged in activating an archetype. If you regularly record your dreams, look for archetypal figures in them. Often these figures are compensatory, expressing in your dreams what is missing from your life. As you identify these figures, they enter your conscious mind. A process then begins that creates the preconditions for expressing the archetype in your waking life.

In Jungian dream analysis, you might be encouraged to start reading about the mythic patterns that have emerged in your dreams. Even if you haven't been told to do this, it is not unusual for people to pick up intuitively on patterns in their dreams and begin to read books and see movies that express the same plot line. They may not notice that, after some time, this archetype is expressed naturally in what they think and do and say. For many, this is a largely unconscious process, yet it works.

You also can look for archetypal patterns in your doodles, day-dreams, fantasies, and journal entries. Any habit or practice that helps you stay conscious of your own inner life can keep you from getting stuck by revealing the archetypes that are knocking on your door, waiting to enter your conscious awareness. Remember that the archetypal figures that recur in your dreams and in spon-taneous art are asking to be expressed in your life. If you let them, they do not have to create symptoms or problems to get your attention.

Exercise G: Keep a record of your dreams, doodles, and other imaginative expressions. Pay attention to which archetypes are calling for your attention in these ways.

You may notice archetypes that are not included in this book. If so, do some research on them and, as you understand their meanings, experiment with integrating their perspectives into your life.

CHAPTER 10

The Ethics of the Journey: The Code

> Nor should it be forgotten that moral law is not just something
> imposed upon man from outside. . . . On the contrary, it expresses
> a psychic fact. As the regulator of action, it corresponds to a pre-
> formed image, a pattern of behavior which is archetypal and deeply
> imbedded in human nature.
>
> —Erich Neumann, *Depth Psychology and a New Ethic*

The crisis of values in our culture today is the shadow side of an advance in consciousness. Unless we recognize this character revolution and articulate its rules to the young, the moral life of the culture will continue to be chaotic. In the past, most people have just followed the rules—or at least gave them lip service. They saw themselves as moral if they did what their parents, teachers, ministers/rabbis, or government officials said they should. Now we expect fulfillment from life. Most of us are resistant to moral codes that do not allow for the journey.

Joseph Campbell was fond of warning people that they can climb the ladder of success only to find that it is leaning against the wrong wall. The very fact that we understand this statement tells us that the moral rules of the road have changed. When character meant following the path laid down by someone else, people did not expect to feel fulfilled by their lives. That is likely why they had to be frightened into doing what was right—by fear of hellfire, social ostracism, imprisonment, or even torture.

Moreover, virtue was defined as doing what authorities told you to do. Today, our very notions of character as well as of success require self-knowledge. If we never learn who we really are inside, we never will achieve true fulfillment. We find ourselves against the wrong wall anytime we are living by standards not our own.

In today's pluralistic world, which brings together people from very different cultures and religions, it often is impossible to gain consensus on what rules we should be following. Even if we think we know what others should do, they are decidedly reluctant to follow our dictums—no matter how benevolent our intentions. In fact, others want their heroic uniqueness respected, just as we do. The result is a revolution in what we mean by character and what we define as success.

It is easy to hang on to your own standards and become increasingly judgmental of those who do not adhere to them. However, over time, this may lead to anger and bitterness, especially if you seem to be the only one taking the high road and others succeed at your expense. You may want to throw in the towel and essentially relinquish having any standards at all. Then one day you wake up and realize that you no longer can face yourself in the mirror.

Those of us who are wise will allow all this moral confusion to thrust them on their journeys. If no one can tell us how to live, we need to find our own way. In doing so, we not only sort out our ethical principles, we also develop the inner resources required for a genuinely heroic life. Heroes always have a sense of social and historical responsibility—to leave the world better than they found it. Thus, individuals who take their journeys build healthier relationships, families, organizations, and communities. This does not, however, mean that we can foist our standards on to others.

In a diverse society, moreover, it is important to learn tolerance. People often judge one another across lines of age, race, and culture, applying their own standards to others who are operating by different, but still moral, precepts. Certainly there are times and places where people act shamefully. I am not suggesting here that anything goes. Virtually all cultures agree that it is not good to cheat or lie or murder. Most also agree that it is virtuous to be loving and wise and to pursue spiritual truths.

People's values differ not only because of their cultural and religious backgrounds but also because of their dominant archetypes:

Inner Ally	Success Is Being	Character Is
Innocent	Happy	Being positive
Orphan	Safe and secure	Protecting yourself from being hurt
Wanderer	Yourself	Acting authentically
Warrior	Triumphant	Doing right, avoiding wrong
Altruist	Good	Caring for others
Magician	Transformative	Living consciously

It is essential to understand that all of us do not necessarily mean the same thing when we talk about living ethically, yet each perspective contributes to the greater good of society.

Archetypes by their very nature transcend culture. Therefore, they give us a way to talk about ethics and values that is not based on any one religion. They provide a way to combine cultural sensitivity with a common commitment to integrity. In your life, you may choose to be faithful to the principles you have learned from your own cultural and religious heritage. However, when we come together across such traditional boundaries, we can find common moral ground in the deep structure of the psyche.

The Warrior helps defend the boundaries against practices that harm us and others. Warriors tend to see moral issues in a clear-cut way. To the Warrior, there is right and there is wrong. The ethical imperative is to do right.

Therefore, it is important to the Warrior within us all that we clarify our values and be true to them. The Warrior knows how easy it is for individuals and groups to rationalize the morality of whatever serves their own interests, and therefore demands that we check our ethical decisions not only against our own honor codes, but also against fundamental principles of morality.

The Orphan, however, understands that none of us is perfect. It helps us see where we have been too weak to be true to our best selves, and to empathize when others fail. While the Warrior might kill, harshly punish, or shame wrongdoers, the Orphan looks to see what caused them to mess up so badly. The Orphan then would try to heal that flaw, helping them to be better next time. In our own lives, it is the Orphan that helps us admit when we have done wrong and try to make amends.

The Wanderer is less interested in general questions of morality than in fine tuning his or her own personal code of honor. The Wanderer also loves to explore difference, so this archetype helps us to learn from others with different values. The Wanderer can be tolerant of differing values as long as people are true to what they believe.

The Altruist prompts us to test our ethical ideals to see if they help or harm us and others. If our thinking is out of touch with human reality, we might subscribe to a belief that seems right abstractly, but in practice creates suffering. If so, the Altruist says it is not moral. In addition, Altruists encourage groups to come together to clarify their common values and seek common ground.

The Innocent finds morality through religious teachings, personal revelation, or divine inspiration. Using Jungian principles, it may see dreams as letters from the soul telling us what it is right to do.

The Magician helps us develop mindfulness, so that in addition to making moral decisions, we pay close attention to their results. In this way, the Magician brings a scientific approach to ethics, seeing life as a moral "laboratory." If the consequences of one approach are negative, the Magician goes inward to reconsider what to do. Magicians also know that ethics are an inside job. If you want to be a positive force in the world, you always must begin by raising your own consciousness.

The archetypes also help us develop the inner strength required to live by a moral code:

- The Orphan helps us process our pain and disappointment when others betray or mistreat us, so that we do not lash out in anger or use addictions to numb ourselves;
- The Wanderer prods us to stay the course of our own values rather than go along with the crowd;
- The Warrior gives us the discipline and moral courage not to succumb to temptation;
- The Altruist requires us to show compassion for ourselves and others, so that we do not want to do harmful things;
- The Innocent provides us with the faith and optimism to believe that we do not need to compromise our integrity to succeed; and
- The Magician helps us see that what we put out into the world always will come back to us, often in magnified form.

Each of the six archetypal perspectives in this book also presides over an important stage of character development. If you have not experienced each stage, you will not yet have the virtue that is its gift. You can achieve that virtue only by overcoming a predictable fear. Thus, if we want people to develop character, we must encourage them to take their journeys. Briefly, the six inner allies described in this book see the world in terms of the following plot structures, which result in the completion of six developmental tasks.

Archetype	Helps Us	Overcome the Fear of	Gain the Virtue of
Orphan	Survive difficulties	Punishment	Empathy
Wanderer	Find ourselves	Conformity	Authenticity
Warrior	Prove our worth	Defeat	Courage
Altruist	Live generously	Selfishness	Kindness
Innocent	Trust life or God	Abandonment	Faith
Magician	Transform our lives	Illusions	Integrity

Exercise A: Write your own code of ethics and share it with a friend or colleague. Then examine any ways in which you have trouble living up to that code. In those cases, identify the archetype that might help you maintain your own standards.

THE HERO WITHIN MORAL CODE

A moral code also goes with the approach described in this book. Essentially, it comes down to one basic premise: honor everyone's heroic journey. In doing so, you should follow five major rules of ethical conduct:

1. See everyone as a hero on a journey.
2. Free yourself from prejudices and stereotypes about others.
3. Recognize the positive potential in negative situations.
4. Model right action by staying true to your own path.
5. Respect interdependence.

Rule 1: See everyone as a hero on a journey. The essential rule of the road for working with this material is to honor yourself as well as others, seeing everyone as a hero or potential hero. These theories should be used with respect for the individual journey, whether it is yours or someone else's. They never should be used to put someone else down for being at the "wrong" place on the journey. It would be better for you not even to have read this book than to use it as more ammunition with which to clobber yourself or others. While this book provides a map to follow, it is the individual journey, not the map, that is important.

Every person in the world has a reason for being here. Each journey is unique, and in that way it is a mystery. It also is useful in working with the material to let go of any sense that we know the next step in the journey—for ourselves or for others.

Respect for the hero's journey requires us never to succumb to the arrogance of thinking that we know what someone can and cannot do. These theories never should be used to pigeonhole someone, as if they always embodied only one archetype. For example, after the first edition of this book came out, I sometimes would encounter readers who believed they could predict other people's behavior based on their archetypes. However, most of us have access to several archetypes simultaneously, and these archetypes shift and change over time. Therefore, it is reductive to imagine that you have someone pegged!

The archetypal progression I have written about in this book is a description—not a prescription. It should not be used to design experiences that try to get people to move lockstep through the same stages. Although the patterns, I believe, hold up in general, individual psyches are very diverse, and their autonomy and uniqueness should be respected. These patterns can help you along by naming the experiences that you or others are going through and can hasten learning and make it less threatening. However, the patterns never should be seen as normative—

as stages one *must* go through or be forever inadequate.

In short, as long as you remember that what is important is the individual journey—and not any theories about it—you can feel free to be as creative as you like in devising ways to use the ideas in this book. They are meant to give people comfort on their journeys and to remind us all that questing is a sacred function. The journey can be described and encouraged but should not be unduly contained and certainly not manipulated, forced, or rushed. Often, the best path may be a winding one, and we may appear to be heading quite the opposite way from where we ultimately will perch. Journeys are not efficient or predictable.

Rule 2: Free yourself from prejudices and stereotypes about others. A number of my colleagues and students read this book in manuscript form and questioned whether taking one's journey might be a realistic expectation for privileged people but possibly irrelevant to the less fortunate. I would ask readers to recognize such a bias as anti-heroic.

I know people with more money, privilege, and access to education and career success than most of us ever will have, but their spiritual poverty is so great that they do not develop. Even in the poorest, most depressed African-American or Latino neighborhoods and on American Indian reservations you will come across old men and women who are as wise and fully developed as can be found anywhere. My claim is not only that individuals can triumph over odds or resist growth in the best of circumstances; it is also that real prosperity is not just a matter of wealth and power. White middle class people have a tendency to see the worth of their own materialistic culture but not of the many subcultures in their midst, especially those that are not materially successful.

Alternately, we sometimes romanticize minority cultures and thereby avoid having to acknowledge the genuine barriers to growth that result from crippling poverty, dependency, and lack of respect from society at large. This is true most blatantly for

Native Americans, but it also is true in varying degrees for all groups that are disadvantaged because of their race, ethnicity, sex, sexual orientation, or class.

It is equally important to avoid romanticizing privilege. Members of advantaged groups—males, Caucasians, heterosexuals, able-bodied persons—often overlook the way the system is biased to their advantage. As a result, their growth is arrested, as they tacitly assume that others should, and will, serve them. Unless we understand that some advantages are won at the expense of other people, our journeys can be limited by the shadow Innocent's unconscious attitude of entitlement.

Rule 3: Recognize the positive potential in negative situations. Anytime we meet the shadow of an archetype in another person, its positive pole has the potential to be expressed. While we must recognize and protect ourselves from anyone who would harm us, it also is important that we mentally hold to a vision of that person living out the positive pole of the archetype associated with his or her current shadow behavior. Consider this a form of prayer—that the positive side can and will emerge over time. If you are embattled in some way—politically, legally, interpersonally—remember that the outcome you want is for your higher self and the other individual's higher self to work things out in a high-minded way. This can immunize you against any desire to use excessive force or push an unfair advantage.

M. Scott Peck's *People of the Lie* defines as evil those who would rather harm another than see the truth about themselves. People also tend to do evil things when they avoid their journeys. Some of them think so little of themselves and feel so needy, they will do anything to gain a competitive advantage over others. If we think of "sin" as being off the mark (which is what the word really means), then they simply have strayed from their own path. If and when they return, they can become a positive force in the world.

The following chart describes the immoral pole of each archetype. Generally, these are expressed when someone has not taken the journey of that archetype. James Hillman tells us that "all our pathologies are calls from the gods." Morality is like homeopathic medicine. The antidote for the illness is from the same archetype—only in its more positive form. In each instance, individuals might do something illegal or immoral, but their attitude about it is different: they may lie, steal, deal drugs, or be emotionally or physically abusive, but they rationalize their behavior differently. If others can recognize the deep structure of these rationalizations, they may be able to help the wrongdoer identify the archetype seeking expression and rectify his or her behavior.

Archetype	Motivation for Wrongdoing
Orphans	Feel they have to do it to survive or protect themselves
Warriors	Take immoral action to get greater power or a competitive advantage
Wanderers	Think they are above ordinary laws and don't allow anyone to tell them what to do
Altruists	Lash out in anger after they have sacrificed too much; shame others and make them feel guilty
Innocents	Use the excuse that everyone does it, or just don't think about what they are doing
Magicians	Manipulate others to get them to do what they want

It is important to hold the boundaries and not let others harm you or anyone else. However, you can help others become more moral by seeing their negative behavior as a symptom and calling them to find the positive pole of that archetypal journey. Understanding this can keep us from writing people off.

Exercise B: Do you know people or groups who are doing things that really are wrong? If so, what are they doing and why? Which archetype is calling to them (and possibly also to you) through that behavior?

Rule 4: Model right action by staying true to your own path. Most true liberation is caught, not taught. If you truly want to help others, you must model fidelity to your own path. Then recognize that what can be taught is the process. The content of your path will not necessarily be similar to that of others', and vice versa. I am sure you know people who have had a major impact on your life—less because of what they did than who they were. Every time you are true to the hero within, you help transform the world.

Exercise C: Think back over your life to any times you strayed from your authentic path. What did that feel like to you? What were the results? How did you get back on course? What was the most helpful thing anyone else did (or could have done) to help you?

Rule 5: Respect interdependence. Most people think of individuals as isolated entities, separate from the communities of which they are a part. This failure to think systemically causes us to conceive of people as the problem when the real issues are structural. I was talking recently with a management consultant who expressed a fear that teaching executives about archetypes might lead them to want to hire or retain only people who evidenced the "right" archetypal qualities. I replied by explaining that no one who actually understood the archetypal dimension of life would engage in such unethical and inhumane applications of this theory.

Archetypes emerge from the collective unconscious and strive for balance in organizational and family systems, just as they do in the individual psyche. A college president who attended one of my workshops explained this phenomenon with reference to her personal experience. Like many strong leaders, she found the Orphan annoying and kept getting rid of staff who whined or found fault with everything. Eventually she discovered that this did no good, because soon someone else would begin reciting a litany of complaints. In other words, she realized that in any system, someone has to express the Orphan. If such voices are silenced or devalued, the result will be an increase in low-level (or shadow) expressions of the archetype. The leadership issue is not to get rid of the Orphan, but to create an environment that encourages its more positive expression.

In utilizing archetypal theory ethically, it is important to remember that we all are radically interdependent—with our families, our friends, our co-workers, our communities, and the natural world. If an archetype is active around us, we are issued an invitation to enter its story. Generally, we cannot refuse to do so unless we leave the situation altogether. For example, if anyone in our vicinity is oppressed, we will have to deal with the Orphan archetype. We may feel too far along on our own journeys to need to do so, but the truth is that life is a communal experience.

Individually and collectively, we eventually have to pick up the pieces if our own actions harm others. If a business pollutes the environment, someone has to clean up the mess. If the cleanup falls to government, corporate taxes may increase and businesses may discover that the bottom line is, in fact, affected by their ethics. When groups demonstrate an overabundance of one archetype, someone suffers the consequences. Too much Warrior, for example, and we run the risk of wiping out whole species (to whom we feel superior), oppressing people who do not measure up to our standards, and increasing economic disparities between the rich (winners) and the poor (losers). Such outcomes set in motion a process that begins to awaken the archetypes needed for an appropriate response. The individual and collective psyches are inherently self-correcting. For example, the Altruist and Magician archetypes now are emerging into human consciousness to help us explore ways to value interconnection as much as we do competition. The more conscious we become about our own imbalances, the less time we spend creating problems we then have to solve.

When we think archetypally, we also can recognize the deep structure behind ideas in different fields that predominate in any historical period. When the Warrior archetype was dominant in Western culture, theology focused on the struggle between good and evil, biology emphasized the survival of the fittest, meetings were run along authoritarian lines by majority rule, and organizations took on hierarchical structures, like the military. As the Magician archetype emerges into consciousness, we see theologies emphasizing oneness, biology stressing ecological interdependence, meetings run according to rules of consensual decision making, and organizations becoming flatter and more egalitarian in structure. When archetypes are strong in the culture around us, we must be open to them or risk becoming irrelevant.

Moreover, unless an archetype is expressed outside us in some way, it is very difficult for that archetype to be active in *our* lives. The hero within always is in dialogue with the hero without. Although the great majority of us are limited in what we can achieve by what is happening in the collective, any advance we do make affects the world way beyond ourselves.

The journey may feel very lonely at times, but the truth is that we all are traveling in a caravan together. Whatever you are thinking or feeling, you have company. Archetypes do not emerge only in one person; they come first to a number of societal pioneers and more slowly to cultural leaders and others. Knowing this can give us courage. We live in a round world. It is not possible to step off the edge.

Most of our social systems lag behind human consciousness. As a result, they often can be transformed as quickly and unexpectedly as the falling of the Berlin Wall. All that is required is for us to stop censoring ourselves, to let go of our fears that others are not ready to hear what we know. For example, the gay pride movement showed how breaking silence often is all that is necessary to change attitudes. Many people questioned their stereotyped views of gays and lesbians only after they realized that they knew some!

Recently I have heard some people complain about the lack of spirituality in the workplace. There is, of course, no lack of spirituality in our organizations. They are full of people with highly developed spiritual lives. It is just that to be taken seriously, most workers believe that from nine to five they have to pretend this is not so. All we need to bring spirituality back to the workplace is to break the ban on talking from our hearts, souls, and spirits. We stop being complicit with "Holdfast the keeper of the past" when we are open about the truth of our own lives.

If you have awakened all six archetypes in this book, you are ready to be an agent of change in the world. Taking a leadership role in your family, school, workplace, or community may not seem so daunting if you remember that no single one of us needs to do it all.

If we let go of grandiosity and recognize that we all are partial and thus necessarily interdependent with others, we can share the diversity of our gifts and voices. You learn from me and I learn from you. That is how we grow, and that is how we can solve the great problems of our time. Your individual life is one stream pouring into a river of humanity. You never can know exactly how much difference your life makes, but you can know that you do matter, immeasurably.

We all do.

Appendix A

The Heroic Myth Self-Test

The Heroic Myth Self-Test is designed to measure the archetypes present in both their positive and negative forms in your life. In responding to this questionnaire, you will be asked to reflect on your own archetypal qualities—as you see yourself and as others see you—and to identify the archetypes that affect you because they were active in your family of origin when you were a child or are active at present in your current family, school, and/or workplace.

PART I: HOW I SEE MYSELF

Check all the words or phrases listed in both column A and column B that describe the way you see yourself.[1]

Column A:
(I see myself as . . .)

Column B:
(I see myself as . . .)

1.

Column A	Column B
____ resilient	____ suspicious
____ a survivor	____ negative
____ realistic	____ cynical
____ empathic	____ a whiner

2.

____ individualistic	____ a loner
____ a pioneer	____ a rebel
____ autonomous	____ afraid of closeness
____ a divergent thinker	____ having trouble fitting in

3.

____ assertive	____ ruthless
____ a winner	____ overly competitive
____ disciplined	____ stubborn
____ tough-minded	____ inflexible

4.

____ caring	____ a martyr
____ conscientious	____ intrusive
____ willing to sacrifice	____ guilt-tripping others
____ generous	____ controlling

5.

____ optimistic	____ seduced by easy answers
____ trustworthy	____ gullible
____ trusting	____ naive
____ morally good	____ goody-goody

6.

____ visionary	____ too far out
____ creative	____ weird
____ powerful	____ manipulative
____ a catalyst for change	____ too great a risk taker

The numbers 1 through 6 correspond to the six archetypes in this book. Column A lists archetypal traits that generally are viewed positively. Column B lists archetypal traits that generally are viewed negatively. Count each check as one point and add up your subscores in each column as follows. Your scores will range from 0 to 4 on each scale.

Archetype	A. Positive Total (0–4)	B. Negative Total (0–4)
1. Orphan	_____	_____
2. Wanderer	_____	_____
3. Warrior	_____	_____
4. Altruist	_____	_____
5. Innocent	_____	_____
6. Magician	_____	_____

You can create a bar graph of your subscores on the following chart. Fill in your A score going up and your B score going down for each archetype. Shade in the box of your positive score above the zero and the box of your negative score below the zero. Then connect the two by shading in the boxes in between.

CHART A						
A	OR	WN	WR	AL	IN	MG
4						
3						
2						
1						
0						
1						
2						
3						
4						
B						

PART II: HOW OTHERS SEE ME

The hard part of assessing one's own archetypes is that most of us do not see ourselves accurately. Some people emphasize their positive traits and minimize their faults. Others tend to stress their faults and miss their virtues. Almost all of us have a self-image that is somewhat out of date (that is, we see what we were, not what we are). Therefore, it is useful to take a look at how others see you. There are two ways to do this. The easiest way is to fill out this part yourself, focusing on what others tell you (or even complain to you) about yourself. If you do it this way, follow the instructions in Part I, only focus on how you are seen rather than how you see yourself. The more time-consuming but accurate way is to make copies of this part of the instrument (crossing out the second set of parentheses below the column titles) and give it to three other people (ideally, one relative, one friend, and one co-worker) who know you well and will be honest with you. Then compare your self-appraisal with the appraisals done by others.

Instructions to friends, relatives, and colleagues giving feedback for _____. You have been asked to fill out the following checklist to help a relative, friend, or co-worker accurately appraise the archetypes active in his or her life. Therefore, be as honest as you can. Simply check every word or phrase that applies to the person in question.

Column A:
(I see _____ as . . .)
(I am told I am . . .)

Column B:
(Some people see _____ as . . .)
(I am told I am . . .)

1.

____ resilient   ____ suspicious
____ a survivor   ____ negative
____ realistic   ____ cynical
____ empathic   ____ a whiner

2.

____ individualistic	____ a loner
____ a pioneer	____ a rebel
____ autonomous	____ afraid of closeness
____ a divergent thinker	____ having trouble fitting in

3.

____ assertive	____ ruthless
____ a winner	____ overly competitive
____ disciplined	____ stubborn
____ tough-minded	____ inflexible

4.

____ caring	____ a martyr
____ conscientious	____ intrusive
____ willing to sacrifice	____ guilt-tripping others
____ generous	____ controlling

5.

____ optimistic	____ seduced by easy answers
____ trustworthy	____ gullible
____ trusting	____ naive
____ morally good	____ goody-goody

6.

____ visionary	____ too far out
____ creative	____ weird
____ powerful	____ manipulative
____ a catalyst for change	____ too great a risk taker

The numbers 1 through 6 correspond to the six archetypes in this book. Column A lists archetypal traits that generally are viewed positively. Column B lists archetypal traits that generally are viewed negatively. Count each check as one point and add up your subscore in each column as follows. Your scores will range from 0 to 4 on each scale.

Archetype	A. Positive Total (0–4)	B. Negative Total (0–4)
1. Orphan	_____	_____
2. Wanderer	_____	_____
3. Warrior	_____	_____
4. Altruist	_____	_____
5. Innocent	_____	_____
6. Magician	_____	_____

You can create a bar graph of the subscores on the following chart. Fill in your A score going up and your B score going down for each archetype. Shade in the box of your positive score above the zero and the box of your negative score below the zero. Then connect the two by shading in the boxes in between.

CHART B						
A	OR	WN	WR	AL	IN	MG
4						
3						
2						
1						
0						
1						
2						
3						
4						
B						

PART III: THE INFLUENCE OF MY FAMILY OF ORIGIN

Our families of origin provide the basic road map for the journey. The following checklist is designed to help you identify your family legacy. In Column A, check all the traits your family said they valued. In Column B, check all the traits that were frowned upon, punished, or kept secret—in short, the ones you were not supposed to have!

Column A:
(I was supposed to be . . .)

Column B:
(I was absolutely not supposed to be . . .)

1.

____ resilient

____ a survivor

____ realistic

____ empathic

____ suspicious

____ negative

____ cynical

____ a whiner

2.

____ individualistic	____ a loner
____ a pioneer	____ a rebel
____ autonomous	____ afraid of closeness
____ a divergent thinker	____ having trouble fitting in

3.

____ assertive	____ ruthless
____ a winner	____ overly competitive
____ disciplined	____ stubborn
____ tough-minded	____ inflexible

4.

____ caring	____ a martyr
____ conscientious	____ intrusive
____ willing to sacrifice	____ guilt-tripping others
____ generous	____ controlling

5.

____ optimistic	____ seduced by easy answers
____ trustworthy	____ gullible
____ trusting	____ naive
____ morally good	____ goody-goody

6.

____ visionary	____ too far out
____ creative	____ weird
____ powerful	____ manipulative
____ a catalyst for change	____ too great a risk taker

The numbers 1 through 6 correspond to the six archetypes in this book. Column A lists archetypal traits that generally are viewed positively. Those you checked were especially valued by your family of origin. These qualities were your family legacy to you, telling you what they wanted you (and others) to be. Column B lists archetypal traits that generally are viewed negatively. Those you checked were actively discouraged by your family. These scores show your family's shadow. It is your challenge to find the gold in the shadow. (You can do this by allowing room in your life for the more positive traits associated with the respective archetype.) Count each check as one point and add up your subscore in each column as follows. Your scores will range from 0 to 4 on each scale.

Archetype	A. Positive Total (0–4)	B. Negative Total (0–4)
1. Orphan	_____	_____
2. Wanderer	_____	_____
3. Warrior	_____	_____
4. Altruist	_____	_____
5. Innocent	_____	_____
6. Magician	_____	_____

You can create a bar graph of the subscores on the following chart. Fill in your A score going up and your B score going down for each archetype. Shade in the box of your positive score above the zero and the box of your negative score below the zero. Then connect the two by shading in the boxes in between.

CHART C						
A	OR	WN	WR	AL	IN	MG
4						
3						
2						
1						
0						
1						
2						
3						
4						
B						

PART IV: THE INFLUENCE OF MY CURRENT FAMILY

The following checklist is designed to help you identify the influence of your current family, however you define it. (*Note:* If you still live with your family of origin or you consider them your primary family at the moment, skip Part IV and go right to Part V.) In Column A, check all the traits your present family now encourages. In Column B, check all the traits that are frowned upon, punished, or kept secret—in short, the ones you are not supposed to have!

Column A:
(I am supposed to be . . .)

Column B:
(I am absolutely not supposed to be . . .)

1.

____ resilient

____ a survivor

____ realistic

____ empathic

____ suspicious

____ negative

____ cynical

____ a whiner

2.

____ individualistic   ____ a loner
____ a pioneer   ____ a rebel
____ autonomous   ____ afraid of closeness
____ a divergent thinker   ____ having trouble fitting in

3.

____ assertive   ____ ruthless
____ a winner   ____ overly competitive
____ disciplined   ____ stubborn
____ tough-minded   ____ inflexible

4.

____ caring   ____ a martyr
____ conscientious   ____ intrusive
____ willing to sacrifice   ____ guilt-tripping others
____ generous   ____ controlling

5.

____ optimistic   ____ seduced by easy answers
____ trustworthy   ____ gullible
____ trusting   ____ naive
____ morally good   ____ goody-goody

6.

____ visionary   ____ too far out
____ creative   ____ weird
____ powerful   ____ manipulative
____ a catalyst for change ____ too great a risk taker

The numbers 1 through 6 correspond to the six archetypes in this book. Column A lists archetypal traits that generally are viewed positively. Those you checked are valued especially by your current family. Column B lists archetypal traits that generally are viewed negatively. Those you checked are actively discouraged by your current family. These scores show your family's shadow. It is your challenge to find the gold in the shadow. (You can do this by allowing room in your life for the more positive traits associated with the respective archetype.) Count each check as one point and add up your subscores in each column as follows. Your scores will range from 0 to 4 on each scale.

Archetype	A. Positive Total (0–4)	B. Negative Total (0–4)
1. Orphan	_____	_____
2. Wanderer	_____	_____
3. Warrior	_____	_____
4. Altruist	_____	_____
5. Innocent	_____	_____
6. Magician	_____	_____

You can create a bar graph of the subscores on the following chart. Fill in your A score going up and your B score going down for each archetype. Shade in the box of your positive score above the zero and the box of your negative score below the zero. Then connect the two by shading in the boxes in between.

CHART D						
A	OR	WN	WR	AL	IN	MG
4						
3						
2						
1						
0						
1						
2						
3						
4						
B						

PART V: THE INFLUENCE OF MY CURRENT WORKPLACE (OR SCHOOL)

Workplaces also encourage certain traits and see others as taboo. (So do schools. If you still are in school or have returned to school as your primary endeavor, answer the questions in Part V with your school rather than your workplace in mind.) Do the checklist again. This time check, in Column A, all of the traits that are particularly encouraged by your boss or work team (or your teacher or classmates). Then check all the traits in Column B that they particularly discourage.

Column A:
(I am supposed to be . . .)

Column B:
(I am absolutely not supposed to be . . .)

1.

____ resilient

____ a survivor

____ realistic

____ empathic

____ suspicious

____ negative

____ cynical

____ a whiner

2.

_____ individualistic   _____ a loner
_____ a pioneer   _____ a rebel
_____ autonomous   _____ afraid of closeness
_____ a divergent thinker   _____ having trouble fitting in

3.

_____ assertive   _____ ruthless
_____ a winner   _____ overly competitive
_____ disciplined   _____ stubborn
_____ tough-minded   _____ inflexible

4.

_____ caring   _____ a martyr
_____ conscientious   _____ intrusive
_____ willing to sacrifice   _____ guilt-tripping others
_____ generous   _____ controlling

5.

_____ optimistic   _____ seduced by easy answers
_____ trustworthy   _____ gullible
_____ trusting   _____ naive
_____ morally good   _____ goody-goody

6.

_____ visionary   _____ too far out
_____ creative   _____ weird
_____ powerful   _____ manipulative
_____ a catalyst for change   _____ too great a risk taker

The numbers 1 through 6 correspond to the six archetypes in this book. Column A lists archetypal traits that generally are viewed positively. Those you have checked reflect the traits explicitly valued in your workplace (or school). Column B lists archetypal traits that generally are viewed negatively. Those you checked reflect the shadow of your workplace (or school). The total scores let you know the relative presence of each archetype in your workplace (or school). Any archetype with a large score is calling you to take its journey and gain its gifts. Count each check as one point and add up your subscore in each column as follows. Your scores will range from 0 to 4 on each scale.

Archetype	A. Positive Total (0–4)	B. Negative Total (0–4)
1. Orphan	_____	_____
2. Wanderer	_____	_____
3. Warrior	_____	_____
4. Altruist	_____	_____
5. Innocent	_____	_____
6. Magician	_____	_____

You can create a bar graph of your subscores on the following chart. Fill in your A score going up and your B score going down for each archetype. Shade in the box of your positive score above the zero and the box of your negative score below the zero. Then connect the two by shading in the boxes in between.

CHART E						
A	OR	WN	WR	AL	IN	MG
4						
3						
2						
1						
0						
1						
2						
3						
4						
B						

PART VI: PUTTING IT ALL TOGETHER

On the chart below, place the names of the positive archetypes and negative archetypes that received the highest scores in each category of Parts 1 through 5. Compare the scores on the five parts of this self-test, looking for any patterns that emerge.

Parts I–V	Top Column A (Positive) Archetypes	Top Column B (Negative) Archetypes
How I See Myself		
How Others See Me		
Influence of Family of Origin		
Influence of Current Family		
Influence of Current Workplace (or School)		

1. Do you see yourself similarly to the way others see you? If not, you might speculate on the differences. Do you hide parts of yourself so that others do not see the real you? Are people seeing parts of you that you miss? Other ideas?

2. What are your strongest archetypes? Where do you express these archetypes in your life?

3. What archetypes are evident in a more negative form in your life? Can you imagine how to express them in a more positive way?

4. Take a look at the virtues your family of origin encouraged. Are you now, or have you in the past, evidenced these virtues?

5. What traits did your family disapprove of? Have you lived these in some way—in either their negative or positive forms (see the equivalent A list)?

6. Compare the traits your current family values and discourages with those of your family of origin. (If your spouse or other family member also is filling out these checklists, you may find it interesting to share results.)

7. What traits does your current workplace (or school) most value? Are these easy traits for you to exhibit?

8. What traits does your current workplace (or school) most discourage? Is the corresponding archetype now active in your own life? Are you able to express its qualities in your work (school) environment? What happens if you do so?

9. Realizing that your family of origin was responsible for your initial socialization and your current family and workplace (or school) are influencing you now, what are the positive and shadow forms of the archetypes that have called or are calling you from these environments?

10. Be aware that you may experience stress because of the difference between your own inner archetypal structure and that of the systems of which you are a part. This stress can be

a stimulus to growth if it motivates you to awaken an archetype or its more positive aspects. What archetype, if awakened, could decrease the stress in your life?

11. You also might experience stress because some important archetype is in shadow (repressed, punished, etc.) in any of the systems of which you are a part. What might that shadow archetype have to teach or tell you?

12. Write a brief autobiography showing what you have gained from each major environment of your life.

You may find it useful to introduce your family members, friends, or co-workers (or classmates) to *The Hero Within* model. If they also fill out these checklists, you will have an opportunity to get to know each other at a deeper level by sharing your results. In addition, you can check your assessment of each family, organizational, or school system with one another. Having such support can further your journey and enhance your ability to express your more heroic self and to do so in more and more situations.

Appendix B

Guidelines for Heroic Journey Support Groups

Readers may find it useful to form Heroic Journey Support Groups. People in such groups can read and discuss chapters, do exercises together, and support each other's journeys. Support groups can be formed by or through:

- Friendship networks
- Families or extended families
- Character development or school-to-work programs in education
- Out-placement programs aiding people in job transitions
- Recovery groups as an aid to second-stage recovery
- Peer groups in workplaces facing major transition
- Therapy groups in preparation for termination
- Poverty prevention programs as an aid to personal empowerment

GUIDELINES FOR PARTICIPANTS

Take full responsibility for your own journey. Others can guide and support you, but only you can find your own grail, your own truth.

Whether or not the group has a leader, take your own share of responsibility for the effectiveness and health of the group. This means helping to keep the group focused on its task; it also means paying attention to the group process to be certain that the task does not get done at the cost of healthy relationships between members.

Honor your own process and that of others. Let it be okay for members to be in different places and to see different truths. Remember, if any absolute truth exists, it certainly is beyond our subjective understanding. We are all like the proverbial blind men, each touching a different part of the elephant and trying to describe the whole animal. We need all our perceptions. In any case, it is wise to respect where people are even if you do not share their views.

Use "I" statements. Say "When you say . . . , I feel . . . ," not "That is wrong/stupid," or worse, "You lousy . . .".

Try to be mindful of others' likely feelings or reactions. This does not mean you should avoid conflict. However, you may need to reassure others of your respect, regard, or even affection when sharing a perspective that they might take as hostile to their own stance. Or you simply may need to remember to be tactful. If you feel hurt or crazy or angry in response to what someone else says or does, tell them directly but also as empathetically as possible. Never talk about group members behind their backs. If something bothers you, be forthright in raising it in the group.

Sometimes it is not appropriate to be tactful. Perhaps you are experimenting with a new way to behave—for instance, you want to break a family taboo against acting angry or bitchy. Then tell the group what you are doing, so people will not be thrown unnecessarily by your actions.

Talk with and to one another, not just to the leader (if you have one). Help one another when you feel someone needs comforting, reassurance, support, challenging, or encouragement to be more honest or confrontational.

Take responsibility for trying to get your needs met. Do not assume that others (including any leader) can read your mind. Say what you want and need, but also be aware that you cannot always have everything you ask for (although asking certainly ups the chances of success).

Journeyers are equals. Even if your group has a designated leader, bring your full wisdom to the group. Do not disempower yourself by waiting for someone else to know what you know or see what you see. Often what we find missing in any group is what we alone could provide.

Take responsibility for group decisions. If the group decided to do something you did not want to do, take responsibility for not speaking up (if you didn't) or not being persuasive enough to change the decision (if you tried). In short, take responsibility for being part of the decision-making process. If you would like things to go a different way, don't just complain. Bring it up to the group as persuasively and constructively as you can.

Take responsibility for your own participation or nonparticipation. Do what fits for you and not what doesn't. Use your creativity to tailor exercises or activities to your own style, priorities, and needs. Ask for assistance from others when you need it.

Stay in touch with your deeper, wiser self to know whether or not you should be in this particular group. If you believe you should, then be as fully present as you can. If not, go where your heart leads you.

Appendix C

Creating Heroic Environments

Organizations and whole societies tend to become as dysfunctional when they are out of balance as do individuals. Righting the balance in our individual lives creates a magnetism that attracts systems back into balance. We also can utilize our knowledge of the six archetypes to create environments that foster heroism in ourselves and others.

HEROIC FAMILIES

The healthy family faces difficulties directly (Orphan), is open to new possibilities and perspectives (Wanderer), achieves enough to feed, clothe, and protect its members from poverty or other harm (Warrior), shows care and nurturance both within the family and toward the larger community (Altruist), demonstrates trust in some higher power (Innocence), and acts with integrity to be a positive force in the world (Magician). Such families also provide ample room for each member to feel free to express all of these (and other) archetypes.

In such families, parents show their approval of all six archetypes by the way they treat their children. For example, children are:

- Comforted and nurtured when they are hurting (Orphan);
- Positively reinforced when they express their individuality (Wanderer);
- Encouraged to buckle down and study, but also to stand up for themselves and others (Warrior);
- Praised for sharing and caring for others (Altruist);
- Kept safe and encouraged to believe in the world and themselves (Innocent); and
- Treated with respect so that they learn they are important enough to act on their power to change the world by standing up for their principles (Magician).

HEROIC SCHOOLS

Schools help children grow when they provide environments that balance their archetypal roles. Such schools:[1]

- Protect children from physical harm, harassment, or abuse, and demeaning notions about their potential (Orphan);
- Promote individual gifts and talents by holding up a magic mirror that shows them how they are special (Wanderer);
- Encourage and reward discipline, focus, and achievement (Warrior);
- Provide opportunities for sharing and collaborative work (Altruist);
- Assume positive intentions, whatever a child's behavior (Innocent); and
- Offer students opportunities for genuine choice (in what they study and in school governance), so they begin to practice having an impact on their own destinies and on larger social systems (Magician).

Preparing students to become productive workers, caring family members, and engaged citizens requires a balance of experiences and perspectives. Too often, we get caught in debates about whether competitive or cooperative learning is best; whether equity or quality is more important, etc. Such debates can lead us down a dead-end road if we think we have to choose one of these polarities at the expense of another. The issue is not deciding between opposite alternatives; it is finding the proper balance between and among collaboration, competition, equity, and quality. Only then are truly miraculous results possible.

HEROIC WORKPLACES

For an organization to work optimally, the following must be in balance.

- Employees need to feel as secure as possible; ideally, they will have health insurance, retirement plans, and a sense that as long as they do a good job, the organization will do its best to keep them employed (Orphan).
- Employees want to find and express their genuine talents, their wisdom, and the full range of their humanity; this means matching people to roles that reflect their authenticity (Wanderer).
- Employees thrive in settings that provide reasonable incentives (raises, bonuses, recognition) for exemplary achievement and help for rising to meet new challenges (training, equipment, etc.) (Warrior).
- Employees feel ennobled when they work for an organization that is doing something positive for the world and when all stakeholders (including employees and customers) are treated well (Altruist).
- Employee morale typically soars when the organization and their role in it is congruent with their values and principles (Innocent).

- Employees need to believe that they have a voice in what happens in the organization; ideally, each person feels as though he or she is at the center of the organization and everything he or she does matters to its future (Magician).

When all these are in place, the result is: high productivity, good morale, and a positive impact on families, the community, and the larger society. This ideal leader also furthers these ends by modeling positive aspects of all six archetypes. Various theories of leadership current today emphasize different archetypal strengths:

Leadership Approach	Archetypal Perspective Encouraged
Advocacy leadership	Orphan
Pioneering leadership	Wanderer
Strategic leadership	Warrior
Servant leadership	Altruist
Visionary leadership	Innocent
Transformative leadership	Magician

The ideal leader actually would have a bit of all of these archetypal qualities. Organizational development interventions tend to shore up some archetypes and depress others: If your organization is not functioning optimally, identify which archetypes are expressed in their positive forms, which are repressed, and which are shadowy or negative. You can choose what kind of training or consultation makes sense based on archetypal organizational analysis.

Any intervention, no matter how well conceived and executed, can end up doing harm if the overall balance is thrown off—either because the intervention is reinforcing a part of the organization that already is too dominant or because the new approach is implemented ineptly or incompletely. For example, if your organization is strong on the Altruist or Orphan archetypes, you and your colleagues may prefer to spend most of your time bonding, to the detriment of other archetypal elements of success. When things go wrong, you may decide automatically that team building is the answer. But that is just what you prefer, not where the weakness is in the organization. It is like a doctor treating the heart when someone has a broken leg.[2]

HEROIC PSYCHOTHERAPY, COACHING, AND COUNSELING

Heroic psychotherapy, coaching, and counseling pays attention to the six archetypes, recognizing, building, or enhancing the strengths of each.

Step One: Find your clients' archetypal strengths. Most helping professionals are trained to diagnose pathology. However, if you constantly imply that your clients are sick or wounded without acquainting them with their strengths, the therapeutic process may undermine rather than help them. That is why many people remain in therapy for years and years. They begin to think of themselves as dysfunctional. Once you have found clients' inner allies, you can safely explore areas of wounding or dysfunction.

Step Two: Diagnose what archetypes are traumatized or wounded— not only in childhood but also by present realities. You may then help clients move through their pain, so they can become free to live in the present and choose more supportive situations in the future. Also, work on ways to awaken or heal the relevant archetypes (Orphan).

Step Three: Promote strategies to explore the inner life. Encourage your clients to analyze their dreams, write in a journal, take part in active imagination exercises, or simply talk about what they like, what they value, and who they are inside (Wanderer).

Step Four: Develop strategies to set and achieve client goals. Stress cognitive approaches and behavioral strategies to help clients be more successful in their relationships, work, and other endeavors (Warrior).

Step Five: Help clients become more caring and responsible members of a family, group, organization, or community. For clients to understand and communicate with others more effectively, couples counseling, family therapy (including the whole family), T-groups, team building, and other group interventions can be very useful (Altruist).

Step Six: Encourage your clients to clarify and act on their values and/or spiritual beliefs. You, as the counselor, should not have a spiritual program you are trying to sell. Instead, help clients clarify their values and find their own authentic spiritual path (Innocent).

Step Seven: Support clients in transforming their lives and environments. The ability to transform one's life generally requires that the other five aspects of the therapeutic journey be in place. Once they are, you can provide support for your clients to fine tune skills of personal mastery so that they become adept at creating positive change from the inside out (Magician).

HEROIC RECOVERY
The Twelve Steps and the Heroic Journey

The Twelve Steps have saved many lives. Because they are so effective, some people even think they are divinely inspired. All twelve-step programs use variants of the original Alcoholics Anonymous steps, which appear on the next page.

THE TWELVE STEPS OF A.A.

1. We admitted we were powerless over alcohol—that our lives had become unmanageable.
2. Came to believe that a Power greater than ourselves could restore us to sanity.
3. Made a decision to turn our will and our lives over to the care of God *as we understood Him.*
4. Made a searching and fearless moral inventory of ourselves.
5. Admitted to God, to ourselves, and to another human being the exact nature of our wrongs.
6. Were entirely ready to have God remove all these defects of character.
7. Humbly asked Him to remove our shortcomings.
8. Made a list of all persons we had harmed and became willing to make amends to them all.
9. Made direct amends to such people wherever possible, except when to do so would injure them or others.
10. Continued to take personal inventory and when we were wrong promptly admitted it.
11. Sought through prayer and meditation to improve our conscious contact with God *as we understood Him,* praying only for knowledge of His will for us and the power to carry that out.
12. Having had a spiritual awakening as the result of these steps, we tried to carry this message to alcoholics, and to practice these principles in all our affairs.

Twelve-step programs may succeed, in part but not entirely, because various steps support archetypal balance in the psyche. For example:

Step One: People activate their Orphan archetypes by admitting powerlessness over any addictive substance and reaching out for help.

Steps Two–Three: Turning one's life over to God activates the returned Innocent.

Steps Four–Ten: Admitting and atoning for one's own misdeeds activates the integrity of the high-level Warrior. The knights of the Round Table adhered to a noble code that helped them survive great battles. Similarly, these steps help the alcoholic or addict survive the battle with addictive substances.

Step Eleven: Seeking to learn the divine will for our lives helps us to know who we are and hence awaken the higher-order Wanderer.

Step Twelve: Serving others activates the Altruist.

The archetypal model contained here is not designed to return people to sobriety unless used in conjunction with a twelve-step program that addresses the individual's situation directly. However, this model can be immensely important in second- and third-stage recovery because it helps people pick up missed life lessons. For this reason, the approach in this work is useful as well to adult children of alcoholics (ACOA) or to anyone from a dysfunctional home. *The Hero Within* model also can help prevent addiction, because fully developed people are at much less risk than those with fewer inner resources and less self-awareness.

HEROIC POLITICS, ECONOMICS, AND GOVERNMENT

The ideas in this book translate into personal terms what it means to live in a democracy. One person, one vote means that theoretically, at least, we all have equal political clout. Of course, people cannot rise to the occasion to live into this power unless they also claim their personal power. That's why it would be ideal if everyone could have access in some fashion to the hero's journey. Democracy is at risk when people take it for granted and fail to exercise the authority of citizenship. For democracy not only to survive but to serve all of us, we need to get involved in the political process, to support and vote for the people and policies that reflect our views.

One can use the six-archetype model to illustrate the attributes of a balanced system, and to appreciate how different groups today are educating us about each piece of the puzzle.

- The Orphan tells us that we need to provide safety nets when people really need help, and some protective legislation to keep people from being victimized by others and the earth from being ravaged and despoiled. The consumer protection, peace, and environmental movements as well as all liberation movements help identify where democracy is not working and for whom, thus pushing for needed change.

- The Wanderer enjoins us to protect the civil rights of all citizens and to uphold the individual's right to life, liberty, and the pursuit of happiness. While all believers in democracy espouse these values, Libertarians articulate this position in its most extreme form.

- The Warrior tells us that we need enough competition to increase quality and productivity and a large enough military to protect us from genuine threats. Generally, political conservatives give voice to these values.

- The Altruist tells us that competition is not enough. Sharing our time, talents, and resources to promote the common good and provide common services is the only way to restore community to our lives. These are the understandings nurtured by political liberals and progressives.

- The Innocent tells us it is important, while preserving freedom of religion, to understand that spirit and soul are part of civic life. While no group has the right to impose its form of religion on another, recognizing the spiritual dimension of all life is intrinsic to realizing the great dream of democracy. It clearly is inappropriate to expect Jews, Christians, Muslims, Hindus, Buddhists, Sufis, or other religious groups to accept the theology and practices of any other religion. The challenge is to find a genuinely pluralistic way to incorporate spirit and soul into public life.

- The Magician tells us that we cannot rely on any one archetypal political perspective to the exclusion of the others. Rather, we must find the optimal balance for the historical moment. The Magician also helps us know what political virtues to emphasize at a particular moment in history to reestablish balance in the system.

Appendix D

The *Awakening the Heroes Within* Twelve-Archetype Model: Notes and Resources

Awakening the Heroes Within: Twelve Archetypes to Help Us Find Ourselves and Transform Our World is a more advanced and complex treatment of the archetypes related to the individuation process—that is, the process by which we find out who we are and what we have to contribute to the world—than *The Hero Within*. Published in 1991 by Harper San Francisco, it has inspired a number of instruments, workbooks, and books designed to further its use by helping professionals. It is available from Harper Collins Publishers or through your local bookstore.

Advance readers of the manuscript of this edition of *The Hero Within* asked for information about the relationship between archetypes in the two books. Some archetypal names are slightly different. Archetypes are not bounded entities that are easy to pin down and label. The same essential energy can take a slightly different form in a different mythic story or human context. I have tried as best I could to use names that communicate the level and style of the archetype appropriate to each book's theme and concerns. The Altruist archetype in *The Hero Within* combines elements of the

Caregiver and the Destroyer archetypes from the twelve-archetype model. The name Altruist also emphasizes public generosity rather than private care.

The Hero Within: Six Archetypes	Awakening the Heroes Within: Twelve Archetypes
Innocent	Innocent
Orphan	Orphan
Wanderer	Seeker
Warrior	Warrior
Altruist	Caregiver
Altruist	Destroyer
	Lover
	Creator
	Ruler
Magician	Magician
	Sage
	Fool

I recommend *The Hero Within* as an introductory text. It also can be used by younger readers and those seeking to apply the ideas to social, political, or organization contexts. *Awakening the Heroes Within* is appropriate for therapeutic use, for application to mid-life and beyond, and for more advanced readers. *Awakening the Heroes Within* differentiates archetypes that help people prepare for the journey (by strengthening the ego), undertake a journey of transformation (by connecting with their souls or deep authenticity), and return to make a contribution to the culture (in the process finding wholeness and fulfillment).

The following training materials and books can be used in conjunction with *The Hero Within* and/or *Awakening the Heroes Within*. All are available from the Center for Applications of Psychological Type (CAPT), 2815 NW 13th St., Suite 401, Gainesville, FL 32609 or online at www.capt.org.

Books and Instrumentation:

Adson, Patricia R. 1999, *Finding Your True North and Helping Others Find Direction in Life.* Explores how to utilize the 12-archetype model in psychotherapy with others or in working on your own issues.

Adson, Patricia R, 2004, *Depth Coaching: Discovering Archetypes: For Empowerment, Growth, and Balance.* Explores how life and executive coaches can use the archetypal models to enhance their practices and their own lives.

Corlett, John G. and Carol S. Pearson, 2003, *Mapping the Organizational Psyche: A Jungian Theory of Organizational Dynamics and Change.* A good primer for organizational consultants and leaders who wish to understand and improve organizational and team cultures.

Mark, Margaret and Carol S. Pearson, 2001, *The Hero and the Outlaw: Building Extraordinary Brands Through the Power of Archetypes* (McGraw-Hill). A guide to authentic and ethical archetypal branding.

Pearson, Carol S. and Hugh Marr, 2002, *Pearson-Marr Archetype Indicator*™, an instrument that assesses archetypes active in an individual's life. Available online or in a self-scored print version. Supporting pamphlets and a manual are also available.

Pearson, Carol S. and Hugh Marr, 2007, *What Story Are You Living? A Workbook and Guide to Interpreting Results for the Pearson-Marr Archetype Indicator.*

Pearson, Carol S. 2003, *Organizational and Team Culture Indicator*™, an instrument that assesses archetypes in organizational and team cultures. Supporting publications include a manual and supporting client guides.

Training Seminars:

For information on training seminars for professions wishing to utilize these theories and models in their work, go online to www.capt.org or www.academy.umd.edu.

Carol S. Pearson, Ph.D., is the Director of the James MacGregor Burns Academy of Leadership and a Professor of Leadership Studies at the University of Maryland, College Park, MD. Her publications include *The Hero Within: Six Archetypes We Live By, Educating the Majority: Challenging Tradition in Higher Education,* co-edited by Donna L. Shavlik and Judith G. Touchton); *Awakening the Heroes Within: Twelve Archetypes that Help Us Find Ourselves and Transform Our World; Magic At Work: Camelot, Creative Leadership and Everyday Miracles; The Hero and the Outlaw: Building Extraordinary Brands Through the Power of Archetypes,* co-authored by Margaret Mark; *Mapping the Organizational Psyche: A Jungian Theory of Organizational Dynamics and Change,* co-authored by John Corlett; and *What Story Are You Living?* co-authored by Hugh Marr. Her books are widely translated. She lives with her husband of 33 years close to her three married children and four grandchildren.

Suggested Reading

SELECTED CLASSICS ON JUNGIAN
PSYCHOLOGICAL THOUGHT

Edward F. Edinger, *Ego and Archetype: Individuation and the Religious Function of the Psyche*. New York: Penguin, 1973.

James Hillman, *Revisioning Psychology*. Dallas, Texas: Spring Publications, 1985.

———. *The Soul's Code: In Search of Character and Calling*. New York: Warner Books, 1997.

C. G. Jung, *Collected Works*. Edited by Sir Herbert Read, Michael Fordham, and Gerhard Adler. Translated by R. F. C. Hull. Princeton: Princeton University Press, Bollingen Series, XX, 1954–1967.

———. *Memories, Dreams, Reflections*. Edited by Aniela Jaffe. New York: Pantheon Books, 1963.

———. *Modern Man in Search of a Soul*. New York: A Harvest Book, Harcourt Brace & Co. 1933.

June Singer, *Boundaries of the Soul: The Practice of Jung's Psychology*. New York: Doubleday, 1972.

Edward D. Whitmont, *The Symbolic Quest*. New York: G. P. Putnam's Sons, 1969.

BASIC BOOKS ON ARCHETYPES
IN OUR DAILY LIVES

Patricia Adson, *True North: Finding Direction for Ourselves and Our Clients in Psychotherapy*. Gladwyne, PA: Type and Archetype Press, 1998.

Angeles Arrien, *The Four-Fold Way: Walking the Paths of the Warrior, Teacher, Healer and Visionary*. San Francisco: HarperSanFrancisco, 1993.

Jean Shinoda Bolen, *Goddesses in Everywoman*. San Francisco: Harper & Row, 1985.

———. *Gods in Everyman*. San Francisco: Harper & Row, 1989.

Joseph Campbell, *The Hero with a Thousand Faces*. New York: World Publishing Co., 1970.

———. *The Power of Myth*, with Bill Moyers. New York: Doubleday, 1988.

Allan Chinen, *Beyond the Hero: Classic Stories of Men in Search of Soul*. New York: Jeremy P. Tarcher/Putnam, 1993.

Clarissa Pinkola Estes, *Women Who Run With the Wolves*. New York: Ballantine, 1992.

David Feinstein and Stanley Krippner, *The Mythic Path: Discovering the Guiding Stories of Your Past—Creating a Vision for Your Future*. New York: G. P. Putnam's Sons, 1997.

Matthew Fox, *The Coming of the Cosmic Christ*. San Francisco: HarperSanFrancisco, 1988.

Jean Houston, *The Search for the Beloved: Journeys in Sacred Psychology*. Los Angeles: Jeremy P. Tarcher, 1987.

Robert Johnson, *Inner Work: Using Dreams and Active Imagination for Personal Growth*. San Francisco: HarperSanFrancisco, 1986.

———. *He*. New York: Harper & Row, 1989.

———. *She: Understanding Feminine Psychology*. New York: Harper & Row, 1989.

Robert Moore and Douglas Gillette, *King, Warrior, Magician, Lover*. San Francisco: HarperSanFrancisco, 1990.

Maureen Murdoch, *The Heroine's Journey*. Boston: Shambala Publications, 1990.

————. *The Heroine's Journey Workbook*. Boston: Shambala Publications, 1998.

Carol S. Pearson, *Awakening the Heroes Within: Twelve Archetypes to Help Us Find Ourselves and Transform Our World*. San Francisco: HarperSanFrancisco, 1991.

————. *Invisible Forces I: Harnessing the Power of Archetypes to Improve Your Family*. Gladwyne, PA: Type and Archetype Press, 1998.

————. *Invisible Forces II: Harnessing the Power of Archetypes to Improve Your Career and Your Organization*. Gladwyne, PA: Type and Archetype Press, 1997.

————. *Magic at Work: Camelot, Creative Leadership, and Everyday Miracles* (with Sharon Seivert). New York: Doubleday/Currency, 1995.

————. *Pearson-Marr Archetype Indicator* (with Hugh Marr). Gladwyne, PA: Type and Archetype Press, 1995.

————. *The Female Hero in American and British Literature* (with Katherine Pope). New York: Bowker Book Co., 1981.

Murray Stein and John Hollwitz, *Psyche at Work: Workplace Applications of Jungian Analytical Psychology*. Wilmette, IL: Chiron Publications, 1992.

Jeremy Taylor, *Where People Fly and Water Runs Uphill: Using Dreams to Tap the Wisdom of the Unconscious*. New York: Warner Books, 1992.

Part 1

Introduction

1. Jessie L. Weston, *From Ritual to Romance* (Garden City, NY: Doubleday, Anchor Books, 1957), pp. 12–24.

2. Dorothy Norman, *The Hero: Myth/Image/Symbol* (New York: New American Library, 1969), p. 12.

3. Joseph Campbell, *The Hero with a Thousand Faces* (New York: World Publishing Co., 1970), p. 12.

4. Robert E. Quinn, *Deep Change: Discovering the Leader Within* (San Francisco: Jossey-Bass, 1998), p. 45.

5. Box-Car Bertha, *Sister of the Road: The Autobiography of Box-Car Bertha*, as told to Dr. Ben L. Reitman (New York: Harper & Row, 1937), p. 280.

6. Annie Dillard, *Pilgrim at Tinker Creek* (New York: Bantam Books, 1975), p. 278.

Chapter 2

1. Charles L. Whitfield, *Healing The Child Within* (Deerfield Beach, FL: Health Communications, 1987).

2. Anne Wilson Schaef, *Beyond Therapy* (San Francisco: HarperSanFrancisco, 1996).

3. Patricia Adson, *True North: Finding Direction for Yourself and Your Clients in Psychotherapy* (Gladwyne, PA: Type and Archetype Press, 1998) and Bill O'Hanlan, *Frozen in Time* (Omaha, NE: Possibilities Press, 1997).

4. Samuel Beckett, *Waiting for Godot* (Cambridge: Cambridge University Press, 1989).

5. Julia Cameron, *The Artist's Way* (New York: Putnam, 1992).

6. Elisabeth Kübler-Ross, *Death: The Final Stage of Growth* (Englewood Cliffs, NJ: Prentice Hall, 1975).

Chapter 3

1. Carol Gilligan, *In a Different Voice: Psychological Theory and Women's Development* (Cambridge, MA: Harvard University Press, 1982), passim.

2. Daniel J. Levinson, *The Seasons of a Man's Life* (New York: Alfred A. Knopf, 1978), passim.

3. Erica Jong, *How to Save Your Own Life* (New York: Holt, Rinehart, and Winston, 1977), p. 243.

4. Jean M. Auel, *Clan of the Cave Bear* (New York: Bantam Books, 1980), passim.

5. Jean M. Auel, *Valley of the Horses* (New York: Bantam Books, 1982), passim.

6. Tom Robbins, *Even Cowgirls Get the Blues* (Boston: Houghton Mifflin, 1976), p. 43.

Chapter 4

1. James George Frazer, *The Golden Bough* (New York: Simon & Schuster, 1996), pp. 1–2.

2. Chogyam Trungpa, *Shambhala: The Sacred Path of the Warrior* (Boston: Shambhala, 1978), pp. 33–34.

3. Susan Griffin, *Women and Nature: The Roaring Inside Her* (New York: Harper Colophon, 1978), pp. 193–94.

4. Tom Robbins, *Even Cowgirls Get the Blues* (Boston: Houghton Mifflin, 1976), p. 130.

5. Howard Gardner, *Frames of Mind* (Cambridge, MA: Harvard University Press, 1993).

6. Thomas Moore, *Care of the Soul* (New York: HarperCollins*Publishers*, 1994).

Chapter 5

1. Carol Ochs, *Behind the Sex of God: Toward a New Consciousness—Transcending Matriarchy and Patriarchy* (Boston: Beacon Press, 1977), pp. 31–46.

2. Robert Wright, *The Moral Animal: Evolution in Psychology and Everyday Life* (New York: Vintage Books, 1995).

3. Robert E. Quinn, *Deep Change: Discovering the Leader Within* (San Francisco: Jossey-Bass, 1998).

4. Joseph Heller, *Catch-22* (New York: Dell, 1955), p. 414.

5. Jessie Bernard, *The Female World* (New York: Free Press, 1981).

6. Riane Eisler, *The Chalice and the Blade* (San Francisco: HarperSanFrancisco, 1987).

7. Jane Jacobs, *The Death and Life of Great American Cities* (New York: Vintage Books, 1961), pp. 74–88.

Chapter 6

1. Paulo Coelho, *The Alchemist: A Fable About Following Your Dream*, trans. Alan R. Clarke (San Francisco: HarperSanFrancisco, 1993), pp. 176–77.

2. Harriette Arnow, *The Dollmaker* (New York: Avon Books, 1972).

3. Gerald Jampolsky, *Love Is Letting Go of Fear* (Millbrae, CA: Celestial Arts, 1979).

4. Ntozake Shange, *for colored girls who have considered suicide when the rainbow is enuf* (New York: Simon and Schuster, 1983), p. 63.

5. Paulo Coelho, *The Alchemist*, p. 44.

6. Paulo Coelho, *The Alchemist*, p. 134.

7. Claremont de Castillejo, *Knowing Woman: A Feminine Psychology* (New York: C. G. Jung Foundation, 1973), p. 178.

8. May Sarton, *Joanna and Ulysses* (New York: Norton, 1968), passim.

9. Shirley Gehrke Luthman, *Collections 1978* (San Rafael, CA: Mehetabel and Co., 1979), p. 14.

10. Shirley Gehrke Luthman, *Energy and Personal Power* (San Rafael, CA: Mehetabel and Co., 1982), pp. 33–34.

11. C. G. Jung, *Synchronicity: An Acausal Connecting Principle* (Princeton, NJ: Princeton University Press, Bollingen Paperback Edition, 1973), passim.

12. Matthew Fox, *Whee! We, Wee All the Way Home: A Guide to a Sensual Prophetic Spirituality* (Sante Fe, NM: Bear, 1981).

13. Margaret Drabble, *The Realms of Gold* (New York: Alfred A. Knopf, 1976), p. 29.

14. Suresh Srivasta and David L. Cooperrider, *Appreciative Management and Leadership: The Power of Positive Thought in Organizations* (San Francisco: Jossey-Bass, 1990), pp. 119–24.

15. Mary Staton, *From the Legend of Biel* (New York: Ace Books, 1975), passim.

Chapter 7

1. Shakespeare's otherwise beautiful play has a subplot with elements that reflect the colonialist and perhaps also racist attitudes of his time. My comments should not be interpreted as condoning this unfortunate aspect of the play.

2. Eric Butterworth, *Discover the Power Within You: A Guide to the Unexplored Depths Within* (San Francisco: Harper & Row, 1989).

3. M. Scott Peck, *People of the Lie: Hope for Healing Human Evil* (New York: Simon and Schuster, 1983).

4. Ursula Le Guin, *A Wizard of Earthsea* (New York: Bantam Books, 1968), p. 180.

5. Ursula Le Guin, *The Farthest Shore* (New York: Bantam Books, 1972), p. 180.

6. Philip Ressner, *Jerome the Frog* (New York: *Parents Magazine*, 1967).

7. Madeleine L'Engle, *A Wind in the Door* (New York: Dell Publishing Co., 1978), p. 205

8. Madonna Kolbenschlag, *Kiss Sleeping Beauty Goodbye* (New York: Bantam Books, 1981).

9. Margaret Atwood, *Lady Oracle* (New York: Simon and Schuster, 1976).

10. Tom Robbins, *Even Cowgirls Get the Blues* (Boston: Houghton Mifflin, 1976), p. 43.

11. See Carol S. Pearson and Sharon Seivert, *Magic at Work: Camelot, Creative Leadership, and Everyday Miracles* (New York: Doubleday/Currency, 1995).

12. Margaret Wheatley, *Leadership and the New Science: Learning About Organization from an Orderly Universe* (San Francisco: Berrett-Koehler Publishers, Inc., 1992), pp. 56–57.

13. Ursula Le Guin, *The Dispossessed* (New York: Avon Books, 1975), p. 242.

Part 2

Introduction

1. See Jeremy Taylor, *Where People Fly and Water Runs Up Hill: Using Dreams to Tap the Wisdom of the Unconscious* (New York: Warner, 1992).

2. Marie-Louise von Franz, *Projection and Re-Collection in Jungian Psychology* (London: Open Court, 1980), p. 57.

Chapter 8

1. Carol Gilligan, *In a Different Voice: Psychological Theory and Women's Development* (Cambridge, MA: Harvard University Press, 1982), passim.

2. For more details about archetypes and families, see Carol S. Pearson, *Invisible Forces I: Harnessing the Power of Archetypes to Improve Your Family* (Gladwyne, PA: Type and Archetype Press, 1998).

3. For more information about the archetypes of organizational cultures, see Carol S. Pearson, *Invisible Forces II: Harnessing the Power of Archetypes to Improve Your Career and Your Organization* (Gladwyne, PA: Type and Archetype Press, 1997).

Chapter 9

1. This insight comes from conversations with psychologist Pat Adson, author of *True North: Finding Direction for Yourself and Your Clients in Psychotherapy* (Gladwyne, PA: Type and Archetype Press, 1998). Dr. Adson worked for many years in a treatment program for sex offenders.

2. See Carol S. Pearson, "Women as Learners: Diversity and Educational Quality," *Journal of Developmental Education*, vol. 16, issue 2, Winter 1992.

3. See *A Course in Miracles* (New York: Foundation for Inner Peace, 1975).

Appendix A

1. The Heroic Myth Self-Test is provided to help readers reflect on their lives. The checklists included have not undergone instrumentation testing, such as reliability and validity studies. The *Pearson-Marr Archetype Indicator* is a well-researched instrument. See Appendix C for more information about it and its availability for use.

Appendix C

1. See Patrick and Eileen Howley, *The Inner Life of Leadership* (Gladwyne, PA: Type and Archetype Press, forthcoming).

2. See Carol S. Pearson, *Invisible Forces II: Harnessing the Power of Archetypes to Improve Your Career and Your Organization* (Gladwyne, PA: Type and Archetype Press, 1997) and *Magic at Work: Camelot, Creative Leadership, and Everyday Miracles* (New York: Doubleday/Currency, 1995).

PERMISSIONS

The following publishers have generously given permission to use extended quotations from copyrighted works.

From *Whee! We, Wee All the Way Home: A Guide to Sensual Prophetic Spirituality* by Matthew Fox. Copyright © 1981. Published by Bear & Co.

From *The Hero With A Thousand Faces* by Joseph Campbell. Copyright © 1949. Bollingen Foundation, Inc., renewed 1976 by Princeton University Press. Reprinted by permission of Princeton University Press.

From *Appreciative Management and Leadership: The Power of Positive Thought In Organizations* by Mr. Suresh Srivasta and David L. Cooperrider. Copyright © 1990.

From *The Collected Poems of Wallace Stevens*, "The Idea of Order at Key West" by Wallace Stevens. Copyright © 1954. Published by Alfred A. Knopf.

From *Women and Nature* by Susan Griffin. Copyright © 1978. HarperCollins Publisher.

From *The Realms of Gold* by Margaret Drabble. Copyright © 1976. Published by Alfred A. Knopf.

From *Projection and Re-Collection in Jungian Psychology* by Marie-Louise von Franz. Copyright © 1980. Reprinted by permission of Open Court Publishing Company, a division of Carus Publishing Company, Peru, IL.

From *for colored girls who have considered suicide when the rainbow is enuf* by Ntozake Shange. Copyright © 1975, 1976, 1977 by Ntozake Shange. Reprinted with the permission of Scribner, a division of Simon & Schuster.

From *A Simpler Way* by Margaret Wheatly and Myron Kellner-Roberts. Copyright © 1996. Barrett-Koehler Publishers, Inc., San Francisco, CA. All rights reserved. Reprinted with permission of the publisher.